Dag^pe by Beckers & Piard. Eng^d by A.H. Ritchie.

Ever your loving
Mother.

AMERICA

AS I FOUND IT.

BY THE

MOTHER OF MARY LUNDIE DUNCAN.

"That great country, the United States."—*Sir Robert Peel in the House of Commons.*
"May Great Britain and the United States move hand in hand as brethren in the regeneration of the world."—*E. D. Smith, D.D., New York.*

NEW YORK:
ROBERT CARTER & BROTHERS,
No. 285 BROADWAY.

1852.

T. B. SMITH, STEREOTYPER,
216 William Street, New York.

R. CRAIGHEAD, PRINTER,
53 Vesey Street.

Preface.

About thirty years ago, articles appeared "Quarterly" in a London Review, which filled the surrounding atmosphere with their evil odors, and whose venom was unhappily not spent when it had crossed three thousand miles of "blue water," so that they excited swellings and high disdain as they spread in the United States. Yet it is probable all the articles dropped from one pen, filled with gall. The pen, one may suppose, of some ancient Tory, whose ancestors had suffered in the War of Independence, or whose political creed admitted not of safety except in feudality and hereditary government, and who therefore was embittered by hearing of prosperity beyond it.

These splenetic articles originated or prolonged animosities in their day, though they probably emanated from the pen of a person sufficiently insignificant. That day is past. But, if injurious impressions were made by one insignificant character, it is possible that contrary impressions may be produced by another. It was a little mouse, according to Æsop, that gnawed the net which entangled the lion, and set the forest monarch free. The mouse would have missed a fine opportunity, had it at the moment refused to gnaw. It possessed industry and influence, and used them. Every one is possessed of some degree of influence; if it be met by energy, and leisure to put it forth, it must not lie inactive, though it be but small.

The unpretending traces of what fell under every day experience, here offered to the public, come from one who visited America with cordial feeling and ardent expectation, and was not disappointed. Of course many subjects, such as literature and politics, run in parallel lines with such as are treated here. But they have been plentifully delineated by others, and this affords a plea for their entire omission, which the incompetence of the writer willingly embraces, while religious and social habits fall naturally within the range of her remark.

The diversities between America and Great Britain are only sufficient to add the raciness of novelty to the observer's enjoyment. America is the country in which to form rapid and cordial acquaintances, and from which to carry friendships against whose continuance even the last enemy has no power. Character comes forth naturally there, and is therefore *piquante* and charming. Heart flows out fearlessly, and is therefore ardent.

A nation so prosperous does not need, or condescend to wish for adulation. It is far above flattery—but it demands justice, and in several cases has failed to obtain it from English tourists.

The light pages which follow, design to be just, candid, and kind—not "hinting a fault, and hesitating a dislike," but admiring and blaming with equal simplicity.

Every one admits that the present condition of things on the earth is not what it ought to be, either as it respects nations or individuals. None of my readers would say they are perfect, or that their country is perfect. We are, or ought to be, trying to improve. If I have, in some one or two painful instances, been obliged to allude to that which is evil, and ought to be changed, I say no more than what millions of the citizens of the "freest country in the world" think. If my small meed of approbation were of any value, it would be reduced to worthlessness by the absence of sincerity, in reference to circumstances which I must mourn over or disapprove. Let me be true—or nothing!

The time is on the wing, which will reduce all nations, with all their various governments, into one vast monarchy. Whatever we are under now, whether a despotism, a monarchy, or a republic, then those who have accepted the covenant of peace, will find themselves under the gracious dominion of Him on whose head are many crowns. His throne is the holy hill of Zion. Under His government there are neither bond nor free, for all are His willing subjects—freemen whom His truth hath made free. Those who are given to Him out of the world, will all be subjects in the KINGDOM THAT ENDURETH FOREVER.

EDINBURGH, February, 1852.

Contents.

Introductory.

THE English traveller who, having crossed the Channel, steps on shore at Calais or Ostend, finds himself much more decidedly from home and removed to a foreign land, than he who, having crossed the ocean, lands at New York. The identity of language, though not the only reason, is the most powerful cause of this. Sensible people, accustomed to explain themselves with perspicuity, find themselves when using a foreign language reduced to an incapacity, childish in appearance, and painful because of its uncertainty.

A humorist, describing his landing in France, said the ducks in the hen-yard were the only things he was sure he understood, for they quacked in good broad Scotch.

The language, then, is a great point of affinity, and a wonderful convenience. But there are a thousand other points which give a home-feeling to the British visitant of the United States. Some are obvious and striking, and some not the less attracting, because they are among the finer chords which elude the eye of the careless observer.

Man, in whatever climate he dwells, and under whatever modifications of habit, progress, and institution he is met, still identifies himself with his race, and claims to have sprung from the same Creator's hand. Born in what zone soever, he has a mind which will do some thinking work, and will have its conjectures about the future prospects of the immortal part that he feels stir within him. His object of fear or worship may be some monster of terror, or some pleasant myth. It matters not which, for either indicates the presence of a spiritual part, which seeks a spirit to have sprung from, to trust in, to return to, when the struggle of life shall be ended.

When man is enriched by divine revelation, and gives himself to its guidance, he has found a compass to steer by; he falls into the track that leads him safely and uniformly, and in it he meets with fellow-travellers. Introduce the light of revelation, and his vain fancies fall out of view; philosophical and painful conjecture folds its weary wing, and he reposes on that which commends itself to his mind as common sense, and to his heart as simple truth.

Christianity is the electric chain which unites communities, whatever be their external diversities, and, however their mere temporal advantages may be opposed, it combines their highest interest. It produces uniformity of motive, of sentiment, and action. It is the parent of peace.

This is the bond which to the British Christian renders America a second native land. Whatever he has found of holy aim and zealous effort to attach him to his home, he will find there, in a form slightly varied, but imbued with the same spirit,—and thus he combines safety and improvement with travel, he finds sympathy with strangers, and enjoys confiding trust in the midst of all the gratifications arising from novelty.

Diversity of clime, complexion, manners, and even of tongue, cannot separate, if the great pulses of the heart beat in unison. A Welsh missionary from Ohio, on the platform at the Tabernacle in New York, mentioned a Welsh woman who walked often six miles to worship, though she did not understand English. The reason she gave for this was, that the name of Jesus Christ often occurred in the service, and the sound of it warmed her heart. So, people from all lands, *who know Him*, are united in heart, under that name which is above every name.

It would be a dull world, and not much worth exploring, were there no national and peculiar characteristics, and he is a dull traveller who only admires and approves in proportion as things resemble his home. The organ of comparison is useful when in enlarged and generous exercise, but is poor and contemptible when it leads us only to depreciate and censure. And patriotism, that generous instinct productive of a happy preference for, and contentment in, our own land, dwindles into narrow-minded selfishness if it leads us to regard the success and prosperity of other countries with a jealous eye, or to desire to depreciate the excellencies which they possess. We may each hold our preference for our own country with a grain of allowance, and be willing that each should think

> "The land of his birth
> The loveliest land on the face of the earth,"

if he only willingly discerns the loveliness of other lands. The worn-out colored man crying,

> "But now I'm old and feeble too,
> I cannot work any more,
> O carry me back to old Virginia, to old Virginia's shore,"

though singing of a place of bondage, yet loves the home of his childhood, and is exercising the same sentiment which swelled the heart of Sir Walter Scott, when in decrepitude and infirmity he almost flung himself out of the carriage on coming within sight of Abbotsford. And again, the same sentiment, multiplied a thousand-fold, burst from the hearts and lips of the German army, returning weary and worn from Bonaparte's wars, when, on reaching the mountain top, they rent the air with one long shout, "Am Rhein! am Rhein!" Let us love our countries, but let us also love our friends; let us be faithful patriots, but also enlarged citizens of the world. Let us honor worth wherever it exists, and delight to recognize true sympathies wherever we can find them. Those petty criticisms of manners and of "notions," which are no more dignified than the squabbles for precedence of rival Misses at a ball—how unworthy are they of two great nations who know that each, after their own model, are free—how lowering to men who have a higher than human tribunal to stand before, and a loftier object than man-pleasing to aim at!

Much has been said and written of the United States by English men and women, and unhappily, there has been more displeasure excited, and temper shown on both sides, than the occasion warranted. Diedrich Knickerbocker has quizzed, and Cooper has censured and criticized, and Mrs. Kirkland has described, each saying according to their fancy, things more keen than most of what has been said by English tourists—and their countrymen have borne it well, and confessed, when called upon, the truth of their censures. But let a remark much less pungent drop from an English pen, and one would think that the ghosts of the Stamp Act, the Tax on Tea, and all the long horrors of a war amongst brethren were risen up to revive ambition, wrath, jealousy, and every evil thing which wisdom, brotherly love, and Christian charity, would wish to plunge deep into the caves of the ocean, which divides and yet unites us. It has been said of flattery, that it is so pleasant, that if it be but administered warily, the wisest man living could bear it laid on in shovels-full, and such is self-complacency or love of approbation in many, that probably there is truth in the saying. But in the abstract each person of common sense and common observation will admit that, as no individual, so also no nation is faultless. And it does not become a great nation like the United States, possessing much to rejoice in, and much to be thankful for, to condescend to covet flattery, or to yield to irritation at the statements of passing observers. Part of them haply mistakes, while some of them are undoubtedly true. Moreover, in such a wide country, society is made up of numerous circles, which as little resemble each other as do the people of different countries. Therefore, a description of one circle may appear over-colored or absolutely false to another, but be quite true nevertheless. What points of assimilation would be found between the accomplished judge on the bench or the divine in his study, and the man of suddenly-found fortune working off his exuberant spirits by trotting fifteen miles an hour up the Third Avenue, and calling to his peers (though mayhap not his acquaintances) as he scours past them, "Go ahead, boys! go ahead!" The judge or the divine might suppose this an exaggeration, as their pursuits keep them apart from such lively youths—and yet they are their townsmen.

If a "lady," whose associates have been strolling players or backwoods people in a very *raw* settlement, tells all the vulgarities she met with in such society, why should it ruffle the plumes of the dove-like dwellers among persons of refined taste in a civilized state? The same "lady" if it suited her to enter into minutiæ about home, could probably tell you similar tales—or if a gentleman takes it into his head to imagine that his readers will be interested in his descriptions of the use of tobacco, and its disgusting consequences in such rough conveyances as canal boats, or amid such unpolished members as are some of the congressional representatives from the newly settled and "far, far west," why let him do it *if it be true.*—Perhaps were he himself engaged in clearing an untrodden forest, or draining an impracticable swamp, or dwelling on a misty stream where fever and ague prevail, he also might find a use in departing from his tobacco horrors, and instead of exciting displeasure, his hints might be improved into a more cleanly use of the preventative. He might set up for a pattern tobacco eater, and teach the world. It is not for me to question the reality of such descriptions. The things happen as all admit they do, but, as they did not happen in my circle, I never saw them.

A captain bold being carried to a missionary meeting, came away laughing to see the Yorkshire folks so "humbugged," for he had been eighteen years in India, and had never heard of, much less seen, a missionary. The man was honest in his statement. There are missionaries in India nevertheless!

Looking back on the ancestry of the United States, and considering brother Jonathan as a well-grown and thriving youth, who knows his own affairs, and does not feel any want of paternal government, one understands that a degree of jealousy and displeasure may arise against criticisms, which prevents their being profited by, even where they are known to be just. Yet many a brother has been cured of biting his nails, and many a sister has been broken of some awkward trick by a little good-natured bantering at the family fireside; and if Jonathan could cure John of his self-sufficient pride, and John could subdue in Jonathan his love of boasting, each would have done the other good service. We are all of one blood, Saxon to the core, and perhaps it is because we resemble each other so nearly that we stand each other's criticisms so ill. What a much better game have we discovered to play at when Jonathan is exerting all his ingenuity to pick John's cunning lock while the Bank of England is ordering transatlantic locks for his strong box, or when the English Yacht and the American Clipper are speeding together through the waves, and the one learning from the other how to form his keel, so as to cut them more deftly.

It is in our power to help and to teach each other in a thousand ways, were we but in the vein for it—and why should we not be? I lay no great emphasis on the limited cousinship arising from the old story of the three brothers that came all over in one ship, and how three came from Shropshire and settled in one state, and three from Warwickshire and settled in another, &c., &c. That is a relationship whose footprints are presently lost sight of amid the sands of time—but there are holier and nobler points of affinity, which, feel as we may upon it, proclaim us brethren. Are there not the institutions and aspirations of freemen? Are there not the mutual efforts of industrious and ingenious men? Have we not the raw material in the one country, and the manufactures in the other? Are there not the genial and balmy outgoings of hospitable men? Are there not the skilful and untiring exertions of benevolent and philanthropic men? Are there not the contritions, the faith, the hope, and the walk of Christian men, that unite the bravest and the best of both our countries proclaiming us brethren, at present, and preparing the way to unions in the world, that is wide enough, wise enough, and holy enough to make a final home for us all, and where—if we cannot before—we shall see and feel distinctly that "all we are brethren?" The heart of America at this very juncture beats in unison with the heart of England, in regard to the European struggle for liberty; and the hand of America is stretched across the Atlantic in defiance of the oppressors, and in aid of the oppressed. Have we not been gladdened to see the exile and the refugee find a free home in the United States? and is it not a generous rivalship that has been practised by both countries in seeking who first should welcome and sustain Kossuth, the hero, who if he bring with him the heart and hopes of Hungary, meets where he comes the heart and hopes of freemen?—Sacred is the deposit of freedom, Great Britain and the United States have that deposit in charge for the relief of a despot-ridden world. They must not, they dare not dissipate their influence in petty rivalries and family quarrels. They are bound to unite to make its weight felt in the kingdoms of oppression and imprisonment.

More than thirty years have elapsed, with their clouds and sunshine since the first American whose society we had an opportunity of cultivating, strayed in upon us. His fine metaphysical head, his rich conversational powers, the freshness and piquancy of his opinions, the novelty of his information—for wars and stormy seas alike rendered the United States at that period a far country to us—and above all his Christian principle, formed a whole which attracted and charmed us. I have not forgotten the tears which flowed, when this unlooked-for stranger poured out at our evening worship confessions, petitions, and gratitudes exactly our own, and how from that hour the wide Atlantic seemed bridged for us by sympathies which the world could not interfere with.

After him came another and another, each new guest in the course of years introducing his friend, the characters of all in degree fraught with those principles which prepare the mind for exalted intercourse, based on plans and hopes which will live when the world and its life are extinct.

Our earliest specimens of men from the other hemisphere were not merchants, but pastors exhausted by their labors in pursuit of health and relaxation, and students in pursuit of knowledge. And noble specimens they were of keen investigation, lively perception of novelty, acute dissection of truth, and bold assertion of Christian principle, as the rule and guide of their motives. It is not to be wondered at that such associates should engage and enliven the mind, and that after long years of distant contemplation, an opportunity of seeing them at home should be embraced with willingness. Neither is it surprising, that such being the character of our first transatlantic acquaintances, their successors should have been like-minded, or that when these welcome visits were at last returned, they should have opened for the guest whom they so generously cherished, a vein of ore precious and rich in its rewards to the feeble and unworthy hand that worked it.

Others have described the festivities, the political institutions, the energetic mercantile pursuits of the Americans. Perhaps a path yet scarcely trodden may furnish some points of interest, from one who numbered amongst her early and valued friends, J. M. Mason, D.D., and his young friend Bruen, who acted as the keys to open Society's gate for her. One whose attention has been directed as much to the Christianity and philanthropic exertions of the people as to their noble rivers and rich plains, and as much to the lively and influential Christian sentiments of their women, as to their domestic virtues and personal loveliness.

It is to the Christian and social habits of this interesting people that access has been chiefly afforded, and with them chiefly that sympathies have been exchanged. Abhorring the vulgar soul that uses the hospitalities of a country to go home and criticize domestic habits, as much as the treacherous, seeming reserve, which points its tale so as to mark infallibly the parties alluded to, while it affects to withhold the names, my remarks and details are sincere and affectionate as are my feelings; accompanied by that respectful reserve which becomes a friend, pledged as much by grateful regard as by sympathy to feel and act as becomes brotherly love.

A passage in the conclusion of Dickens' "American Notes," one of the best in the book, is quoted verbatim as the best expression of my own sentiments, only adding to "cultivation and refinement" a more essential quality which he has omitted—I mean Christian principle.

"The Americans are by nature frank, brave, cordial, hospitable, and affectionate—cultivation and refinement seem but to enhance their warmth of heart and ardent enthusiasm, and it is the possession of these latter qualities in a most remarkable degree which renders an educated American one of the most endearing and most generous of friends. I never was so won upon as by this class; never yielded up my full confidence and esteem so readily and so pleasurably as to them; never can make again in half a year so many friends, for whom I seem to entertain the regard of half a life."*

* *Dickens' American Notes,* vol. i. p. 288.

The Children.

Our ancestors are the root of the tree, our aged the trunk, our youths the branches, and our children the coronal of leaves and blossoms—and who that anticipates the future prosperity of a country can fail to cast a lively observation on the blossoms, and to watch the spring-time? Who that has experienced the parental instincts, which are interwoven with the very life of the heart; who that has seen children grow out of infancy into manhood, and out of ignorance into maturing wisdom, can dwell in a country and be admitted into its domestic scenes, without casting an earnest eye over the little ones, the light of the dwelling, the source of its freshest interest?

English children in the presence of strangers are reserved and shy. They feel that the nursery and school-room are their proper spheres of action, and that they are only brought out at times, as it were, to be *shown* to particular friends.

Scotch children are bashful and awkward, and as if constitution or climate had not done enough for them in that respect, their parents too often repress them as if they were ashamed of them, or afraid of some outburst of ill-manners, when the poor things are behaving their very best. This partly arises from the reserve of the mothers, who, with hearts flowing with affection, press it down and cover it up, as if they feared it might be suspected by a stranger.

Most unlike to these is the sentiment of the American, both parent and child. The little citizen seems to feel at a surprisingly early age, that he has a part to act on the stage of the world, and is willing enough to act a little before his time. And the parents, full of frank, simple emotion, bring their little treasure under notice, and ask you, with pride and joy, "Don't you think my Charley is a brave little fellow?" or, "Did you ever see such a quick eye as my Austin's?" or, "Is she not a pretty little darling?" or, "Did you ever see such a cunning little thing?" (The word *cunning*, according to some old English use of it, meaning in this application nothing like sly, but neat, tidy, or expert-looking.) If the children are not at home, you will be shown their pictures, or told their histories,—or if the arrow of death has stricken any of them, the stroke, the manner of it, how it was borne, and how the bereaved were sustained under it, will be all poured out with a confiding certainty of your sympathy that is most winning and touching. How often have I envied that self-command which enables them to relate such events with unshaken voice, and to dwell on deep sorrows without tears. And how often have I with shame contrasted my own long past concealment, nay, almost negation of powerful sentiment, with this its beautiful outflows.

The little ones seem to partake from the first of the exciting effect of the climate. I know not what philosophers or medical men may say to it, but it seems the only easy way of accounting for the hasty and impulsive character of the people, to impute it to the climate. All partake of it alike. Even the very horses have a spring about them, which makes them run without driving, and gallop as soon as the rider is fixed in his stirrups. Strangers who bring with them the dulness of more weighty atmospheres, presently become enlivened, and even the drooping and half-clothed Milesian, recovers his wit and doubles his spirit amid the dry air, and under the pure blue sky.

It is very true that another cause exists. The new settler, as well as the native, feels that there is room enough and food enough for all. So that, a man does not look on his enlarging family with an eye of care, and cast about, as in "the old country," for openings through which each may make standing room, and find bread. Each new babe is a new source of delight, and should the number surpass that of a common family, you cannot but smile in pleasant emotion with the father, who will tell you that he has the round dozen, or he can produce you "any quantity" of little ones; and then they come, not with a "make your bow," or "courtesy to the lady," that is not republican fashion, but with a becoming courage, looking straight into your eyes, and extending the right hand for a cordial shake. Frank to answer, and ready to ask a question, you soon find you have not got a timid creature who needs your encouraging patronage, but a companion who will do you a service, get you information, or ask it from you, as the case may be.

The first impression produced by their manner is, that they are brave, bright, pleasant, little "impudent things." But this, like many first impressions, turns out to be erroneous. The "impudent thing" is gradually dropt, and instead of the bad word you adopt "intelligent" or "independent." I have smiled to see a little fellow, who had certainly not been quite seven years a traveller in this world, lead the way in stepping into an omnibus, and walk up to a convenient position for reading the regulations. Then placing his hands behind him—I dare say in the very attitude of papa if one saw him—read, turning to the two younger brothers who seem to listen with understanding, "Constructed to carry twelve inside. Children who take seats pay half price;" upon which information, the small ones scramble on the laps of the ladies who accompany them, and the leading youth adjusts himself to stand at a window, without visible direction from the ladies. I have also seen a child, a year older at most, according to the rule of politeness and consideration for females which pervades all ranks in such of the States as I have visited, calculate how many sixpences he wanted from his ladies, and how many cents for himself, collect them, reach up with some help to pull the driver's string, and then on tiptoe give the money to the driver through the little hole in the roof. With us, such children would have been guided and paid for. There is no air of assumption in the doing of such small services. It seems natural, and expected by the seniors. A bright little fellow, it may be about nine years old, was asked in my hearing if he had been to Mr. ——

this morning. He said, "No, he thought it better not to go until his return from school." I was a good deal surprised to learn that this visit, so easily and pleasantly planned, was to a dentist, for the purpose of having a tooth extracted; having seen a good deal of fuss, and much unnecessary fear excited on such occasions among children of that age at home.

But much earlier than this, even in early infancy, does this precocity show itself. At six weeks old, a babe will cock up his small capless and nearly hairless head, and observe the new-comer into the nursery, and smile if pleased, or scream if the "countenance likes him not." And you will see a little being that has not seen the sun make one circle of seasons, lay hold on a toy, not to cram it in his mouth and look stupidly at it, but to turn it curiously over, open it if he can, and peep in with a look as wise as that of a raven peeping into a marrow-bone. One mark of early observation and comprehension never failed to excite my wonder. Little creatures feed themselves very neatly, and are trusted with cups of glass and china, which they grasp firmly, carry about the rooms carefully, and deposit unbroken, at an age when in our country Mamma or Nurse would be rushing after them to save the vessels from destruction. My surprise has also been excited by the lengths they are permitted to go in mischief, without punishment, or scarcely admonition. I heard a grandmamma relate with complacency, how her boy had locked himself in the drawing-room and deliberately thrown a large set of china, piece by piece, over the window. His "reason" was, because he liked to hear the "*crash*" as it fell. I inquired what she said to him. The indulgent parent had explained to the small man that "she did not choose to have her pretty china broken, as that rendered it useless." A very reasonable advice to an unreasonable performer. It reminded me of an incident in the early days of Charles James Fox, whose father had given him a gold repeater. The boy said he must throw the watch against the wall. "Why must you?" inquired Lord Holland. "O just that I may see what will happen." "Why it will break!" "Well, Papa, I just want to see how it goes when it breaks." "Well, Charles, if you must you *must*, I suppose." The watch was thrown, and, as was expected, flew into many pieces. Whether destructiveness was very large in the boys or correctiveness very small in the parents, we leave each one to settle according to their fancy.

The more rapid are the children in the early unfoldings of the powers both of mind and body, the more do they require wise guidance and wholesome restraint. And here arises the parental difficulty. It seems to require as much self-denial in the father to refuse his boy anything as it can require in the boy to be refused. And thus, as each obtains a seat at the family table at meals as early as they can be trusted in an elevated chair, they are used to ask for and to receive all manner of varieties of food. Breakfasts, like all other meals in a country richly prolific in luxuries, are made of many dishes and many kinds of cakes, and it is common to feed the little ones on fish, flesh, and game; fruits, salads, and hominy; Johnny-cakes, corn cakes, buckwheat cakes all hot, with molasses; toast swimming in butter, and mayhap a little plain bread and milk; tea or coffee, if it is acceptable. It may be but a taste of many of these things, but thus is the foundation laid, I doubt not, of many a poor dyspeptic's pining life. How often have I run over in my mind the many brave and wise men of my own country, who grew to health and strength on simple fare, and remembered Sir Walter Scott's list of "lads" who, like himself had breakfasted till they were fifteen on porridge and milk.

The same danger meets them at all meals, and

especially when they are allowed. to sit up, as they commonly are, to see the guests at evening parties, and share oysters, jellies, and ices, fruits and preserves, not in the moderate way that contents grown-up persons, but with all the heartiness and excess of "frugivorous children."

In spite of melting summer suns and the keen pursuit of objects, to which it is common to impute the exceeding lack of flesh which renders many a fine profile no better than the edge of a knife when the face is turned to you, might it not be that a more abstemious and simple diet in early years, might be the means of adding to both the strength and beauty of the full-grown man?

Children's diseases are hasty and come with a fell swoop, desolating cities and hearts—Oh, how desolating! Who can compute the pungency of the parents' grief when the nursery is the scene of such visitations. Many a young heart, that in its first love and early marriage and early maternity, scarcely knew any throbs but that of joy, by a visit of death to her nursery has suddenly been taught the solemn truth, that the world is a blighted place, and that the passage is through a wilderness—and also the deeper lesson, that there is a world of spirits, a treasure-house for those who are gone.

Our departed friend, Hewitson, beautifully wrote on that subject: "God has taken from you, as it were, a pledge that you will live for eternity. The bereaved soul goes across the border of time in quest of the departed spirit, and so acquaints itself better with eternity and its unseen realities. How real is the distant isle to which a friend has gone, though formerly it seemed but a dim fog on the sea! How real is eternity, when one that we have loved, and *love still*, is there! 'One that I love is there,' that gives our hearts a local habitation in eternity. This event tells us that we are nearer our journey's end now than we were yesterday. The Jordan is not far off—a few breathings of the air of the wilderness, a few steps across the dreary sands, and then we reach home."*

It is very touching to listen to many parents, who will tell you it never entered their apprehension that their first dear child was mortal, till on being weaned it fell sick; or, convulsions in teething, or that wide-wasting destroyer, "summer-complaint," swept it away.

This loss of children seems to me the rod under which the Good Shepherd gathers many a sheep into his fold. It is precious to hear them tell how

* *Hewitson's Memoir*, p. 238. New York: Carter & Brothers.

they first turned to Christ, when they followed their departed lambs to his bosom. Sweetly and confidingly do they entrust you with their soul's secret, and amid the riches of their new-found hopes, mingle their sweet smiles and tears with your sympathies—and precious it is to hear of little disciples, taught early by the Great Teacher, who never made a soul too young to receive His influences, speaking words of resignation, of love and peace to the weeping parents whom they are about to leave, and of hope and joy of the welcoming Lord whose presence they are about to enter. On listening to narratives of such early Christians, I have felt it difficult to abstain from congratulating the mourners with a "blessed are the dead who are already dead, more than the living who are yet alive."

There never was better material of which to make good and wise citizens, than these children, so quick to understand, so keen to feel, so prompt to act. But the very metal in them renders the use of breaking bridles in childhood, and a tight rein in youth, of great importance. They receive education with facility and smartness, but those who are destined for commerce are so generally mounted on a tall desk seat as early as their fourteenth or fifteenth year, that they much require exact and strict moral discipline before. Obedience, that grave self-denying quality, is never so easily nor so fitly learnt as in childhood—self-will never gains strength more rapidly than in the nursery. If the child does not learn submission to his natural guardians with the first shooting up of his own will and desires, how shall he later in life, learn obedience to the divine will?

One perceives a perplexity in the parent's mind sometimes, between a consciousness that he ought to rule his son, and a notion that the little rebel's escapades are the natural result of "Liberty." Liberty! that sacred name under which many a crime has been perpetrated, and many a dangerous and ruinous mistake committed. There is no fear of the child born under free institutions and destined to exercise a freeman's privilege, becoming too tame by means of just parental discipline—and it is certain that he will render the more healthful obedience to the laws of his country, and more reverential observance of the laws of God by his being accustomed to observe the laws of his earliest protectors and loving friends. To see sensible people smile with secret admiration of the "spirited" exhibition of rebellious will on the part of their offspring, excites, in an English mind, a sense of lurking danger—as also to hear pupils asserting boldly what they "will never learn," and what they "will learn," and to see teachers using all manner of adroit flatteries and timid expostulations, with a view to obtain a slender influence over the pupils, leads one to look out anxiously for ultimate results.

Natural quickness enables persons to discern methods of "getting along," and to pass well in social life, who have lacked thorough training. Many a man finds himself in a position which forces him to guide or influence others, who has not acquired the difficult art of governing himself, and many a girl is placed in the centre of maternal cares, with all the duties and responsibilities of rearing a family, who feels herself at a loss on many points, because of her own undisciplined childhood; or what is worse, feels herself at no loss, but thinks she knows all about it.

It happens frequently, also, that persons attain wealth, who have not themselves been well educated, and they, in the United States as in England, mistake the important objects of instruction, and omit them in favor of the showy or amusing. In this way only can I account for the listlessness or even the impatience that I have seen manifested in school-examinations, when the subject is a solid branch of education. Thus at an exhibition of the attainments of the children who were brought in from the "Orphan Asylum," to the Apollo Rooms in New York for examination, a well-dressed and animated audience, began to thin away in an alarming manner, under an examination on geography and arithmetic, so that the sagacious directors "stopt that," and immediately seats were cheerfully resumed to listen to choruses, solos, and amusing dialogues—and, though printed in the programme, grammar, and parsing, and lessons in geometry were not ventured upon, but gave place to "Dirty Jane," "the Handy Lad," and the "Grand Banquet." When I remarked this to more than one sensible and well-educated matron, I was told that, not only at an examination of strangers, and orphans, but of their own children, the parents often exhibit weariness when the subjects of investigation are solid. It is pleasing to see severer studies diversified by moral songs, hymns, and music, and a touch of elocution may be very wisely bestowed on the embryo stump-orator, or future senator, but that these should be the all of education which excites an interest, is an unsound and unsafe state of things. I am not a judge of how much may be enjoyed by

Americans in such matters, being myself used to the ways of a slower and more enduring people, who can sit out long sermons, long lectures, and long school examinations—but I feel assured that it is not the well-informed part of the audience who become weary of the substantial and useful portions of instruction; and it might be wise in the less-instructed parents to remain and see if they can learn something of what their children are acquiring. In no country shall we find more lovely examples of cheerful domestic union, or more honorable and self-denying exertion on the part of parents, in sharing and lightening the studies of their children—any one might feel with me enriched for life by having been admitted to such family circles, and formed friendships with such parents; but in the ever-changing mass of people in the maritime and commercial cities such steadfast and enlightened characters are far from being the majority. Yet how rich are the rewards of those who lay themselves out to indoctrinate the young immortal, and to strengthen while they prune the budding energies of the future citizen.

Though it is years since in my remote Scottish home, my eyes often overflowed as I read the speeches of John Quincey Adams, and pictured the venerable hoary-headed friend of his country day after day standing on the floor of the Senate, breasting alone the opposition of the many, and asserting alone the right of petition, yet it was not till I recently read his mother's letters to him, that I comprehended whence he derived his solitary courage, or how he was so deeply imbued with the principle which sustained him still in old age. Was not Mrs. Adams as truly serving her country, in rearing such a son, as was her husband in his long years of separation from his family, amid vexatious and ever-varying negotiations? The generous enthusiasm, the reasonable and life-giving patriotism which glowed in her bosom, was transferred into that of her children, and was expended in cheering and strengthening her husband under a separation, which, to her devoted heart, was but one long pang of suffering.—It is most interesting and amusing to see her complain that the paper she writes on cost a dollar a sheet, and beg for an importation of pins, as there is not one left in the town, and of needles, for the tailor has the cloth still, but no tools to make it with, in the same letter in which she wisely comments on the history of her new-born country, cheers on the patriot to greater endurance and firmness, and selects parallel cases, on pattern characters from Greece or Rome. Bravely did she live through many painful trials and dangers, and was after all, in spite of much privation, as happy in her strenuous exertions for the good of her large family, and her wide circle, as she could ever have been after, even when she saw first her husband and then her son elevated to the Presidential chair.—She was a *Mother!*—suited to the trying times on which her lot fell, and nobly fulfilling her part to her children and her country. Such a mother as Napoleon said France needed, but such as France has not yet found.

But America had still a higher style of parental discipline in the parents of her Washington, which she most justly appreciates. Every school-room has rung with the story of that father who embraced his erring boy, because he spoke truth even though he accused himself; and every parish library can produce the narrative of the patriot's early training. —When, as its fruit, we find the self-denying hero and brave warrior retiring to the forest to seek a place of prayer, which the throngings of a restless camp denied him; when we see him refusing the perpetual honors and government which his grateful country pressed upon him, we gladly trace back all these heroic virtues to parental training, and to the early reception of those Christian principles which made him what he was, and enabled him so well to accomplish the work for which God raised him up —and do we not sympathize with the quiet confidence of his wife, when asked if during his long absences in such stirring times she were not wretched with anxiety, she replied, "I know that wherever George Washington is he is doing his duty, and thus I am calm." Happy and honored wife, successor of happy and honored parents. Who would not exert themselves to produce such fruits as these?

To rule a household well, and to rear children with the view of the early home being the nursery ground from which plants will be removed first to flourish as trees in the church on earth, and again to grow forever by the river of crystal, and under the glorious tree with its twelve manner of fruits, whose leaves are for the healing of the nations—these are objects worthy of the noblest ambition, and the most indefatigable pains.

Prayerful teaching accompanied by the earnest eloquence of a full heart, and the original illustrations of a yearning spirit, never passes unrequited on this side the Atlantic or on that—in the wilderness on this side the Jordan, or on the glorious shores of the Promised Land.

The Common Schools and Free Academy.

From observing the smiling crowd, which is to form the men and women of the succeeding generation, we turn naturally to the means of Education. In this department it is very pleasant to adopt the language—at which one is apt to smile when you hear its mistaken application on some other subjects,—and to say gladly, that "no country in the world" has a more just appreciation of the importance of universal instruction than the United States—and also that the Eastern States, have been surpassed by "no country in the world," in the extent and energy of their educational schemes.

The knowledge which is reckoned necessary to every man, no matter what his business or position, and which forms the subject of instruction in the common schools, is to "spell accurately, read well, write legibly, understand the principles of grammar, have a fair knowledge of geography, arithmetic, and the history of the United States." One of the annual reports of the Board of Education for the city and county of New York, gives its judgment on the subject thus—"The education of no citizen should fall below this standard, whether his interests and happiness as a man, or his influence as the head of a family, or a member of society be alone regarded," and at this object the Common Schools aim. It may be needful to state that the word "common," in the designation of the schools, does not mean schools for the common people, but schools, common to and suited for all. The basis of education is satisfactory so far as it goes; but while for the multitude this is as much as their destined occupations permit them to reach, for those whose prospects, ability, and leisure may induce them to desire to go further, more is wanting—and in consequence the Free Academy has recently sprung up in the city of New York, which receives youth who have attained all that the common school offers, and who wish to advance to classical, mathematical, and scientific studies. This Free Academy is founded by the city, and like the common schools, sustained by a self-imposed tax. The Board of Education took up the initiative in this matter—a committee was appointed to report, and ultimately a memorial was laid before the legislature. By it an act was passed under which the institution was established, but with the provision that the question be submitted to the people at the ensuing school and judicial election. The result of this election is interesting as showing to which side the balance for ignorance or for instruction turns. There were votes *for* establishing the Free Academy 19,404, against it 3,409, giving the enormous and honorable majority in favor of instruction of 15,995—and thus the scheme went on, and the beautiful new edifice was opened in the beginning of 1849, with the following staff of professors :—

Mathematics and Natural Philosophy.
History and Belles Lettres.
Latin and Greek Languages and Literature.
Chemistry.
French Language.
Spanish.
German Language and Literature.
Drawing.

No government is so much in need of universal enlightenment, or so much in danger from popular ignorance as the republican. Each member of it ought by having a certain store of knowledge laid up in his own mind to be sheltered from the overpowering influences of eloquence, the hasty and unweighed opinions of talking demagogues, and the misleading sympathies of popular cries. He requires to discern the liberal from the selfish, the just from the unjust. Not only his own but the general welfare is concerned in his being able to take a part in carrying on its government; he may be required to enact laws, or to aid in their execution when enacted. If he understands his own rights as a citizen, and those of his neighbors, and takes any part that may fall to him in carrying on the government, he will gain a useful ascendency, and may by means of superior cultivation become a help, an honor, and a blessing to his country. Therefore it is pleasant to consider that the largest proportion of those who enjoy the advantages of the Free Academy are sprung from parents who could not well afford to give them such an education—and that the only barrier against their admission, is deficient attainment in those lessons which they ought to have previously acquired in the Common School.

It is curious to remark the grounds of dissent from the plan of the Free Academy propounded by Horace Greeley—a kind of republican run mad, who objects to learning the dead languages, because science and art are of far greater practical importance, and refuses to afford to a part of the youth a more costly education, because it cannot be provided for and freely proffered to all.

If the Free Academy were to abridge the powers and extent of the Common School, the objection might be valid, but as it only offers the deeper cup of instruction to the lip which has already drained the shallower, and as it only passes it from those who, from position or slow attainment, have not leisure or relish for it, one apprehends that the objection is unsound, or mayhap insincere, and got up to serve some political turn.

A republic possesses a sacred trust in the talents of its citizens, and ought to cultivate them for the public good—and the more that the average of talent is low, ought those who rise above the average to be cared for. As you would select the strongest to bear the standard, and the bravest to man the breach, so should you cherish him of powerful intellect to deal with the laws and executive of his country. Self-educated and self-raised persons are apt to despise the ladder to learning, from a notion that if mind is worth anything it will find its level. But what an advantage to remove early difficulties and suggest pursuits that may be selected according to taste. These self-raised know not how much higher they might have risen, or how much better they might have acquitted themselves had they been early placed amid the facilities which education furnishes. New York may bravely lift up her head and say she has not left the "step-children of nature and fortune, the outcast, the benighted, the brutalized, and the homeless," to flee to a rock for shelter. She has generously opened her arms, and is opening them wider and wider still. She has instructed thousands, and will instruct thousands more. Besides the very extensive benevolent institutions sustained by voluntary subscription, the report for 1850 shows at least nearly 11,000 dollars contributed by the City to aid in sustaining orphan houses, blind asylums, and places of reform for juvenile delinquents. How poor and dangerous a plea is it for depriving the few of the refining and expanding influences of good scholarship that the same boon cannot be conferred on the masses—and how much need has a republic of leading minds, well imbued with principles of justice, and enriched with the histories of other ages and other nations, and with their experience, under a just and wise Providence, of past failures and successes! It is easy to raise a popular cry which may frustrate the wisest purposes. Such a cry about liberty of conscience has hooted all catechisms and creeds out of the present scheme of instruction—and in virtue of the City having at present an inheritance of children, whose parents as Romanists dare not, or as infidels will not read the Scriptures, the Holy Book and all teaching founded on it are sparingly used in the common schools. How this comports with the order of a country calling itself Christian, and essentially Christian in most of its institutions, it is not easy to see, while it is very easy to see that a cry raised about encroachment on liberty of conscience was sure to tell on a people so jealous for liberty as are the Americans.

It is melancholy to observe bright children, capable of all manner of impressions, well versed in the brief history of their own country, but utterly ignorant, so far as the school-teaching goes, of the history of the world they live in, its creation, the path by which they may pass safely through it, and, above all, of how they may go well out of it.

It will be said that this statement is not fact, and that a portion of Scripture is read each morning, and the Lord's prayer said, or sometimes chaunted, at the opening of the school. This is optional, and, judging by delicate admonitions in the reports, it would appear is omitted by some teachers. If reading the Scriptures were steadily observed, it could not be said that some classes after learning to read pass on to other things, and never read any more, or at least read a little history so seldom that the inspectors complain of reading not being cultivated as an art, and say there is no reason why the pupils should not read as well as Miss Fanny Kemble, to listen to whose "readings of Shakspeare" the taste and cultivation of the city were thronging.

It is an excellent rule to begin the day by the habitual reading of the word of God. Let it be without note or comment, if that be necessary to security against the teacher's peculiar dogmas, but still let it be—solemnly and soberly. How many whose hours are hereafter to be spent in earning a livelihood may thus stow up sacred sentiments to fall back upon when the time of reflection or of retrospection comes. And if there is to be no more extended petition than what is found in the Lord's Prayer, at least let that be *said*, not *sung*, with deliberation and reverence, each in the attitude of prayer.

Were the vote reconsidered, apart from any false excitement about encroachment on liberty of conscience, one cannot but hope, that even in New York —where numerous recently-arrived Irish emigrants have, by some evasion of the laws, been permitted to exercise the power of voting—they would lay it down as a rule, that the Scripture History be read and questioned upon, at least, as diligently as that of the United States. It seems to me grievous to see the real Christian influences which would be shed from many of the teachers, neutralized by this vain cry of liberty of conscience. Children do not learn arithmetic and geography without teaching—but they are supposed to know Christianity by intuition, and to exercise conscience before it is enlightened. Liberty of conscience! Poor dear ignorant offspring of fallen Adam! Let it be called liberty of sin, liberty of forgetting God, liberty of neglecting the Saviour, liberty of slaying their own souls,—but let not the citizens be deluded by supposing that training which omits instruction in reference to God and his thoughts towards themselves is honest genuine liberty.

Protestants have thus heedlessly in keeping with the constitution of their government as they reckon it, slighted the means of conveying early knowledge of the Bible, and are not awake to the proceedings of the enemy, who, with unsleeping eye, discerns where and how he may insinuate his baleful influences. Amid many pleasant moral songs which form the peculiar attraction of a school examination, you may not hear one Protestant hymn. No strain of adoration or of love is put into those young hearts. But watch, and when you inquire what are the words of that noble and striking air? you will discover that it is the chaunt of a Popish pilgrimage. What those sweet cadences of thanksgiving? they are praise for the pleasant rest to be obtained before the little shrines which stud the deep and *meritoriously* stony ascent, crowned by the image to whose sacred fane the pilgrims are climbing on their knees. Think we such strains are adopted by accident? They are certainly by carelessness in some quarter, but it must be of purpose and by Popish influence in some other. In England we are sufficiently accustomed to such wiles, and we have seen music made the plea for the introduction of many an "ora pro nobis" to the Virgin, which the unthinking have accepted because of its beauty.

Another mode of insinuating mischief is the prize books, which are distributed on a day of examination. Many are good and useful, many are pleasant, but, if one may venture to say so, too juvenile and silly, and some are unwholesome and dangerous. In selecting a set of books, when an eye must be turned to the cost, and to the attractive aspect of the prize, it is not difficult for the designing to introduce mischief under cover of blue and gold. In such a livery have I found, in the hand of a girl of fifteen, the "Beauties of Festus," as her reward for attainments in the highest class. Festus! a work which in spite of all its talent and fine thinking, I threatened to burn on account of its blasphemous tendencies, when a young person proposed to leave it on my table. Festus—which introduces among its dramatis personæ the Sacred Three, and daringly inserts in the margin the holy names, mixed up with its other interlocutors. I turned over the "Beauties of Festus" with eager fear, and found that no delicate omission had been made; as is the book, so are its beauties—and this the reward of a studious girl! Surely an enemy hath done this!

Another painful effect of this liberty-of-conscience scheme struck me again and again in attending the Inspector's examinations, viz., the abridgment of his liberty and that of any Christian minister's who might be present, so that their final addresses were limited to stories of obedient boys, good morals and good manners, and not a word hinted of the divine law, of the gospel, and of the bright prospects which the gospel unfolds. The rewards proposed to them are that they may be respected, may become magistrates, governors, senators, or even President of the United States. One grieved to see the Christian sentiment kept down in the speakers, and the Christian motive withheld from the listeners, and as one looked over the pleasant, orderly, ductile-looking youth, one felt how much finer things are in store for those who love the Lord, and how delightful it would be, instead of senators and presidents, to tell them of crowns and palms, and harps, and of the city where there is no night, no pain, no difficult tasks, and no death. The idea also arises, that there is an over-tenderness in the examinators. If a whole class blunders over a question, as I have repeatedly remarked to happen more in English grammar than in any other branch, it is glided by, some loophole for excuse is found, so that neither teachers nor pupils feel the deficiency sufficiently to be put on the alert in correcting it. Why not say simply, this needs to be amended? The general tenor of remark is of a complimentary character. Is this lest free pupils should take offence and leave the school? Then surely the pupils are much more free than their examinators. One expects genuine freedom to use great plainness of speech, and that in cases of this sort, the performance of duty demands it—a painful evidence that in New York city liberty is sliding gradually under an influence which domineers over conscience wherever it reigns, is found in the blackening of one page in a whole edition of a school lesson-book. And what is this page bearing so condemning a mark? Nay, it is carefully obliterated, and so past my reading, except that through its gloom the name of Martin Luther is dimly perceptible. Is there liberty of conscience here, or is there not rather incipient papal domination?

With these exceptions, but they are grave ones, the Common School is an admirable institution, furnishing the fundamentals of all learning, and the books employed in teaching, to every rank of children. No one need be uneducated if willing to be taught. The school-houses are, in general, erected by the district, which also elects trustees who manage the school for one year and appoint teachers, while the teachers are paid from the general school-fund. A difficulty about obtaining steady attendance, arises from the very liberality of the plan. Caprice leads to leaving one school and entering another. Or a new and airy school-house in the next ward, may thin the benches of the school in this. It is our experience in Britain that we prize less what we get freely, and therefore, the mother who sends her penny with her infant on Monday morning, will have more scruple about keeping the child at home for a trifling reason, than she would have if she paid nothing. We need not weigh the penny against lost time and opportunity, and the contraction of idle habits—any one who can "calculate" sees that, and the absence of charge is hinted at as a difficulty with the common school teachers as well as with our own.

There is a very becoming courage in the manner the pupils give out their attainments, and a pleasant music in their recitation, and at times a swelling feeling of the sentiments they utter, or a suppressed consciousness of the drollery of the dialogues which they recite on exhibition days, which always drew forth my heart to the young people. In no country does one feel so clearly that courage exists apart from boldness, and that frankness has no necessary connection with forwardness, as in the United States. That movable excitabilty which "turns at the touch of joy or woe, and turning trembles too," is inexpressibly lovely in youth—and I have never more admired young countenances, than some of those that I have seen turned to beloved teachers, and stirred by the zeal, ambition, or animation of a favorite lesson.

The education, if we except the classics, embraces a wider range than that of our parish schools, and is very thorough, if it be not the pupil's own fault. One sees the higher classes of girls quite "au fait" in astronomy, square and cube root, &c. Another striking difference is the employment of Female Teachers, not in the industrial department only, nor for girls alone. They seem more numerous than the Male Teachers, probably because they are obtained at a cheaper rate. Why the rate should be cheaper does not appear. Their labor is not less, neither are their attainments and success inferior. I have never admired calm authority and sensible dignity more than in the person of an American female teacher, while she drew forth the attainments of fifty big boys in Mathematics and the Latin rudiments. Her class was in perfect order, and her pupils evidently observed her with affectionate respect. She was not teaching in one of the Common Schools, as the Latin lesson proved. But such female teachers are nearly as common as the schools.

As past experience generally passes in the mind in a sort of panoramic review while we are busily observing the present; or rather, what we witness now forms the foreground, while what we have seen elsewhere forms the background of the picture, so it is inevitable that comparison should be in active exercise. One difference which met me everywhere was, the mode of addressing pupils at an examination, showing what is expected of them. They are not treated as machines upon whom the Teachers are to act, as they unfortunately sometimes are in England; but as members of the community, who have a part to act themselves, and who are as much interested in the credit of the school as the Teachers. The effect of this is to excite a common interest between teachers and taught, and to give superior manliness and energy.

The fittings-up, or "fixings," as our brethren call them, of some of the more recent school-rooms are very worthy of imitation. Instead of one long, dreary bench in front of a desk, which forms a barrier to be climbed over, each pupil has a rounded seat, which turns a little on a pivot and has a low back, so that he glides gently into his place, instead of clambering into it with an unsightly scramble; and when seated, he has a rest for his spinal column, which saves him at once from oppressing and contracting his chest by leaning forward, and from the lateral curvature which so frequently is the result of attitudes chosen to relieve the weariness of a long unsupported seat.

There is much ingenuity and spirit in the songs and recitations which awaken patriotic sentiments in the very dawn of life, and give each child a personal interest in what he is engaged about. A selection of these things might form a curious and characteristic publication, letting one into the very heart and spring of the national character. The stanza or two here presented are only fragments :—

THE COMMON SCHOOL.

* * * * * * * *

I'll sing the hours of sweet content,
Of innocence and toys,
When to the Common School I went
With other girls and boys.
'Tis a happy theme ; like a golden dream its memory seems to be,
And I'll sing with joy and gratitude—The Common School for me.

* * * * * * * *

Then blessings on our Common Schools,
Wherever they may stand.
They are the people's colleges,
The bulwarks of the land.
Thus in our songs we will them praise
With loud and joyous glee,
And Yankee Doodle we will raise,
And tell the world we're free.

'Tis a happy theme; like a golden dream its memory seems to be,
And I'll sing while I have voice or tongue—The Common School for me.

This fell the more cordially into a Scottish ear, because of the familiar air, "There's nae luck about the house," to which it was sung with great spirit.

There is a very extensive Temperance Society, which bears the name of their great General as its rallying word. There is practical usefulness, both to the cause of Temperance and that of Patriotism, in teaching the children a strain like the following, which, we need not say, is not introduced because of its poetry, but because of its influence:—

"Through all the wide creation,
This glorious reformation*
Must spread to every nation,
So nobly speeds it on.
Then let the cause speed on.

Let the name of Washington
Be rung through all the land, boys,
Oh, boldly take your stand, boys!
Come join us heart and hand, boys.
Remember Washington.

He bared his noble breast, boys,
To give his country rest, boys,
Because we were oppressed, boys.
Then let the cause speed on.

* Temperance.

Let the name of Washington
Excite each youthful heart, boys,
To act a generous part, boys,
When in the cause you start, boys.
Remember Washington.

If a few heart-stirring rhymes were introduced into those of our schools at home, where the art of singing is practised, they might produce a happy effect in awakening the patriotism, and quickening the loyalty of our juvenile citizens, and worthily supersede "Little Tom Tuck," and his tribe.

What has been said of schools refers chiefly to the City and County of New York, but might be equally said of all the counties and cities in the State. In all the Eastern States, the impulse to furnish education is vigorous.

In Connecticut there is an extensive school property, consisting of Bonds and Mortgages, Bank Stock, Cultivated Lands and Buildings, and Wild Lands, which is portioned out according to the claims and wants of the several counties. The arrangement is probably nearly the same in all the New-England States, and in the other *Free* States. The management varies with the places, but all have schools with libraries attached. Some have Committees to examine and select books, and where no Committee exists, the good people in the district do what they can to form useful libraries, and happily by a common law, positively bad books are excluded from all public libraries.

The United States delights to call itself the Model Republic, and is a fair field for proving the republican form of government. In this world, where perfection is not found, we are often glad to do the best that circumstances admit of, and to yield points for the sake of unanimity, but this exclusion of religious instruction from the common schools is a very great thing to yield. They talk of the purpose of some religious bodies, to erect church schools, and take the superintendence of their own children, and they are very right if better may not be. But a distant spectator, who is ignorant of the adverse power which may arise to prevent a change, should it again be put to the vote, cannot but wish the matter were reconsidered before the most pious of the community withdraw from the present system entirely. If a more decided duty were made of Scripture-reading, if questioning on that, in the same manner as on other reading, were introduced, and if a few passages of the Bible and a few hymns, from the copious collections which exist, were committed to memory, and if a little sacred singing were added to the morning prayer, it would give solidity to the whole fabric, and form a foundation for all the moral lessons which it is the duty of the teachers to inculcate. To expend all the pains on preparation for this short life, and leave an eternity of happiness or misery unthought of, uncared for, is not the act of a truly kind and reasonable government.

A little French pamphlet, entitled "Le Palais de Cristal," contains a few sentences that apply but too well to this subject—they are here translated: "It seems as if all would work without the influences of religion, and without having recourse to its aid. They never call it to help them, and even, they think to do, or to be able to do better without it than with it. They pretend that it has failed of its aim; that it has not succeeded, and they leave it on one side in the positive expectation to accomplish their design. They will not mention it, because they fear in doing so, to introduce a source of quarrels, of divisions, and animosities, as the past has proved, for men have quarrelled and gone to war and strife as much for religion as for politics and other things. No, Jesus Christ and his religion go for nothing in modern plans and projects. The religious amelioration of man is of no moment. The sole object is the temporal, corporeal, material, and a little the intellectual good of man. All belongs to this world, and all is for this world. As if they supposed that man is not immortal nor fallen, and responsible before God. Here, man and his glory are the sovereign, nay, almost the sole object."*

* *Le Palais de Cristal, par le* REV. Z. V. CACHEMAILLE, page 11.

Sabbath Schools.

When the lack of religious instruction in Common Schools is mentioned, pious parents generally advert to Sabbath-schools and try to console themselves with them as a substitute. And so they might, in some degree, were the influence all-pervading, and the attendance steady—and did not the heart require "line upon line and precept upon precept," before the truth sinks into it.

Were all who venture to take charge of classes themselves enlightened Christians, had all the gift of teaching, and all the zeal and love which would induce them to accompany lessons with their prayers,—then one might comprehend how the tender mother who has begun to teach the sweet story of Jesus, and has delighted to hear her little ones lisp hymns in his praise, can venture to resign her office to another. Then one might see the father confide the charge which is given him of God, to a youth who in the common course of things, is not likely to be as experienced a Christian as himself. Then one might hope that mollifying Sabbath influences would subdue young hearts and bring them home to their parents, what they wish them to become.

One cannot but question whether this is the natural result, if the natural guides withdraw entirely from the office of ordering their children well themselves. There is a uniting power, a respectful affection, an elevating sentiment, which if it be awakened at all, is lost by the parent and transferred to the teacher. The years in which the young and helpless draw their support from their parents, are also the years when their sympathies may be interwoven, so as to make a life-long web of mutual help and unfailing concord. Why should this be sacrificed? and a gap made of the intervening time between the nursery lessons and their entering on public life.

It is said, if the well-qualified parents withhold their children from the Sabbath-school, the ill-qualified will not send theirs. If this be so, it must arise from a maistake lying somewhere as to the origin and use of such schools. When Mr. Raikes first assembled a few children in the city of Gloucester, he did not go to the most pious people in the city and ask for their children, that he might instruct them in addition to the little vagabonds of the high-ways and hedges—but he filled his benches with the uncared-for, and his example was quickly followed by thousands.

An unfortunate consequence of children, who might be at least as well trained at home, going out for religious instruction, is, that they are often seated with the school in church; and thus another bond with their own family is not formed. They do not walk to the house of God in company; they are not under the parental eye during the service, and the hoard of remembrances is not treasured up which might come over the heart in after-life, like a breeze from the sweet south, fanning the flame of love, or awakening the drowsy conscience.

There is no more tranquil use of Sabbath morning hours than to enrich the memory with the word of God, and no more social way of passing its evening than in reading and catechizing the domestic circle. In a country where sociality is so lively, and natural buoyancy so excitable, a stamp of domestic tranquillity may be placed on such use of the sacred hours, which may steady the character for life.

No one can suppose, from these remarks, that

Sabbath-teaching in schools is meant to be rejected. To the Christian artisan who is glad of the unwonted delight of an hour for repose and meditation, what a privilege to send his young ones to the care of pious teachers who act under the inspection of his pastor or elders. He is glad that they are better taught than he could teach them, and that they procure from the library books which he could not seek for them, and he prays for a blessing on the teacher and his efforts. While to the children of the ignorant and regardless, the Sabbath-school is a boon of whose worth they are as yet unaware.

It would be a decided advantage if the young people were to remain a year, or even two, longer under instruction than they usually do, so that they might ascend from mere juvenile recitations to the proving of doctrines or the collation of Scriptures, such as the prophecy in one book, and its fulfilment in another; or the conversion of an apostle in one city, and his planting of churches in another.

If a looker-on who confesses not having attended more than a dozen Sabbath-schools in various cities may venture an observation, it would be, that in Scotland more pains is taken to lay in a store of Scriptural knowledge, and give the understanding food which may work upon and guide the conscience, while in America more pains are taken to arouse the conscience and address feeling. If the latter method succeed at present, and a permanent change be wrought, it is well; but should it prove but a momentary flash of feeling which expires, it is not so likely to return, for it has no firm foundation in the mind. The recollection of an emotion is not potent like the return of a Scripture truth, coming with an authority which cannot be gainsayed or resisted.

Many there are who carry a grateful love for their teachers through the church during life, and many young ones who entertain a respect and confidence for their Sunday guides, but still the fear arises that amid the multitude there be young guides who require to be themselves guided, and that the calm consistent walk of their fathers is painfully departed from by some who venture to be Christian instructors. The admonition to the pupils to beware of being "lovers of pleasure more than lovers of God," falls powerless from the lips of a teacher who crowds to juvenile parties and passes evenings in music and dancing. And it is very painful to see loving mothers watching their offspring plunge into a sea of folly, which they do not seem to hope to control, and their turning with a moistened eye and asking, " Ah! do you think they will be drowned?" Who shall solve the question? Prayer may be answered for them—God may in mercy arrest them, and show them, perhaps by a stroke of his chastening rod, that what they pursue is unsatisfying, and leads to dreariness and vanity. At any rate it was not such early occupations that made the parents such advanced Christians, and it is probable that more domestic union in divine teaching, and less herding together in smiling throngs on the Lord's day, might prevent the ardor for and extent of vain social pleasures, over which Christian parents mourn, and from which they forebode evil.

Some small arrangements which might be easily changed seem inconvenient, and pernicious in their consequences. Such as that of laying the " Christian Messenger," or other religious newspapers, in the pews, and distributing the Sabbath library-books to the children just before the service commences. The temptation is great, and is yielded to without reserve, of occupying time previous to the commencement of divine worship in reading and diverting the mind by religious *news*, or so-called religious tales, which might be fitly employed in petitions for the pastor, and for power to unite the heart to fear

God's name. It is very painful to see the paper scarcely thrust aside to make way for the hymn, and the little ones devouring the narrative portion of their book—carefully passing by the "sermonizing"—while the man of God is pouring salutary instruction into their unlistening ears.

The question was gravely put in a Southern city, whether, seeing parents are *indulged* with a portion of worldly matter in the "Presbyterian," "Observer," and "Evangelist," it would not be right to *indulge* the children in the same way in their "Record" or "Messenger." Do you refer to a Sunday or religious paper? was the question in reply. "Yes; of course pious children would pass the news by until Monday." "But you teach them to pray, 'Lead us not into temptation;' would not this method lay a snare before them?" "Those who have any fear will see and shun it." "But those who have not will fall into it, and get the habit of lax employment of sacred time, acquired by means of you who wish to do them good. Believe me, Sir, in Scotland your question would admit of but one answer."

This little colloquy indicates a degree of slightness with respect to the use of sacred time and happy opportunities, which may lead to painful consequences.

Many solid Christian people feel so deeply that the libraries are flooded with trifling and insipid would-be religious stories, full of vague and unsound theology, that the evil must speedily be corrected.

There is a degree of sensibility in the Americans in all matters of taste, which often calls forth admiration, and which mingles with occasions of sorrow as well as of joy. At times perhaps the tasteful might with advantage be restrained, lest it occupy the room of some more precious thing.

One simple example of what is meant, may be exhibited without a breach of delicacy. A gentleman past the meridian of life, with manners and countenance beaming with benevolence, enters a room where he is hailed by the children with loving welcomes. But especially the little girl, who is his pupil, places herself on his knee, and twines her fingers through his half-hoary hair.

The mother, with grateful expression, relates that he is the teacher, and most beloved by all his class, in school and out. The gentleman mentions how many years he has kept a Sabbath-class of children at the age reckoned most liable to distressing deaths, and how he never had a death amongst them, but kept them on till ready to be promoted to a higher class. It was remarked "that this was happy for him, and for parents; yet sometimes the removal of a school-mate by death, impressed the young mortals with a new and important view of the eternal world." "You would not wish for a death, for the purpose of giving the children such a lesson?" inquired the mother. "Surely not; but at the moment I remember a large school, in silence, and many in deep emotion, when the children by their own motion selected a hymn and recited it after the death of one of their number, the effect of which remains with some to this day. The poem began thus:—

> 'Death has been here, and borne away
> A sister from our side.
> Just in the morning of her day,
> As young as we she died.'"

Well, Madam," said the excellent man, with his loving, smiling countenance, "we have not been so many years united, without opportunity to send the lesson of mortality home to the heart. We lost a beloved lady, one of our teachers, some time ago. She was very dear to her own pupils, and they sincerely mourned her; and I led my own little train to the funeral, dressed in white; and when we came up the centre aisle in a double column, they divided and passed up each side of the coffin, and each laid a bunch of roses upon it. They then seated themselves on each side of the wide pulpit stairs, which they nearly filled."

It was easy to say, for it is true, that the scene must have been touching and pretty, but there was a want of fitness. It would have been touching and pretty at a wedding or a baptism. It was not so easy *not* to say, "Were you not sacrificing the solemn to the picturesque, and diverting thought from the judgment throne and the world of glory, on behalf of the merely graceful and beautiful?"

The "Boys' Meeting."

In every crowded community, there is a circle which from profligacy, ignorance, or poverty in the parents, falls below the educational degree; and, if that circle is to be taught at all, it must be led and raised by the hand of Christian benevolence. New York has a crowd of such persons who linger about the docks half employed, because intemperate, not to mention the newly-arrived and desolate-looking emigrants, and is quite as able to furnish out a few "ragged schools" as are the Trongate of Glasgow, and the Cowgate of Edinburgh.

I am not sure, that with the exception of that of Mr. Pease at the Five Points, any such week-day gathering of forlorn creatures has been made. Several Sabbath ragged-schools, however, have been assembled by means of the energy of individual compassion. Intelligent and spirited young Christian men have permeated the throng, and coaxed them within the sound of instruction. By what ingenious devices they influenced the wild little denizens I am not aware—Perhaps by some such as the poor shoemaker, John Pounds, on Plymouth dock used, whose pot of hot potatoes on a cold day used to furnish a bribe by which the boys were drawn within the circle of instruction. The good youths must have had many a fruitless or at least disappointing stroll on the docks, and around Hudson and Greenwich Streets, before they assembled the nucleus of what are now very flourishing schools.

And here we find gathered "the step-children of nature and fortune, the outcast, the benighted, the brutalized, and the homeless." Surely here we shall find Horace Greeley and some of his brave three thousand toiling with might and main to raise the motley crowd to the level of the common school. They *may* be there, but I did not hear of them—well, but the children are assembled. What shall we call them? There's much in a name! Though every knee and elbow testifies that it is a ragged gathering, though every mop-head unconscious of a comb, and many a shirtless neck buttoned round by the collar of a coat big enough for father, proves that they are uncared for, yet "it is not right to have it thus set down."—Ragged school indeed! Which of all those four hundred tatterdemallions would

enter your door, in spite of the temptation of a dry seat and warm stove, if you give it such an opprobrious name. Benevolence is ingenious. It will not be baulked by any obstacle that can be managed, and so to publish itself in the district without offence, it hangs out its cotton placard, on Sundays only, with "THE BOYS' MEETING," in capital letters for guidance to the wanderers.

Here they come pell mell! but a composed person meets them at the door, whispers a calm word or two, admits them one by one, and turns them over to another, who seats them. And now look along the benches. Here are four hundred creatures full of grimace, restlessness, trick, and temper, ready to fly to buffets, if but their neighbors touch them.—A good man with fire in his eye and zeal in his heart, tells them a little of Him who made and preserves, and can destroy or save them, and asks the open-mouthed, unintelligent throng to join him in prayer. He directs an attitude and act quite new to them, and seeing them all down on their knees he closes his own eyes, and addresses a few simple petitions to his reconciled Father in heaven; but when again he looks up what does he find? That the occupants of the front seats, out of sheer ignorance and fun, have crept under the benches, till they have actually reached and stood up at the lower end of the room, laughing at their exploit, and as busy as may be tugging, knocking, and struggling with each other.—Oh! hopeless crew! Shall the good man turn you out, and resign his attempt? By no means. The ingenuity of benevolence is not so soon spent. He tells them if they will replace themselves, he and his friends will sing for them, and if they like it they may learn to sing too. The wondering and diverted mob flows back, and distributes itself once more over the seats. The good man recites twice or thrice the words of a single verse, and he and his associates raise a lively tune. We have all heard what it is that music has charms to soothe. It is wonderful that power. After two or three repetitions of that one verse, one and another takes up the strain, till all the musical ears which happily are always nine tenths of any company, have caught it, and are engaged in following the air. Now he has got them interested—their leader says, "If you will learn the words we will sing it together," and thus is the point of the wedge inserted. Presently it is driven deeper. "Now, if you will be quiet, I will read you a story, and then we will sing our verse again before we part," and so perhaps the "Prodigal Son," or "the man that fell among thieves," is read, and at least a third listen, and the hymn is repeated, the blessing prayed over their neglected heads, and off they go, amused and surprised with the novelty, and chiming the new tune, and newer stanza as they run.

They had been some months under training when I saw them—steady and quiet by help of a little admonition from their teachers, who, it was observable, did not venture to exact much mental effort from them. They sung two or three hymns, answered as many questions, listened with tolerable decency to a passage of Scripture and its explanation, and with lively interest to a narrative which was related in a way that could not fail to fix their minds. They were steady at prayer, and although I could not but observe that the distributor of the singing-books, took a very exact account, lest any should be smuggled away, they were treated kindly and respectfully, and gave kindness and respect in return. There were many clean faces and smooth heads, and even a few tidy suits of clothes, which doubtless owed their origin to "the Boys' Meeting." Some countenances, bright and beaming, turned earnestly to the teachers, and gave promise of springing from the slough where they were found, not only to respectability in society, but to a home beyond the skies, and to the society of just men made perfect. It was delightful to observe hope sustaining the good men through their labor, and the love and energy with which they were borne forward.

I regret not having thought of the story so as to write it in the graphic manner in which it was told. Its outline is this:—A boy who feared not God, nor obeyed his mother, set out to roam with others on a Sabbath afternoon, several years ago—when the spot on which we were now seated was a green field. The field was enclosed by a ragged paling, with here and there an upright plank. On one of these planks was written in chalk, "Remember the Sabbath-day to keep it holy." The boy observed the words. They smote his conscience,—he feared to go on, but was ashamed to tell his companions why he turned back, so he gradually dropt behind and slipt away. The tale went on, how a kind person invited him to go to church, how he afterwards went voluntarily to school—how he was apprenticed, and pleased his master by his truth and industry—and how at last, taking pity on boys who might not see a chalk text on the paling as he had done, he had now become a Sabbath-school teacher. He left the "Boys' Meeting" to draw any inference it pleased, but one might guess the inference was that the person spoken of was their kind teacher himself.

As we entered the door of this meeting, two little fellows who were seated on the steps, were invited by the visitors to go up to school. They replied quite civilly, "So they would if they found it suited." "Nay, now, no fear of its suiting, just come with me." "We will see about it." "What need to wait and see about it, come along now." "We will come if we find it convenient." "But please to go up with me, I am a stranger, you can show me the door." They arose, and one pointing, said, "I would go up if it were necessary, but it is the first door, you can't miss it." The quiet independence of the little chaps was a mark of national character. A Scotch boy would have run away, or said something impudent if he were resolved to refuse. The American had made up his mind, and merely stated it with perfect civility. My curiosity was excited, and by watching I made out their reason. A band of Odd Fellows with all their quaint array of flags, belts, music, and all the profane bustle with which they disturb the Sabbath-day, was expected to return from a funeral. They came presently, and when a rush of boys came into school after the pageant had passed, my resolute acquaintances having seen what they had made up their minds to wait for, "found it convenient" to come up also. Does the superior courtesy of the less cultivated classes arise from the sober certainty that you cannot in fact interfere or constrain them, so that, "I don't feel like doing it," is the quiet reply, instead of the Scotch "what is your business," or, "what need you care whether I do it or not?"

In this meeting we saw the encouraging results of a few months' labor. In another quarter of the city a similar meeting, which had been convened for two years, exhibited a much advanced condition. There were girls and female teachers, as well as boys and males. The hand of industry and kindness was visible. Neat, clean, and cheerful was the pleasant crowd. Many a tunic was there which had been—

"Turned upside down, and outside in,
And made a braw new cotie of."

And many a cap, bonnet, and frock, reminded one of Burns' mother, "wi' her shears, who made auld things look a' maist as guid as new." This order and comfort among the garments is the result of the united contributions and industry of the female teachers, and many a complacent eye ran over a row of little scholars fitted up for the school by means of many hours of labor. It was Christmas-day, so the recitations were rather more of a discursive nature than on the Sabbath, but all of useful tendency. There were interspersed hymns sweetly sung, and passages of Scripture remarkably well recited. The toil of collecting the children, and the responsibilities of teaching them, have for their incentive Christian love alone, seeking neither fee nor reward save that of seeing the children walk in the truth. And when we know, that two years before they were as wild and rough as uncared-for children could be, even the present fruit of the labor was a most pleasing reward.

I understood the female teachers met occasionally to make clothing in concert, while one read aloud —an excellent refreshing sociality, not exercised by fine ladies, who might leave their embroidery to unite in this way—but some who had hastened through domestic cares, to procure the time, and others who had passed the regular number of hours in teaching in the Common Schools.

Sustaining the Sabbath Schools is with many church-members, a duty observed with as much care as any private devotional exercise. On remarking to a zealous teacher that one could hardly hope Senator A. or Governor B. to have leisure from their duties, political and public, to attend still to their class, for they must enjoy the repose of the Sabbath; I felt justly rebuked by the hearty reply, "Why, Madam, don't you believe the teaching hours are nearly the most refreshing hours of the week?" and so it is. Wherever the mollifying power of the religion of Jesus is felt, there flows into the heart with it a spirit of hopeful benevolence, which turns the man into the protector of the feeble, and the elevator of the neglected and debased. Be he Senator, Governor, or City Missionary, his object and his pursuits will, allowing for difference of circumstances, be the same, and none will be found too low to sink beyond his loving effort, none too debased, to pass the line of his faith and hope—as witness Mr. Pease at the Five Points. Its rows of miserable dwellings, whose creaking stairs, broken palings, and rag-stuffed window-panes, sufficiently indicate that honest and cheerful industry have long since fled the precinct, while its dull and besotted, or loud and brazen tenants, render it prudent for a respectable female to seek protection in threading its streets in broad day. Yet there has Christian benevolence raised its hopeful standard, and there have some immortals been lifted from the depths, and entered on the path that leads to peace.]

The process of commencement, as related by the zealous operator, is worthy of a record. He was Missionary of the District, and many a day his heart fainted as he toiled from den to den, and found none to care for his Scripture readings, none to accept his tracts, none to value his prayers. "We are hungry—give us bread—away with your preaching!" "Why don't you work?" One profligate replies, "My eyes are dim." Another, "Me work! if I could do it, who would trust me with it?" "I will, if you will come to me at the room in the corner of C—— Street to-morrow morning." The new idea had entered the man's mind, and his almost electric energy was instantly applied. His room was opened, and the necessary preparations made. A few poor shaken, miserable women dropt in; and poor work they made of it, yet the effort was wholesome. After the day advanced a little, their employer said, "Now, I will pay you for what you have done, that you may go and buy your breakfasts; and if you return and work again, you shall have what will procure your dinners." This went on, and presently little children hung about the door, peeping in at their mothers, and morsels of the purchased meal were shared with them. Immediately the mercurial mind seized another new idea. "Little ones, if you will wash your faces and hands, and smooth your hair, and be as neat as you can, you may come to me to-morrow, and we will begin Infant School," and thus shot forth a new branch from the prolific stem.

By and bye some of the sempstresses fell into their old snare of inebriety, and when searched for by their faithful friend, whose hope seemed imperishable, they told him, if he would lodge and take care of them they would be kept, but they could not escape if they returned at night to their old neighbors. Here sprung forth another branch. With such friends as he could raise, the philanthropist has added room to room, till in the spring of 1851 he had three houses, with communications enabling him and his wife to pass through them all, and locks preventing the passage and too free communication with the inmates.

At his Sabbath-school many parents and other grown people are auditors. He pointed out several who were seated before us, and mentioned to what condition of wretchedness and misery they had sunk. All the cases were very interesting. One we select as an example:—A still strong and rather fair man, whose hair began to exhibit a streak of silver, and whose face recently weather-beaten was now placid and pleasant, and who had the air of a decayed gentleman, was seated near a class, listening eagerly to the instructions of its teacher. He had come to Mr. Pease at night, and begged to be admitted to the Inebriate's Retreat. He was requested to return in the morning, as a test of his being desirous of anything more than a night's shelter. He did return, one sleeve wanting from his coat, shoes that would not stay on his feet, no stockings, or neckcloth, and a miserable glazed cap on his head. Yet withal somewhat of an air and address about the man showed he had lived in other society and seen calmer days. "Where have you been?" "I don't know." "Where do you come from?" "Nowhere." "Why, where is your home?" "I have none." "Where do you sleep?" "Any where." "Tut, man! where did you sleep last night?" "On the steps of the City Hall." "And where the night before?" "On a bench in the Park." "What is it you wish?" "To be taken in here and reformed—I have nothing else between me and death—a miserable, a drunkard's death." He was taken in, bathed, purified, medicated, and, after a few days of repose, he was asked what he could do to maintain himself. He had been once a respectable bookseller in England. His last employment in New York had been the sale of stationery from door to door. He was trusted with a dollar, laid it out in stationery, and returned at night gladly to deposit his earnings with Mr. Pease. When I saw him he continued still in the protection of that retreat. Had paid for all his clothing, and now paid his weekly board regularly, and laid up something with which to begin the world, as soon as he could trust himself out of doors. Clothed and in his right mind, taking an intelligent interest in all the exercises of the school, he was a pleasant sight to see.

At the risk of being thought prosy, I venture to relate the history of another inmate of this Noah's Ark at the Five Points. A stout, burly, red-haired man sat in that school-room with a child on his knee. He had presented himself at the retreat, desolate and wretched, some months before, had gone through the cleansing and cooling process, hired himself out to labor, and brought home his earnings to pay his board. After some time, a woman came in search of him. He had been lost, and she laden with a babe, and a very heavy heart, had sought northward in Boston and southward in Philadelphia, but in vain. At last she traced him, and told her story to

Mr. Pease. He sent for the man, and conversed with him apart. "Are you married?" "Yes." "Where is your wife?" "I don't know." "That is strange—why did you part from her?" "I forsook her when I forsook myself." "And are you content that it should be so?" "*Content!* No." Mr. Pease went out and brought in the child, who trotted across the floor. The man gazed—the little thing could walk—he was uncertain—at last nature's instinct guided him to the truth. "That is my child!" he cried, and snatched him to his bosom. The reconciliation was not difficult to be brought about, and now he supports his family under the wing of Mr. Pease. It was pleasant to see the big man nurse the little one so tenderly till at last it fell asleep, and he resting the head against his broad breast, arose gently and carried it out of the school-room.

In the upper story of that strange wild extempore retreat, I found a Bible-class of women—nearly thirty, two of them from poor old Scotland, all on their knees around a dear Christian lady who regularly passed her Sabbath afternoons amongst them. I also found both the junior and senior Sabbath-schools well filled.

It strikes one used to the close teaching of the

Holy Scriptures and Shorter Catechism, that there was rather too little Scripture and too much hymn-singing. And also, that there is a danger of treating abstinence from drunkenness as if it were the very rock of salvation. However, no stranger, even after a third visit, can judge of the position, and capabilities, and necessities of the people—and taken as a whole, the resolute principle which has assembled upwards of seventy persons, young and old, providing safe lodging for some, work for others, and instruction for a large band of otherwise neglected and forsaken children, is much to be honored, and ought to be sustained, lest the good man faint by the way. On looking back to those dreary and disgusting haunts, the three houses at the corner seem like the leaven hid in the three measures of meal. Would that they might abide there till the whole is leavened.

A young friend went to ascertain the exact position of the school, before he conducted me there. He inquired of a policeman which was the house, and was advised to address some young women standing in the street, who would show it him round the corner. The prudent inquirer hesitated about speaking to women in such a locality, when the policeman said, "A year since I would not have advised you, but you need not fear to speak to them now." A pleasant testimony to the correcting influence already emanating from this Christian establishment.

On last Thanksgiving day, Nov. 27, 1851, seventeen of the hotels in the city provided a dinner of roast beef and turkeys, for the Five Points Mission, which was partaken of first, by the Sunday-scholars, after by the day-scholars, and finally the remnants were sufficient to satisfy a band of "outsiders," who are not regular attendants at the school. The whole numbered 225. They were waited on by their teachers and other gentlemen. They sung "the Happy Land," that never-failing song of children, and afterwards, by way of returning thanks for their food, "From all that dwell below the skies."

It goes right to the heart to see, hear, and feel, the unity of pursuit of our two countries. The same plans—the same motives—the same Bible—nay, even the same hymns lisped by the infants. Is there not much more to unite Great Britain and America than there ever ought to be to divide them?

In America as in Britain, Christian exertion is ever engaged in a race against ignorance and misery

—and ignorance and misery are ever keeping ahead of Christian exertion.

But the runners though beaten, follow on "faint yet pursuing." And though not accomplishing all they hope for, nor the hundredth part of what they see is needed, yet they gain victories, and their hearts are cheered—for when a wreath is plucked from the thronging and flying squadrons, it is a wreath of amaranth—it will bloom in eternity.

Adopted Children.

OBSERVING how easily and frankly children are adopted in the United States, how pleasantly the scheme goes on, and how little of the wormwood of domestic jealousies, or the fretting prickle of neighbor criticisms seems to interfere with it, one is led to inquire why the benevolent practice is so common there, and so rare in England, and also so pleasant there and so difficult here. The *first* reason that presents itself is, that in England we have not an abundance of food and of unoccupied room, but in America it is different, for, according to the burden of a song sung by the colored orphans in their asylum at New York,—

"Uncle Sam* is rich enough
To give us all a farm."

The facility with which enough, and more than enough, is found to satisfy every hungry mouth on

* A quaint name for the United States.

a farm, gives wonderful scope to the benevolent sentiment. Compassion needs but to well up at its spring in the heart, and there is no counter-current of prudence to sweep it away. The wish can be accomplished without a sense of privation, and if the adopted turn out well, it becomes all pure gain, —gain in the exercise of the affections, in the pleasure which always arises from doing a kind thing, and in a fresh hand growing up to aid in their industry. This latter reason, however, is only of weight among the sons of labor, who are quite as ready to adopt a child as the wealthy. In Britain, probably, the *second* impediment is our remnant of feudalism—the right of primogeniture, or the law of inheritance. The "heir at law," be he son, nephew, or cousin ten times removed, feels that the owner holds his property only in trust for himself, and looks with a jealous eye on the emotion of pity that might introduce an interloper to be provided for from the family funds. It is marvellous to observe how many are fettered by the law, and how very many more adopt the fetter of custom produced by the law, and fancy they act in the line of duty when they pass by an opportunity of kindness which they might have gladly embraced, but that the expectant kindred may be displeased.

Even when children are adopted in England, instances are to be seen of reserve among common acquaintances to admit them, and receive them as they would the children of the family.—A piece of injustice, and want of sympathy with a benevolent deed which seems without motive or excuse.

The first examples I saw of this practice of adoption made my heart as full of glad surprise as might be that of the mother in the tribe of Levi, when the Princess of Egypt gathered her babe from the bulrushes, and ordered him to be nursed. To look on a nice curly-headed little thing, whose parents had died of fever, or in crossing the ocean from a far country, tended and cared for, and nestling under a kind arm, unconscious that it was not a mother's, is very charming.—To hear of a childless pair agreeing to go among the orphans, and select one from the asylum, and begin their charge by having it baptized; and to learn that their brother and his wife, who lives near, are so taken with this little one's winning ways, that they are resolved to have their childless home also enlivened, and have taken that orphan's own brother, and are now each and all enjoying their prize, is quite delightful.

The novelty of the plan led me to inquire very carefully as to its results, and the statement was, that if one in a hundred tired or failed to do by the adopted, as they would have done by their own, it was *but* one in the hundred.

In the city of Boston we found two excellent sisters, who not being able to gratify their benevolence by assuming the charge of little ones, had ingeniously discovered a mode of help still more extended.—Carlyle found it an unsolvable problem how to bring the quantity of ready-made shirts and the shirtless together, but these dear ladies have found out a way by which they introduce the friendless to the friendly, and the fatherless to the childless.

Their monthly publication called "The Orphan's Advocate" is interesting, simple, and truthlike. They publish the age, and sex of the children in one column, and the places where children are wanted in another, for example:—

"HOMES FOR CHILDREN.

In *Curtisville* a boy will be adopted ten years old.

In *Leominster*, a girl will be adopted eight years old.

In *Great Barrington*, a girl will be adopted about twelve years old."

The list extends to twenty-six; then comes

"CHILDREN NEEDING HOMES.

A girl five years old.

A boy eleven years old.

A girl two years old.

A boy two years old.

An infant girl four months old; also an infant girl eight months old;" the list extends to twenty-eight.

A paragraph unique in its simplicity and peculiarity we quote as a perfect curiosity in Great Britain; it and the above lists are found in the "Orphan's Advocate," published in Boston, March, 1851.

"WHO WILL FIND THE CHILD.

"Among the many good places for children, we know a superior one for an infant boy twenty months old to fill the vacancy left by the death of an infant of that age in a family of prosperous people. If we mistake not the child should have light eyes and hair; an orphan would be preferred."

The solitary number of the Orphan's Advocate within reach, contains various touching passages; here is a sample:

"INFLUENCE OF CHILDREN.

Many a ray of sunshine has a child shed into a

dark heart. Childhood softens the selfishness of age, and bids the frozen sympathies gush out.—Who has never felt that he had reason to bless children for what they have done for him?

Many orphans owe their happy homes to the influence of other children. We have known instances when a child has persuaded its parents to adopt a little orphan—They have persuaded others to do the same.—They read of the little ones, who need homes, and they seek homes for them."

" CHILDREN'S SYMPATHY FOR ORPHANS.

Children frequently sympathize deeply with orphan children. There are no objects for whom their hearts are so easily or deeply enlisted. We have been frequently told of children who read over regularly the list of children needing homes, in the Orphan's Advocate, and manifest great interest for them."

These excellent Misses Fellowes enlist the services of the benevolent to " search out the children." Besides having ten travelling agents, part male and part female, they urge them not to overlook the poor-houses. " Shall we not," say they, " have our poor-houses emptied of their young inmates? Shall Massachusetts, shall any State in the Union bear upon its brow the curse of young humanity neglected? The older poor can speak for themselves, the younger cannot; but their cry goes up to God, who hears and knows, and who will recompense good or evil to those who search out, or refuse or neglect to search out, the little ones, and see that their wants are supplied." "Applications, especially for young children to be taken by adoption, are becoming daily more numerous." "Our friends will need to be diligent in looking up the destitute little ones, so that there may be a constant supply for those whom this increasing interest shall lead to seek to become foster parents."

I have been assured that the success of this plan is unfailing, and that its benevolent inventors are greatly encouraged to proceed.

One instance of adoption touched me deeply on many accounts. In the graveyard of the first Presbyterian Church in Elizabethtown, the monument is found which tells the dismal story of the deaths of Mr. Caldwell, once pastor of that flock, and of his wife. She was shot, with her babe in her arms, through the window of her own house, by ravening soldiers in search of plunder. He encountered a similar fate more than a year after, when exerting himself like a Christian patriot in the service of his country.

Such deeds have left scars which are calculated to excite national spleen, and such monuments, records so sadly true, aid in fretting and keeping it alive.

Nine children were by these deeds of cold murder left unprotected. After the funeral, the Hon. Elias Boudnot ranged the bereaved offspring around the remains of their father, and with that speaking spectacle before the eyes of a crowd of mourners, asked which of them was going to fulfil the divine promise, that the seed of the righteous shall not be forsaken? which would embrace the opportunity of proving that they valued their patriotic friend and faithful pastor? which would from these forsaken ones rear citizens worthy of their parents? "For my share," said the noble man, "I select this boy for mine, and engage before you, my fellow-citizens, and under the eye of heaven, to rear and train him as my own son, and may our God give his blessing." There was a solemn pause. Many an eye brimful was turned from the dead father to the fatherless little flock. One and another stepped forward and led forth an orphan, till all the nine found parents; and, with the exception of one unsettled character, whose act was that of fleeting emotion, and not of Christian resolution, and who in a short time returned the chosen child to its friends, no one failed of their engagements. Nor did the Father of mercies fail of his; they turned out excellent citizens, who served their country, or who became the mothers of those who serve it now; and nearly—may I not say *all*—came forth in life as real Christians, the petitions which their parents left behind being answered when they had passed by their stormy deaths to the world of eternal peace. And that rejected and returned one was, if I remember right, the very one afterwards chosen by General La Fayette, carried to France, and furnished with the most complete and accomplished education which Parisian skill could offer to sound ability. He returned to do his country signal services in the walks of literature, piety, and philanthropy.

Two of this group of early mourners still survive, one of whom holds an honorable place in the General Post Office at Washington. And it was a Caldwell of the third generation that did me the great kindness to introduce me to President Fillmore.

No plan of charity, when performed in a right spirit, seems more calculated to do good and to receive a blessing, than this. It is a feeble imitation of the manner of the Father of us all; for we, fallen beings, are aliens and parentless until through atoning mercy and converting grace we become the adopted children of our God, and then we are partakers of his love, and heirs of the heavenly inheritance.

Doubtless amid the many, some of the kind purposes are frustrated—some of the parents tire, as in the case of the little Caldwell—and some of the children disappoint and wound, but these cases are the exceptions.

I have seen the parties dwelling harmoniously and helpfully together; and I have seen the adopted, in the old age of the adopter, exercising all the tender cherishing that filial piety could devise. There is a beauty in the pleasing sympathies thus exercised, for there is a blessing on them from on high.

Collegiate Schools.

THOUGH the engagements of past years led me more to concern myself with the education of the working classes, and the friendless, it was impossible to dwell among the cultivated and refined without being desirous of learning somewhat of the plant by which they had been educated.

Most of the Female Institutes seem to be under the guidance of men, or of a man and his wife, when it is understood that most of the solid parts of instruction are conducted by the head of the house. This is a plan not followed in England, and in various cases, when a husband happens to be in existence, he is generally felt to be an incumbrance to the household rather than an assistant. Professors who, it is presumed, are well qualified to teach the one object of their pursuit, attend at stated hours with us. But, judging by advertisements, it would seem that husband and wife teach and manage in unison all over the United States. It is customary to deliver lectures on Astronomy, Botany, Chemistry, &c., to the pupils in both countries, and it is possible that some expansion of mind is thus obtained, even when no real thirst for knowledge induces the pupils to follow up the subjects by private study.

In some of the Female Institutes in America, a plan is pursued which, with the exception of the Normal School students, has not yet been adopted in Britain, within my knowledge. The students "graduate" after strict examination on various branches of learning—a useful and important mark of a certain degree of attainment, the absence of which is often felt with us on occasion of selecting teachers. The graduating is by no means a nominal or slight affair, but is accomplished only on the candidate being able to meet a searching inquiry into her attainments.

Nevertheless, as it happens at home, persons whose previous education and habits have not been calculated to fit them for the office, and whose chief qualification is present misfortune, frequently assume the office of instructors. In consequence it at times occurs that the benevolence of parents interferes with their judgments in the choice of a school; and sometimes a dash of romance or pathos, or elegance of manner, carries the day against substantial attainments and conscientious industrious instruction. One learns in every country to defide "picturesquish" programmes, and to fear the solid instruction of strings of young ladies who are carried about to fashionable lectures and evening concerts.

To have judged by the unsteady attendance at school, and the little solicitude observable among the young people about preparing for their classes, to say nothing of the wilful speeches, such as, "Mama, I don't feel like studying French any more;" or, "Ma, I am going to drop mathematics, they are so tiresome;" one would suppose there are many imperfectly educated women. But meet them grown up, engaged in the useful pursuits of life, and you will find well-informed, cultivated, refined minds, strong in their sense of right and pursuit of duty. Ask them of their early years and you will find they were nearly as idle as their children seem to be, and then you must draw the conclusion that their wilfulness is only seeming or vanquished while it is yet time, and that they acquire as much amid their springy, vivid ways as we do in our more sedate and careful fashion.

The means of education extend continually with the need of it. Yet as food, shelter, and clothing form the most imperative necessaries of life, each new settlement must first secure these, leaving the mental and spiritual supplies to lag behind, and overtake these as they best may. Taking pity on the uninstructed condition of the settlers around them, some young gentlemen have begun to give an hour or two of evening teaching to their young neighbors. Some have employed themselves during the winter months in that benevolent exercise. Some have collected Sabbath-schools, and in a few cases, the log school-house has formed the nucleus of a church, where, at last when the population thickens, a church is erected, a minister of Christ appears, and next comes the colporteur with his load of good books, and a library is formed. How sound is the patriotism, how true the benevolence which, amidst the earnest pursuits of present advantage, step aside from the tumult and the cares of life to enter on such engagements as these ! And how happy the man who falls on that era of his new district's cultivation which enables him to be the founder of useful institutions, which will continue to bless the land when he is resting from his labors ! His stock-in-trade for this kind of usefulness need not be brilliancy of genius, nor high attainment, but simply common sense, with some power of arrangement, and a heart to love his neighbor.

It is not for me to tell of college halls and professors. The names of the first, and the faces or writings of many of the others, are familiar to students in Britain, yet it is pleasant to recall the shades of Yale, the more than half venerable aspect of a portion of its numerous edifices—the extent and excellent order of its museum—the countenances of learned men, and their portraits in its picture gallery, and the interest excited by the living men who study and walk its academic groves. The hours passed at Princeton also, amid the courtesies and hospitalities of the venerable Dr. Alexander, are amongst the hoarded gems of memory.—A powerful interest hangs around that aged man so true of heart, so distinct of mind, so affable of manner. He is full of Christian sympathies, and ready to communicate, so that you require but to put an inquiry and he flows out whether the subject be a thing of sixty years since or of yesterday, and it is your own fault if you are not the wiser for his communings. Perhaps others may have remarked, what added much to the interest that cleaves to the demeanor of this excellent gentleman—his strong resemblance to Wilberforce. Though much more bulky, yet the figure is like that of a twin-brother.—His manner of sitting in his easy chair, of speaking, of smiling, and above all his ready way of giving information, and his edifying Christian remarks, showed a resemblance both in the mould and in the jewel within.*

Princeton! with its troops of busy students, with its historical memorials of battles, showing still with pride the frame, now encircling a portrait of Washington, but once occupied by a portrait of George II., which was hit by a cannon-ball in the hall where it hung.—Princeton, with its lecture-rooms, and libraries, and above all, with its row of monuments, over the tombs of departed presidents,

* How touchingly are those remembrances deepened in pathos by the tidings just arrived, that the Patriarch is with Abraham and Moses, and all the prophets, in glory. It is true he has reached the consummation of his faith and hope, but then his family have lost him—his students have lost him. Princeton will see his face no more. The church will never again appeal to his wisdom and experience. America must number him with her patriots, and heroes, and divines, who have departed—and I a passing stranger, while I prize the more the privilege of having seen him, feel .but the more keenly, that the anticipated "passing away," has begun. One leaves a country where admiration, respect, and love have been awakened, with the conviction that we shall see the faces of most of these estimable persons no more; and that while one's own life lasts, the tidings will come ever and anon, that one and another has entered into rest, and left ourselves and the world the poorer.

amongst whom lie Witherspoon and Edwards.—Princeton seems to surpass most spots in that young country in its claims to classic veneration. It is a gratification not to be forgotten, to have seen and heard the dwellers there, and to have trodden their familiar pathways; but they have been described many times already.

Colleges multiply rapidly, and seem pretty fairly dispersed over the face of the country. In 1800 there were only twenty-five. Drs. Reed and Matheson, in 1835, found ninety-six colleges, and nine thousand and thirty-two students. Dr. Baird, in 1851, stated before the Evangelical Alliance, in London, that the number of colleges in the United States amounted to one hundred and twenty. That these suffice for the wants of so wide a dominion, or that they are all equally sound in principle, or successful in teaching, cannot be said; yet the zeal and energy which has raised so many seminaries of learning, some even in districts which are scarcely cleared of the forest, and where the raising of bread requires the first effort, proves that some members of the community feel keenly the intellectual and spiritual wants of the country. It is also very striking to observe, that however little it was impressed on the minds of some founders of these seminaries, that they ought to be vehicles for conveying Christian views to their alumni, yet nearly the whole of them have so far yielded to the principles which touch conscience and control thought, as to accept of religious teaching.

It has been remarked, that of the three colleges whose founders openly repudiated revealed truth and Christian principle from their scheme, two of them have already been glad to adopt the opinions they have contemned, as the only method by which they could rule their students, and guide their professors. Shut their eyes as they may against the sight of the divine economy which is established for the restoration of an apostate world, yet they are made to feel the powers of the world to come, and the workings of a spiritual kingdom within and around them which they cannot shake off. Cooper's College, in South Carolina, and Jefferson's, in Virginia, are of those marked with the stigma of "no religion," yet they have been gradually led to admit religious Professors as their teachers, and have thereby found good order and peace much promoted.

It was very pleasing, in looking over the long rows of orphan boys in the Girard College, at Philadelphia, to know that the purpose of the man who left his gold (for he could carry nothing away with him) for their benefit, had been so far frustrated.

His very magnificent marble halls, which, according to his last will and testament, are not, on any pretence whatever, to be polluted by the footstep of a Minister of the Gospel, were in the first instance placed under the control of an excellent lawyer who resigned his seat on the bench, that he might bring Christian verities before those orphans. It is pleasant to think of that holy man's exertions, of his reading the word of God, and of his prayers in those noble halls where it was designed they should be prohibited,—of his regular family worship there, and his oral instruction of those lively and promising young people—and now, though circumstances have led to his resignation of that onerous position, his commencement has left an influence behind him stronger than that of him who held and who bequeathed the gold.

There is something in the soul of man, be it superstition if you will, that readily adopts an impression of interference from the invisible world in the case of any daring transgressor. People, to this day, shake the head and tell gravely or fearfully how Grierson of Lagg, the bloody persecutor of the Dumfrieshire and Galloway covenanters, could not get carried to his grave—how the hearse three times broke down, and how the people trembled at the token, and could not be prevailed on to touch it. It may have been a similar connection with the recollection of poor Girard's ostentatious working of his garden in sight of church-goers—the Sabbath being the only day of the week on which he assumed the hoe and rake—that produced this curious paragraph from the Philadelphia correspondent of the New York Tribune: "On the night that the remains of Stephen Girard were disinterred and conveyed to the undertaker's residence, previous to being deposited in Girard College, the coffin was to be opened in the presence of several persons. As they were about removing the lid, a slight explosion was heard and combustible gas escaped from the inner case. No damage resulted, however, except a slight scorching of the coffin-lid. It is not known whether the fear of ghosts had anything to do with it, but it is certain that the occurrence caused the room to be vacated in the shortest possible time!"

It is earnestly to be desired, whatever may have been the designs of the founders, that all such institutions may be overruled to train up citizens to fear God and hate evil.

It has been well for America, and its effects are visible on her educational institutions up to this hour, that her "world's gray Fathers" were not adventurers in search of wealth, but men of wisdom in search of liberty of conscience. In the earliest settlement of the New England Colonies, laws were enacted by which all townships were obliged to secure education to their young members. In cases where no government aid, or contribution from the mother country could be obtained, individual zeal and learning have wrestled with difficulty in a manner alike surprising and honorable.

Dr. A. Alexander's history of the "Log College," which the senior William Tennant commenced during his ministry at Neshaming, N. J., gives a lively view of what may be accomplished single-handed; and the galaxy of holy pastors who issued from that humble edifice to bless the land, and to co-operate with Whitefield in his life-bringing labors, was an enlightening to the State, and a rich reward to the founder. The "Log College," like its founder, has passed away, and given place to grander buildings and more dignified staffs of professors; but the mark of its vital piety, which shook the dead ministers and the formal worshippers from their sloth, remains and continues to descend to the present generation.

Some Colleges are founded and sustained *entirely*

by particular denominations—such as Princeton, which is Presbyterian; New Brunswick, which is Dutch Reformed. Others derive some aid from the State; for example, Cambridge at Boston, and Yale at New Haven, which are both congregational in government; but I fear Cambridge is Unitarian in faith.

States often found Universities; as in Virginia, North and South Carolina, Vermont, Michigan, &c. &c. But the State Institutions are not always found to be the best, and often meet with difficulties in the management. The General Government grants lands to the new States for Colleges and Common Schools, so that they are provided with the means of instruction from their commencement, though to arrange the machinery, and to set it agoing, often requires an impulse from intelligent benevolence.

An experiment has been tried in a few of the Western Establishments, which is thought by those most conversant with them, to work prosperously—the combination of manual labor with study; giving three hours a day to printing, cabinet work, or farming. Lane Seminary, near Cincinnati, which could receive a hundred young men, is the scene where this novel plan seems to have most prospered. But in Illinois, Indiana, and New York, plans nearly similar are pursued, but with vaaying success. Many reasons concur to make this a most suitable plan in a certain condition of society, especially for preparing missionaries and ministers for new and rough settlements. The very great majority of those to whom the gospel is to be preached, are not persons of refined manners, but such as earn their daily bread by daily toil. When a young man of good natural powers amongst them comes under strong religious impressions, and desires to become a teacher of his brethren, on the old plan of *all study* he is exposed to loss of health by a complete overturn of his early habits, and is probably by his new pursuit reduced to a state of dependence; whereas, on the manual labor plan, he secures three hours of exercise, and nearly, if not entirely, supports himself. His hours of study will be all the more vigorous, that his hours of relaxation have been usefully employed; and his manners, he being a Christian, will not be in any degree roughened by such an engagement. If some of our own students had such means of aiding themselves, we should not have so many enter their ministerial lives enfeebled by unrelaxed, and perhaps poorly fed years of study; neither would they enter on their rustic charges less honored, or less suited to encounter country hardships.

On Long Island I met with a Missionary whose scene of toil had been for some years among the new settlers in Ohio. He talked of going from one preaching station to another on foot, leaping from one knob of solid ground to another in a morass, and of being wet through when he reached his post, with no prospect of dry raiment, except as the wet steamed up from his person before a huge fire. And when he asked if he could have some hot tea, the mistress disappeared in the wood, and presently returned with a lapful of herbs, which she infused in boiling water and gave him to drink. Her husband not having got home from the distant mill, she could not make him a cake; and indeed the shrunk, bald old man might have been painted for Shakspeare's starving apothecary. Had his years of preparation been passed in the luxuries of College halls, he would have endured this very hard life much worse than he did. He spoke of having rejoiced to find a nook beside the blazing hearth of two active young men who welcomed him and his message, the description of whose *menage* is strange to those unused to the hardships encountered during the first season by settlers in the "Far West." Their large log dwelling had two doors opposed to each other near the end where was the fire-place. When they wished to replenish their wide hearth, they felled and stript a tree of its branches and yoked a horse to it, which drew it to the proper centre of the fire-place, where the chain was taken off, and it was left to be consumed at leisure with the help of its lopped branches, the horse making his way out by the other door!

Some of the Home Missionaries endure equal privations and hardships with those who expose themselves on foreign shores and in savage islands, without the éclat and sympathy which accompany the foreign missionary, and without being so well provided for. Here was a specimen. One could not but look with reverence on the hoary-headed and weather-beaten man whose heart, full of the invisible treasure, could not rest unless he might, by many a toilsome effort, convey that treasure to the ignorant and famishing.

But while a nation extended and varied as America is, has much use for manual labor Students, and while these are as well read in divinity, and, having the first grand essential of being themselves regenerated men—as competent teachers as others, it does not prevent those who have means and appliances from embracing a more extended range of study, or from exercising architectural taste and raising beautiful buildings at many of their seats of learning. Of these, the most beautiful—one wing of which is not yet finished—is the Smithsonian Institution at Washington. It has been erected by the bequeathed wealth of Mr. Smithson, an Englishman, whose generous wish was to place a magnificent library, museum, gallery of paintings, geographical and chemical apparatus, together with a noble lecture-room within reach of the statesmen of the great Republic. The gold of the edifice is English, but the art American. Two chambers which are finished and occupied, are said to be in the style of the Escurial, and are handsome and perfect in their beauty. Mr. James Renwick, the rising architect, calls the order pure Norman; it does certainly, not come within any of the old Greek orders of architecture, and if Norman be its name it is very fine. The rich mellow lilac-brown of the stone, contrasting finely with the noble gray base and white superstructure of the Capitol and the rather weather-stained marble of the Post Office and the White House.

The Professors in all Colleges are appointed by trustees, whether they be endowed by their States or by private benevolence, and scholarships are frequent, as they are at Oxford or Cambridge, and as bursaries are in Scotland. They are usually the result of private and Christian munificence.

It would seem that all the world over, study and learning do not form the path to wealth, and those who wish to encourage learning and literature must give of their abundance to fill the student's lamp, and to cheer him in his pursuit, which, while it possesses hidden delights, scarcely furnishes the necessaries of life.

The Churches.

Amongst the many errors which are corrected by closer intercourse with the citizens of the United States, one of the most prominent is the general impression received in England of their tendency to boasting. Their high animal spirits which induce them to express the very same self-approving sentiments which we may entertain, although we prudently keep them secret;—their lively emotions, whether of patriotism, friendship, or domestic affection, which are played on as the bosom of a lake is played on by zephyr, while ours are deep and still except when moved to strong and resolute expression;—their sanguine temperament so buoyant and hopeful;—these give birth to utterances which may occasionally wear the air of boasting, but examine them narrowly and you will find it is not so. The gasconading which derives its name from Gascony, is the true bragging. It tells grand tales of what it has done, and to magnify itself, paints, magnifies, or *makes* the self-glorifying story rather than do without it. The American so-called *boasting*, arises from a natural sensibility to successes. It is the joy of victory, the triumph of achieved independence. It has warmed the heart before it flowed out from the tongue.

When a sprightly, polite, benevolent young guide, to whose courtesies we owed much in exploring the city of Boston and its beautiful environs, rushed forth in a tide of exultation as he pointed out the fine monument to those patriots who perished in the battle of Bunker's Hill;—when he related how the English army had made the song and air of "Yankee Doodle," and were used to cast it forth in scorn against the unregimentalled patriots, who fought not for pay but for independence;—when he cracked his whip in triumph as he told that when the invaders were routed, the American band took up the strain and marched to possess themselves of the enemy's forsaken posts, to the mocking tune of Yankee Doodle, and concluded with, "That is how the tune has been adopted as our national quick-step ever since." Could any one that had a heart see and hear him, and apply to his emotions such a term as *boasting?* Nay, it was impossible even to remind him that we belonged to the discomfited side, or to feel anything but sympathy with his gladness.

Yet it is not joy in the past, it is expectation for the future, to which the accusation of boasting is chiefly applied. Their position is progressive, their circumstances are encouraging, and HOPE is the master passion of the whole nation. They seem incapable of entertaining a desponding or alarmed view of any circumstance. When the fate of the fine "Atlantic" steamer was for so many anxious weeks veiled from the deeply interested multitude, it was amazing to hear people, in the face of all manner of probable misfortunes, express conviction that the good ship and her people, and even her cargo, were all safe. If some of those who profess faith in "*clairvoyance*," consulted a modern witch of Endor on the subject, and the oracle was favorable, it was handed about with great cheerfulness. If, however, she saw a wreck on the African coast, or a ship burned to the water's edge, and three forlorn men, one of them of huge proportions, and still undaunted bearing, preparing a slip of paper to be sealed up in a bottle; the consulters turned off in disdain denying the witch's skill. They *hoped* then, hoped on, hope always. And thus, when they speak of their country, the mind rushes on to distant lakes and populations, and prairies, and future ages, and instead of being bounded by the great things already achieved, they tell of what they *shall* achieve. We say they prophesy,—we ought to say they hope. We say they boast!—we ought still to say they hope. It seems easier to extinguish in them the torch of life, than that of hope.

To this great principle in the Christian community does the church owe much of its vigorous effort at extension. Hope animates to energetic endeavor and vivid exertion. The faithful advance courageously, feeling that the deep and permanent wants of the human heart meet their efforts, and that the high objects which they present, have power alike to arrest and influence the aged and the little one.

The emblem of the Church of Scotland, endeared to us by years of oppression and persecution, during which its fitness has been verified, is the "bush burning, yet not consumed." The Motto of the Church in the United States might fitly be, "We are saved by hope." Its whole existence is a history of the pulsations of hope, urging onward to more extended effort, and more strenuous exertion. It is not of its nature to say, "This city is so crowded, that we must leave it alone, we can make no impression on it." On the contrary, a church that is awake and alive will observe, "Here is a district beyond us, filling up with a population who have no religious ordinances; let us draft off two of our elders, and a few of our influential Christian families—let the people be visited and invited to a prayer-meeting in a convenient place—let us offer them the means—let us set them the example—let us set about it *now* with prayer for the influences of the Holy Spirit.—Does the pastor quail under the separation from some of his steadfast people? Does he say, How can I do without you? How can I spare so many pillars and props from my spiritual edifice? Nay, he says, "Go my friends, it is a Christian enterprise, it is our Master's work. I will lend you help as time and strength may serve, and we all shall follow you with our prayers." So armed and encouraged they go. The nucleus gathers around it a few of the sober-minded inhabitants of the new district. The success of the enterprise becomes interesting to them, as well as to those who came there and opened the scheme. In a year they have filled the district school-house, and have regular worship. In two years they have erected a becoming edifice, and got a pastor settled, and all the influences of a well-worked Christian system are brought to bear on the neighborhood.

Here it is a city population that is spoken of, but, allowing for the difference of a fewer and more scattered people,—the process in the country is nearly similar, reminding us of the manner in which a bulbous root propagates itself, swelling and pushing out fresh bulbs on either side. This method of church extension is employed by the various bodies of Presbyterians. The Methodists and Baptists, whose communion rolls are numerically stronger, use similar methods. They are not equal in influence and steadfastness to the Presbyterians if we embrace under that name all the fragments which rest on the presbyterian foundation. The colored population are more generally united with the Baptist and Methodist bodies—and their status in American Society and degree of intellectual cultivation, necessarily place them in a lower grade with regard to influence; so that though the Baptists have nine thousand and eighteen churches, and the Presbyterians only five thousand six hundred and seventy-two, yet the latter are the more powerful body.

The Episcopal Church, which the English would expect to be first and greatest, has only one thousand five hundred and sixty churches and twenty-eight bishops. It loses much in a country constituted like the United States, by its habit of standing aloof from other denominations, and fails in the more expanded exercise of Christian love which would be called into play if it were substituted for the cold formal exclusiveness in which the majority of the congregations encase themselves.

One is at a loss to explain the sectarian trammels in which episcopacy seems in all countries entangled. Not the high church party alone; the tractarians or Puseyites, as we should call them. Their notions of apostolic succession, and baptismal regeneration, account for their exclusiveness; but the low church party, holy, zealous, and faithful though they be, seem not to assimilate cordially with other denominations. In England we impute this chill reserve to their ideas of the dignity becoming an established church, and to an idea that all dissent from it is schism from Christ; but in America it must arise from some other cause. It is not apostolical succession, neither is it baptismal regeneration, for the low church party do not hold such dogmas. Is it then the damping effect of forms of prayer? One feels much disposed to come to that conclusion for want of another, and then to reason upon it as an effect to be expected. What spirit can escape weariness under repetitions that must become monotonous. Or, when prayers are requested for a sick member, how can a heart surcharged with emotion, fail to feel *that* a slender parenthesis to aid the importunity of an anxious spirit, which is limited to the "all sick persons, *especially that one for whom our prayers are desired.*" And one cannot understand how such another poor "specially" can serve for the outpouring of a request for "those who travel by land or by water,"—if it be the missionary, or the emigrant, or the one beloved member travelling away from a weeping family, without damping or deadening the sentiment.

The Liturgy has been altered and much improved in America, without exhibiting any of those alarming results which seem to be anticipated in England when a proposal to modify or in any way to interfere with it is made. It might be a fabric of straw on cards, so great is the alarm felt on that subject. Is not the alarm a superstition? And if the substantial Scripture truths of the Liturgy have suffered no injury by abridgment and verbal alteration in America, why should they suffer elsewhere, if managed with equal judgment; for example, the Lord's Prayer is recited once during morning and once during evening service, instead of four or five times as it is on communion occasions in England;

and the "Gloria Patri" is repeated but once, that is after the last psalm for the day, instead of as many times as there are psalms read. The verbal alterations are numerous and judicious, as well as the correction of all the ungrammatical phrases which we, from long custom, scarcely perceive to be there.

Upon the whole, though the service has been much improved, the disadvantage of being confined to one set form of words still remains. Petitions can never be adapted to the subject pressed on the soul in the sermon. May it not, therefore, check the effect of a preached gospel, and place the mind in the attitude of feeling, that all that is required of it has been done, when a certain form of words has been repeated? This, surely, more than the external government of the Episcopal Church, is the damper which impedes the flame of love and zeal, and reduces even the good and faithful to a chilly level; a level which has no power to vary with the ever-varying circumstances and states of advancement of the people, and which, therefore, may pluck backward the aspiring spirit when it aims at a closer union with Christ, and a more uniform indwelling of the Holy Spirit. That this is the experience of some of her most zealous pastors, may be inferred from the fact, that in week-day lectures, when they have escaped from the "consecrated" edifice, they are apt to employ extempore prayer.

Notwithstanding these anti-form-of-prayer remarks, which may excite displeasure in minds that are often refreshed by the use of the Liturgy, let it be understood, that the Episcopal Church in America is enriched by some men who are not surpassed in holy zeal and ability by the men of any other denomination, and that the feeble soul who may be thought thus rudely or ignorantly to interfere with their ark has many times found refreshment within it.

It appears as if the confusion of sects, which is ever found where many minds are interested in divine truth, resembles the confusion of tongues, impeding the work it designs to promote, and exciting displeasure and disappointment, where it ought to cheer and harmonize. But in spite of all impediments, there is a spiritual kingdom in this evil world, and it makes progress in a wonderful manner in the very heart of obstacles.

The world is exceeding worldly,—yet the spiritual kingdom rushes into it and plucks forth victims who seemed beyond the hope of rescue. The enemy is exceeding treacherous,—but there are unseen guards over the newly-formed subjects, who prevent and preserve them in their allegiance. The gainsayers are full of contempt and mocking, but the feeble are made strong, and taught to stand forth with courage as subjects of the Spiritual Kingdom, and as advocates to enlist others under the Lord's Banner.—"We are saved by HOPE." Well may the Church in any land say so,—but how peculiarly may it be said where the man of sharp speculation, of far-seeing enterprise, or of keen politics, is withdrawn from these which were his first objects, and by a power which is hid from the wondering worldling, is fixed on an entirely new pursuit, which he professes as openly and follows with as much energy as ever he did his old ones.

The frankness and cordiality of the American religious professor is a great gain to him. He confides himself to the sympathies and prayers and all the sweet influences of Christian intercourse, while we in Scotland tremble and shrink, and carefully turn the bushel over our little candle, till its light is well nigh expiring for want of air. They commit themselves to a consistent walk, for they empower all lookers-on to say whether their conduct consists with their profession or not, while we sneak along, and are barely suspected to be perhaps Christians. What is there more honoring to God, or silently admonitory to the worldly, than the Christian life shining as a light in the world. Even Wall-street raised its head from its money calculations, and said, "Brewster dead! Ah, then he is in heaven!"

That faithful man had, for more than twenty years, filled honorably his place in the Church, and met his death hastily by an accident. This, the world's unpremeditated testimony to his consistency, showed that he had been as a "city set upon a hill," and had been observed by the careless.

Such a life is full of light, and such are the men who are sustained for service by hope, and who infuse hope into the bosoms of others. They press on, and exert themselves, for they are "saved by Hope." This strong power of *hope* may, in some degree, affect the settledness of pastors as well as others. It is not very rare to find a minister resting for a year or two from the charge of a flock, and occupied in other—sometimes even in secular—engagements.

When an enterprise is on hand, they are not used to regard any man as a fixture not to be spared from his present station. They draught him off to take charge of a publication, or colportage, or new missionary scheme, feeling that their best men are most in their place in any new and important work.

By such means they fill the eye of the public, and give an impulse that has a powerful effect, on their first movement in any new scheme.

Preaching, though alike in its aims and objects, differs considerably in its method in Scotland and the United States. We are doctrinal—they experimental. We refer continually to Scripture for proof—they found on Scripture, but treat the hearers as if they knew the proof. We are solemn and objurgatory—they solemn and entreating. We draw our illustrations from Scripture, and from past ages—they, without compromising the dignity of the chair, gather illustrations from the events of the time. We feel it a duty to be textual, and often to explain the connection between text and context—they frequently use a text but as a motto, or catch a collateral idea from it, and treat that with great spirit, as if it were the real subject indicated.

One sometimes longed for more bibles in the pews, and more calls to refer to them. It is true the hearers are quick of apprehension, but they might be the better of having the scriptural foundation fixed more clearly in their minds. The more quick and impulsive, the more need of solid instruction. They see the thing, but they do not want to dwell on it. One feels as if "Hall's Contemplations," or Meikle's

"Solitude Sweetened," could not have been meditated by American minds. What a spring would be made in the divine life if more of the contemplative, meditative, self-acquainting, and God-acquainting spirit were cultivated by a people so lively and ardent. The preachers who cultivate these may lack something in early popularity, but will gain in permanent weight and usefulness. While with regard to Scotch preaching the remark may with equal propriety be reversed.

Good specimens of the "motto" text were given by two of the excellent preachers who took share in the New York winter course of "Sermons to Young Men." Dr. Cheever's was, "Son remember;" and Dr. Tyng's, "Run, speak to this young man." By this choice they were left at liberty to "remember" or to "speak" anything, and they used their freedom skilfully and usefully. Yet, when a few weeks after a religious newspaper mentioned that one hearer had ever since had a sound in his ears of, "Run, speak to this young man" following him wherever he went, one felt a wish that the text so fixed had been some thing more definite and instructive—to say nothing of the hasty impulse which had published such an incident. It was true the young man was haunted by a sound, but was he thereby converted? or was the result certain to be sound conversion? If he were, was it prudent thus to hasten before the public? Very likely the avidity of Editors for news, is one reason why the people seem such a "hasty nation," while the judicious disapprove this haste. This young man's spirit of a sound that haunted him, reminds me strongly of a letter from a valued friend, written in the heat and glory of the "Great Unknown's writing the "Tales of My Landlord." The letter ran thus: "Sir Walter Scott told me that he must give utterance to a foolish rhyme that has haunted him for days, hoping thereby to get rid of it. He then recited with great force—

'Cuckoldy moy, my boy, my boy,
What shall I do to give thee joy?'

The words are too absurd, but they in my turn haunt me in bed and out of it, at work or at play, and I now write them to you instead of uttering them, hoping thus to escape from them without inoculating you." This idle tale is not designed to mock at the sound which might prove the forerunner of a salutary change in the young man, but to suggest the imprudence of making a paragraph about it in the Newspaper.

People talk in England of the "aristocracy of

wealth" in the United States. It is true that in a land so open to all manner of enterprise, the acquisition of wealth gives a man influence, not only as its holder, but as the man of skill who obtained it. They who speak thus, however, have set their mark of aristocracy at a grovelling level. There is an aristocracy of moral worth and consistent piety, and an aristocracy of scientific and philosophical knowledge, within whose circle the "aristocracy of wealth," without these higher attributes, can find no standing. The faithful and consistent Pastor becomes *the man* of his circle. His influence is felt in his city and in his State. His presence renders a public meeting more respectable than that of ten men of mere wealth. His influence as a chairman will be of more weight than that of a "real live Lord" in England, while he will escape those complimentary flatteries which our intelligent aristocracy endure as best they may, and estimate at their true emptiness.

If a clergyman speaks at a public meeting he is sure of attentive listening. His Thanksgiving Sermon gives the tone to his people for the year. His inaugural address, or popular lecture, is expected before it is delivered, and discussed after.

Even amongst the very worldly there does not seem such an absence of the religious element as in

Britain. Religion is not a proscribed topic. All treat it as a real thing, and admit the claims of their own souls. The gay, the giddy, and the neglectful seem aware that they must undergo a change before they can enter the kingdom. This may be imputed to the experimental style of pulpit address. We state the principle, and leave it to produce its effect; they draw the inference from the principle, and dwell on it in such a manner as to arrest those who would not dwell long enough on the subject to draw it for themselves. The solemn deep tone from a pulpit in Hartford often still awakens an echo in the cells of memory, "Hear me! sinner, hear me!" and convinces me that there is a moral power far overmastering that of wealth, which rests at the root of American society.

The Prayer-meeting.

There are, it may be, "so many voices in the world, and none of them are without signification." The lion roareth in the forest because he hath no prey, and the young eagles seek their meat from God. Each voice is intelligible to the ear of the Creator, but the most welcome must be the voice of petition from his children, conveyed through the ever-welcome Intercessor. How simple are the words, "Ask and ye shall receive." Every child understands, and acts upon them daily, in reference to its earthly parents. Yet how difficult for the heart to adopt and act upon them with perfect simplicity in reference to our Father in Heaven. It is a great thing to say, "I sought the Lord, and he heard me," or to point to an afflicted neighbor and say, "This poor man cried, and the Lord heard him and saved him out of all his trouble;" but this ought to be, and might be, the experience of every praying heart, were it not for lurking unbelief.

In some of our Scottish prayer-meetings I have felt a degree of distraction of purpose, and want of defined object, which seemed to eat the soul out of the petition. Perhaps an address on some passage of Scripture diverted the mind of the leader, so that the object of the meeting seemed rather to be instruction than petition; and thus a multitude of vague confessions and requests which did not fix the heart, destroyed the idea of a union for prayer. It is true our wants are numerous and varied, and each petition might be suited to the necessities of some one; but the mind gathers strength by fixing on some special subject, and avoid distraction by grasping at no more than it is able to embrace at once.

We cannot forget the solemn meetings of two or three brethren at once to plead for direction, or the mighty outpourings of some hundreds so frequent before the wrench was made which severed the Free Church of Scotland from the Church of its habitual attachment. We were in earnest then, and knew distinctly what we wanted, and that put life into our petitions. And so it is ever. Defined wants produce defined prayers.

I have attended many prayer-meetings in the United States, and been refreshed by the ready outpouring of heart of elders in various churches. At times the home sensibilities have received a lively touch, by hearing the tones and method of approach of a father from Scotland; differing from his brethren in style, yet the same in aim, for there are "many kinds of voices in the world, but none of them are without signification," and all are intelligible to the ear of mercy.

The association for prayer, of which I wish to give a minute detail without the help of anything except the strong impression on memory, was held in the city of Boston, in the lecture-room of the Old South Church.

That "Old South"—hallowed as the only lighthouse, which at one period held up the true lamp of salvation to that city. The "Old South"—where so many pilgrims have been guided, and so many new-born souls have made their first dedication to Christ. My heart was glad, when a lady to whom I carried a letter of introduction, told me of her morning engagement, and most kindly offered to introduce us to that little quiet assembly.

Eight was the hour of meeting, and three quarters of an hour the time allowed, as the numerous merchants and clerks who were present must be in their offices at nine. More than once we enjoyed the privilege of attending, but it is the incidents of one morning which are presented as a specimen of true simplicity, and mingling of sympathy. The gentleman who occupied the chair was a layman, who we heard was then only present for the second time. He selected for singing two or three stanzas of a hymn, and then prayed with fervor and fluency for the great and leading objects of this meeting, viz.: the renewing and refreshing influences of the Holy Spirit on the churches in Boston, and on the city in general. He then read a portion of a chapter in the Acts. At the close of reading, he made some sensible remarks on the minute guidings of Providence, which we often follow without perceiving them, in consequence of our unwatchfulness; and which when perceived, can never be neglected with impunity. His reason for choosing the passage he had read, was that he awoke that morning with the last verses on his mind; and that some thirty, or it might be forty years, since when in the city of Portland, he heard the sermon on those verses which was the means of awakening spiritual life in him. He had not heard the clergyman before or since, nor seen him with his bodily eye again till this morning, but had good reason to remember him and the time with gratitude. He then stated as another reason for addressing them, that he had good news in which all would rejoice. He had heard a report four months since of the conversion of an eminent lawyer of that same city; but when he considered that the man was a keen politician, occupied in party warfare, writing pamphlets on his favorite questions, and mingled up with all the elections, he dared not credit the good news and had kept silence. Now, however, he could on undoubted authority, invite the sympathetic congratulations of the meeting on the sound conversion to God of Mr. John ——, whose standing in society, whose noble mental powers, and whose extensive interest were now all enlisted in the cause nearest our hearts. You should have felt the sentiment that throbbed from breast to breast as the true-hearted man sat down. There was no articulate sound, but the tear drawn quietly from the cheek, the little movement like the rustling among the leaves in autumn indicating that the breeze is there, and then the long breath like an exhalation of thanksgiving, betrayed the universal sentiment. After a brief pause, an aged man arose whose trembling hand had carefully turned his ear-trumpet to the chairman during his address. He expressed gratitude and joy that he had been permitted to hear what he had just listened to. He was the clergyman who remembered well having preached on that passage at Portland all those long years ago, and here was one rich fruit of that sermon, which he joyfully gave thanks for, for the first time, to-day. Again the little sympathetic rustle breathed through the community, and we feasted our eyes on the tall, thin, bending-over pastor, and the glad, grateful, spiritual son, who gazed on the venerable man through tears. He went on to set his seal to what had been already said of the wisdom of following small indications of Providence; saying that if his friend had not awaked with that passage on his mind, he might never have heard the news so calculated to cheer him towards the close of his pilgrimage. He had, however, still another coincidence to point out, as he had borrowed a letter from a friend for the purpose of reading an extract from it to this meeting this very morning.

It was from the lawyer of Portland, Mr. John ——, and entirely corroborated what we had already heard. In it the writer stated that he and his wife had lived in all harmony, and, as they thought, wisdom, trying to do good to their country after their fashion, but entirely without God. Nor had they discovered any defect in their scheme, till their own cherished and highly educated son—"our poor boy," as he was called—had disappointed their hopes and grieved their hearts. Then they asked each other what could have been omitted in his training that could leave him a prey to evil pursuits, and suddenly they remembered that they had, in the midst of many accomplishments, failed to teach him anything of his spiritual relations to God. They opened the Scriptures for themselves, and their hearts were opened by the Holy Spirit, so that they made a thousand discoveries. It was joyful to hear the outflowing upon new objects, new motives, new influences, new purposes; "behold, I make all things new" seemed written on his capacious heart, and if he had served his country zealously as a politician and lawyer, his plan and purpose now was to serve it as a Christian. One felt sorry as a stranger, to have no familiar hand to take in fervent and thankful gratulation as many did. Another gentleman was requested to offer prayer and thanksgiving, which it was most pleasant cordially to join in. We then sung a few more stanzas,—and presently arose a little thin, threadbare, tidy, sweet-looking, but evidently simple man—who said he had something to say to his brethren and sisters—and one might notice ladies tightening their shawls, and gentlemen clearing their throats, as if preparing for the exercise of endurance. Here, thought the interested observer, is a specimen of the effect of a popular constructed meeting. He has a right to speak, and the chairman has no right to prevent him—and why should he? If he is one of the Lord's simple ones, one would like to hear what he has got to say.

And then the mild man, in a silver tone, told us how he had been perplexed by Christ's command to "love his enemies"—for if they were wicked he ought not to love them. "Do not I hate them who hate thee? yea I hate them with a perfect hatred." But at last he discovered that he was to hate the wicked who were Christ's enemies, but he was to love and pray for those who were his own. "And so," said the innocent, modest man, "fearing that any of you, my brethren and sisters, might be perplexed by the same passage, I am happy to help you with my explanation of it." And now, the time being exhausted, we parted with a closing prayer.

In a far country I long to hear of the answer which we expect, even a refreshing time from the presence of the Lord, on the Churches and City of Boston.

The most touching feature of this meeting is, that it had been held daily, with the exception of the Sabbath, for the last four months, and that it consisted of all denominations that hold the head—even Christ—without sectarian inquiry or impediment. Who of all that breathing company thought to inquire with which of the sects that lawyer and his wife at Portland had cast in their lot? It was enough that they were united to Christ, and were gone forth with brethren to labor in the vineyard. If we really have our spirits moved with divine love, and if we dwell in the light of our Saviour's countenance, that ruling sentiment will occupy the room which might otherwise be filled with heart-chilling and deadening influences.

A dream, as it is called, though probably it was a dream by daylight, or rather a very pregnant parable, comes forcibly to mind in this connection.

A man dreamed that his soul was disunited from its earthen dwelling-place, and flew boldly up to "that great city, the holy Jerusalem," and frankly addressing one of the twelve angels who stand by the twelve gates, he asked for admission, as he was a faithful member of the Church of England. "But," said the guardian of the glorious portal, "we do not know any such citizens here." "Why," expostulated the candidate for admission, "that is strange. Who have you here—have you any Baptists?" "I never heard of them," replied the angel. "Any

Presbyterians?" "I know not what you mean." "Any Methodists?" "No such names are known here." "Well, then," asked the baffled and alarmed soul, lingering by the gate, to enter which had been his heart's longing for years, "have you not any members of the body of Christ here?" "Ah! yes —all who enter here are members of his glorious body. If you be one of these, enter and welcome."

If the churches were, according to the beautiful figure of James Montgomery, "distinct as the billows, but one as the sea," how profound would be the Unity of the Spirit beneath, compared to the sectarian undulations on the surface. The "Unity of the Spirit in the bond of peace"—that is what must possess us if we ever dwell in heaven, and therefore what we must aim at even in this carnal world. The mighty ocean which laves our continents and islands is ever the same, and by its beneficent cloud-collecting and wind-diffusing powers, the whole world is fanned and watered—but what is this universal beneficence compared with that of the "fountain opened for sin and for uncleanness?" There must every soul of every denomination have washed before it has learned to commune with God.

And if all are indebted to the same cleansing flood, how can we stand aloof as if we were strangers? If even the ten lepers associated together in their misery, shall not those who are healed associate together in their thankful union?

"Lift high thy banner, Prince of Peace;
Let discords die, and love increase."

The Sacramental Services.

In the dark parts of the earth, we find shadowy intimations of Scripture truths. Some have three united idols for their god. Some have traditions of the original pair who peopled the earth. Some have an account of Noah's flood, not very unlike the truth. All these are valuable as intimating the one source from whence they draw their origin.

They have by tradition a dim representation of what we have by inspiration. Even those things which are distinctly stated in the New Testament, become modified in the course of ages, and under the different degrees of light or liberty of the Christian Church.

Thus, some baptize by immersion, some by sprinkling, some in a house, others in a running stream. But all derive the rite itself from the divine record. And so of the Lord's Supper, which continues to show forth the wonderful sacrifice made for man. It will remain "till He come," but under varied forms. It has been touching to me to observe such variations, and to feel that in spite of them all the believers are one in heart and in hope.

At the communion service, in an ancient village church in Switzerland, the Pastor was raised two steps above us, he took from a small table by his side a long strip of bread, as thick as his finger. From this he broke a morsel which he silently gave to each communicant, who then passed behind him and received the cup from one of the two elders stationed at another little table on the same platform, and passing downward the people returned to their places by entering the pews at the opposite end from that by which they had left them.

In Belgium, on a similar occasion, the church having been lately painted, the elder who had charge of the communion plate was absent and had locked it up. Were the children to fast because of the absence of the regular order of vessels? Nay, verily. Their pastor treated the matter in a more practical way, unfettered by any solemn consecration, and using simple goblets of glass, and a common china plate, the tokens of redeeming love were dispensed to us—and the accompanying exhortations and prayers were never more strengthening or quickening.

Some of these services in the United States had only so refreshing a variation from ours, as to be the more arresting to the mind. One of these which we enjoyed in New Jersey, I shall describe as correctly as memory will enable me.

We had public worship on Friday afternoon and evening, and again on Saturday at two o'clock. It was lively to see the country people congregating from distant hamlets, and to count upwards of seventy vehicles on the green—the number on Sabbath being increased to upwards of a hundred. Each vehicle carried four persons—many of them six—and some children were there above the regular complement. They were chiefly plain country people, who in our own country would walk a few miles to church without weariness. The vehicles comprised many of fashion new to me—the Wagon, the Rockaway, the Dearborn, and so on, up to the comfortable Brougham. The spacious church was well nigh full—the services instructive and edifying. On the Sabbath all who were to join the church for the first time, came up the middle aisle to profess their faith. Their names were mentioned by the minister, and also the names of those who were to be received from other evangelical churches. After reading the covenant, and a short affectionate address from the pastor, the new members took their seats with the communicants. This brought to mind the simple country church in Dumfrieshire, where several years before, those very dear to me had stood in the band of young communicants to receive such welcome and such admoniton.

After this address the minister invited any strangers who might wish to commemorate the Master's dying love, with an affectionate reference to Christian friends from a sister church in a distant country. Next came the baptismal service for those unbaptized. One man and one woman, both of middle age, presented themselves. They advanced to the rail around the elder's seat and kneeled. With us it is so uncommon a circumstance not to have been baptized in infancy, that when it is required, the service is as it were smuggled bye in the session-house or in the Manse. The open profession is the more becoming method, inviting the prayers and the brotherly oversight of the whole flock.

On Saturday afternoon when the children of the church are usually presented for baptism, there stood a mother with her full heart and watery eye, offering her boy—about six—in one hand, and her girl, about three, in the other, awakening the sympathy and petitions of many of us—specially that her heart's wish for the conversion of her husband, might be granted. The boy looked up in the minister's face and smiled when he first poured the water and then laid his wet hand on his head to bless him. The girl gave a startled cry at the shock of the cold water on her face, and then was still. Here was a sight good for a church, calling forth many family and Christian sympathies.

Next approached five or six pairs side by side; the fathers, with that tenderness for the feebler sex which is unfailing in America, carrying the babes, till the pastor took each one in his own paternal arm, named and blessed it in the name of the Lord. The vows as to training in the nurture, and admonition of the Lord were laid on both parents. There was given here a striking testimony to the esteem with which true religion is regarded. The pastor's own family had been called to resign to heaven about ten years before, two lovely children, aged eight and six years, and but recently another lamb of their flock. But the more recently removed was passed by, and the name of the dear child of ten years memory selected, both name and surname, for two of the babes now dedicated to the Lord. The good man's voice trembled as he named the first, but the father's heart within him gave way quite when the second evidence of respect for his little one in glory was given. Her memory is fragrant, and as we learned afterward, nearly a dozen of her name are growing up in that congregation.

On the Sabbath no table was covered, save that on which the elements were placed. On the previous day, an exhortation somewhat like what we call "fencing the tables," had been delivered, so that the preliminary services differed nothing from what is usual on common Sabbaths. The body of the church was filled with communicants. We did not arise and go to a table as in Scotland, but the elements were handed to us where we sat. The service was simple, solemn, and appropriate, detaining us only half an hour longer than usual. We had an afternoon sermon, and at night in the lecture-room an elder's prayer-meeting very well conducted, and thus closed a refreshing and very pleasant Sabbath-day.

The few country churches which I have had an opportunity to attend, are marked by order and neatness, remarkably clean, neatly painted, each having its stove, and aiming at its band of singers. The city churches have a good effect from the taste and uniformity with which they are fitted up. The carpets and cushions are all alike, and the seats have a sloping back which much promotes the ease of the sitter. If the wood be painted white it is banded with a broad border of some rich dark wood, or if mahogany it is banded in the same manner. The divisions are low, the doors sloping gracefully, and the number or name of the proprietor, is engraved on a silver-looking plate on the dark band. Any one purchasing a pew, is bound not to paint or carpet it except in uniformity with the furnishing of the church—and thus the eye is not offended as it may be in old churches, here by a red-fringed cloth spreading over the front of the gallery in one seat, and next to it a brown, and next again a green. A stranger from a colder clime, has the eye drawn to the amazing number of fans sticking between the cushions and the back of the pew. But let him wait till a right hot day, and he will see the wife profiting by the ventilation of her husband's fan; the little ones placing themselves within the gale of elder brothers and sisters; the choir fanning most violently; and the very minister using all occasions of cessation from speech to fan himself, while his tumbler of iced water on the neat marble within his lengthened rostrum, is frequently resorted to in the progress of his discourse.

The buildings of the Reformed Dutch are probably on the exact model brought from Holland at first—nearly square, a façade of steps on which are erected six dazzling white fluted pillars which support a portico, forming a broad piazza, at the back of which open the wide folding-doors into the church. The pulpit at the opposite end, consists also of a long range of steps to a platform, which in the centre has a frontage on which the desk is fixed, while it is without door or interruption, and has at the back, perhaps, a centre chair with a sofa at each side, or three chairs and a small movable table. This is graceful, admits a free circulation of air, and leaves the orator more at liberty than when he is shut up in something shaped like a tulip or a lily of the Nile, with a spiral stair by which to reach it, and an impending extinguisher called a sounding-board; an arrangement, which to a troublesome imagination, calls up paintings of fairy revels, with Oberons and Titanias just emerging from bell-flowers.

Most of churches have an organ and a choir, which might be agreeable if every one would sing. But it is not right to praise God by proxy, nor even wise to withdraw all the fine voices which would be naturally sprinkled over the church and congregate them in one spot, thus leaving the imperfect musicians amongst the worshippers, afraid to make a "joyful noise" in the condescending ear of the Father of mercies, lest they make a discordant one in that of their brethren.

On our return to England we landed on a Sabbath-day. One of the freshest enjoyments of my return to my native land in safety, was on that evening uniting with the multitude in a good old psalm of praise, led by a single precentor. Every one sung their best, and filled the roof with sounds, if not so scientific, at least conveying more of the melody of hearty devotion, than if we had listened to an instrument, or whisperingly and timidly followed a choir. It is painful to be disturbed during prayer, as sometimes happens by the rustle of music sheets, and also by the whispered intercourse of singers during the sermon. This only occurs in churches where the choristers are hirelings, but it is much to be lamented. On the contrary, in some other churches, the amiable willingness to "help along," and the heartiness in the cause, so characteristic of the people, will induce persons of refinement and standing in society, and even married people to forsake their own seat and join the choir. Should any casualty befal the organist, the instrument will not be left mute, but some gentleman or lady will assume the office, with great cheerfulness and simplicity. This comes not only of natural good spirit, but of an independence of "what people will think," which elsewhere paralyzes many who are well-qualified for useful effort.

The method of introducing new church-members to the communion, seems much the same in various denominations, varying only with the temperament of the pastor. I have heard the interesting duty gone through in a matter-of-fact cool manner; again, as in the case described, in a way of practical affectionate interest; and again from a full heart, speaking a thousand welcomes, rejoicing over each soul as one that findeth great spoil, and longing to welcome ten thousand more. Whichever is the manner, the occasion is of profound, it may be of everlasting interest. The frank outflowing character of the people has a very winning effect, as it leads them to hail each new member, and claim brotherhood with him.—A lady mentioned that she came a lonely stranger to Philadelphia, and "heard around" in various churches till she felt sufficiently attracted by the ministrations of one gentleman, to return repeatedly. When she had been observed about three times in the same place, a lady accosted her—"Hoped she liked our minister—would she like to go to prayer-meeting in the lecture-room, she would be happy to guide her next evening—would she like to be introduced to the Rev. Mr. ——— &c."—In short, she found herself taken up, and introduced as one of a goodly company, with whom she has taken sweet counsel now for years. How sociable and comforting this to the solitary, and the stranger, and how fit an office for a Mother in Israel!

A Bee.

Every community in the United States is open to every denomination, and therefore it is not unfrequent that more churches are formed in a new city or district than its population can sustain. Thus they may erect several churches, have several small flocks, and by consequence several poorly paid pastors, when had they limited themselves to two, both might have been in a thriving state. The extravagances of some men have brought even genuine revivals, at least as known by that name, into disrepute. Still the growth of the church proceeds more in the revival form than it generally does in Great Britain. Any symptom of a time of refreshing is the means of calling for extra help; and in that case, ministers of various denominations come to each other's aid. The Episcopalians, alone in their exclusiveness, denying themselves such enlivening engagements. The variety of assistants, who are made useful, this to one soul and that to another, sometimes occasions a little difficulty in "housing the converts," as an intelligent and practical observer calls it; and in this way more denominations are settled than the place requires. Many persons are not so liberal or so punctual in their payments as they ought to be. Many of the pastors, men of good parts and devoted piety, struggle through difficulties with heroic fortitude, which they can derive alone from their zeal in the cause of souls. No other motive could retain them in office, when other means of acquiring an abundant living are spread all around them. They are at times glad to add a little farm to their care of souls, or employ their spare hours in educational engagements. In remote parts money is not very plenty, and the people are accustomed to employ barter instead of our common method of buying and selling. With such people it is much easier to give gifts to their pastor, than to insure him a regular money income. From this circumstance has arisen the plan of having what has got the name of "A Bee," once a year, which if met with as much simple kindness by the receiver of the honey, as it is bestowed by the busy, happy working Bees who bring it, must be productive not of pain, but of pleasure on both sides.

As one not present in the hive on that great day,

I can only tell what has been related by those who have many a time buzzed there with great delight. The plan is in this style: A few of the active, warm-hearted females form a committee and wait on the minister and his wife; or should he be a bachelor, no matter, or all the better. They are not to stop on the threshold for a ceremony. They invite themselves and all the congregation to wait on the parsonage on a named day, or any other that suits the parsonage better. They take all charge, trouble, responsibility, only hoping the family will allow them the privilege of the house. That being negotiated, and the day arrived—first comes the band of waiters, with all the appendages of a table covered and laden with good things. They are spread forth, and who shall count the dough-nuts, and the floating islands, and the piles of cheese, and loads of rich cakes and bread, and oceans of cream, and plates of frizzled beef, and smoking turkey, and fried oysters, and roast chicken, and pineapples of butter, and canoes of brandy peaches, and preserved plums, and ginger, and strawberries. The feast is after the fashion of Abigail, or old Barzillai's gifts to David the King. It is princely. They eat, and drink, and love one another, and are very happy. Drink! did I say? Yes, from urns of fragrant tea, and pots of rich coffee, and, if to be had, from beautiful pitchers of iced water. And the gentle family, cheered by the scene, enjoy it greatly, and some of the minister's jokes hit the nail on its very head, and are recited perhaps till the bees reassemble next year, or may be long after he has passed away. And in the close, they sing praises and give thanks, aad the busy ones gather up their empty vessels and depart—all parties feeling more united in love than they were before.

Then the family explore the house, which had been given up to the friendly invaders. They have been in the larder, and there have left such marks as a side of bacon, a cask of butter, some fine cheeses. They have been in the garret, and deposited a load or two of flour, and a bag of buckwheat, and another of meal. They have been in the study, and placed an easy chair, and a rug before it, for their pastor has left life's meridian behind him. They have been in the pantry, and left a barrel of sugar, a chest of tea, and a cask of molasses. The children find with suprise a nice new great coat hanging in the hall, as if it were quite at home. And on mamma's bed a web to make frocks, a beautiful new gown and cloak, and a piece for jackets for the boys.

In the midst of all the exclamations of joyful surprise and grateful conjecture as to the individual donors, the good man steps to the garden to breathe more freely under this load of kindness, when lo! his wood-house is packed full of winter fuel, and the last wagoner stands at a loss, not finding room for his load. "Take it to my neighbor the baptist minister down the hill there," says the grateful pastor. "I fear he is hardly so richly provided for as I am, and I am as much obliged to my friend as if I had burnt every cord of it myself."

This, Oh! tithe-paying people of England, is "A Bee!" How sweetly could many of your generous hearts fall into the humor of the country, and contribute your own pot of honey, and your blessing with it!

The Wedding.

All weddings are not so bright and gay as that I am about to describe, but every marriage, even amongst the poorest people, ought to be a mixture of the solemnity and the festival. Solemn, because it forms a bond life-long, and coloring eternal things; festive, because love, and hope, and sympathy are all in lively exercise.

Imagine one of the loveliest days of the "Indian Summer," in the middle of November. The sun rising over New York, shaded in his lustre by a thin gauzy haze, which his ardent beams had before eight o'clock drank up, leaving neither shade, nor visible cloud, nor any mark but himself in all that blue vault, the depths of which the eye searched vainly to fathom, or conjecture what might be beyond. It was such a morning as in Britain would have had "the lark blythe waking at the daisy's side," and one would have watched him piercing the vault of heaven, till even the last speck had disappeared from the eye, while his rich warblings still poured down, reached the ear. How is it that neither sky-larks, daisies, nor primroses frequent the lands of this intense blue sky, though they thrive and rejoice in our more cloudy region.

Imagine various households afloat by six or seven, and unwonted toilets and hair-dressings with wreathed lilies and roses before breakfast, and all the sprightly remark and lively anticipations of interested groups, preparing in various dwellings for a pleasant drive, and pleasanter ceremony. Imagine the rough, unsightly broken rocks, unfinished roads, and the half built up brick and mortar litter of the suburbs left behind, and a road gained which carries you from one elevation to another, now in view of the magnificent Hudson, with its flashing waters, its fleet sail-boats, and its steamers; now behind one of the innumerable knolls that rise upon its banks; now sheltered by a grove of noble trees, now fronted by a stern gray rock, and again greeted by a smiling village, a busy hotel, or a tasteful villa. These knobs on the banks of the great river, which whilome were islets that barely lifted their heads above waters which were gradually subsiding into the ocean, are many of them crowned by handsome shining white houses, with wide piazzas, and shading Venetian shutters of bright green. Without a gray curl of smoke in the air, or a yellow stain of it upon the walls, they look very brilliant, and are cheerful and open, so that the eye may often penetrate a whole suite of apartments, till it reaches shrubs, vases, and flowers, on its farther side. These undulating grounds are full of graceful beauty, and when brother Jonathan passes his age of utilitarian furor, and finds a scarcity of Irish laborers to split and tear down the rocks in the nearer environs of the city—in short, when he reaches the picturesque period of his existence, how he will regret some of his remorseless levellings.

"Why," it was inquired of a gentleman of fine taste, as on another occasion we drove through some similar levellings among the spacious and handsome new avenues of Brooklyn, "Why will you remove these lovely eminences? Let them level the avenues as much as they can, but do spare Nature's lines of beauty in those varied heights around. If a tree were scattered here and there on that slope—if that green were smoothed, and some of your touching weeping willows waved their tassels over it—if a grove crowned the height, and formed a background to those houses!" "My dear Madam," replied my friend, "the people would not bear it. They would think we were turning exclusives, and perhaps cut up our trees." "Is this the method by which they preserve their liberty? Is this republicanism?" "It is neither the one nor the other—it is merely the notion of the time." Within half a mile of us there lay a specimen of a lovely green, with its willows, unmolested by any zealous leveller. So I infer my friend uttered but a sentiment born of some momentary vexation. But what a "lie of ground" is there on the Brooklyn Heights! Were it placed in the hands of some *capability man*, it would be found *capable* of all manner of elegancies, as well as easy rising roads, and convenient levels.

But while Brooklyn has risen up in fancy's eye, we have traced several miles of Manhattan Island, and reached a handsome villa which is situated on a height overlooking the river near the commencement of the palisades on the opposite shores.

Many carriages stud the surrounding park, many domestics stand round the stoop, and two or three zealous young Masters of the ceremonies hasten to receive the parties as they alight.

The guests pass through a spacious hall, which is not furnished with mats and high-backed unresting carved chairs, or long antique oaken settles, surmounted by trophies of arms. The American Hall looks like a place to lounge on a sofa in, and cool one's self, or to dine in on a hot day, having all the appliances of a chamber to be used, not of a place of waiting attendants, or of passage only.

In the farther depths of the spacious mansion we entered a fine drawing-room with windows on three sides, all opening on the piazza, giving varied views of the Hudson. At the top stood the pair whose circumstances drew all eyes and all hearts to them. Three bridemaids stood on one side, each with a bouquet rather inconveniently large, and formally arranged, so as to rob the loveliest things in nature of all the graces of bending stalks and flowing leaves. Three groomsmen stood on the other side. There were besides, two pretty little girls, who were held by the hands of two smart boys, not got up for the show, as in the Popish processions, but really relatives and friends of the family. The Episcopal clergyman, in his surplice, was a graceful, nice-looking man, fit to grace such an assemblage. The room was thronged, for not the interested and affectionate friends only, but stewards and house-keepers from all branches of the family were there. Dark coachmen and white house-maids, black cooks and yellow foot-boys, Sunday scholars in their new frocks, Ethiopian Susan, with her ivory-black baby in her arms, and all the other five of them at her feet. Waiting-women, with their ringlets, and their air of mysterious importance, armed with ice-water and essences, in case of need. Aged and withered-looking people leaning on marble slabs next to elegant brocades and diamonds, were all mingled in most admired confusion. The Africans as far up the room, and for once as much mixed with the whites as anybody. The scene, as one could withdraw attention from the modest, sweet-looking bride, or from her beaming, affectionate mother, to consider it, was to an English eye most curious and striking.

And now, all being arranged, the service began. It is abbreviated and improved from the old English original, and was felt to be solemn and appropriate.

> "For the deep trust with which a maiden casts
> Her all of earth, perchance her all of heaven,
> Into a mortal's hand,"

is calculated to fill the minds of on-lookers with sober thought. Our interesting bride went calmly through her part, as if resolved, and gave no use for essences. While her deeply attached husband never moved his eye from her countenance, as if his all were before him. The only movement that seemed to detract from the unity of the heart absorption, was when the bride for a moment pressed a finger on the diamond cross on her bosom. "Is she thinking of her appearance?" No—clearly her thoughts are of a higher tone. "Is she entertaining some superstitious reverence for the emblem?" No—still why does her finger rest there? It was his love-token, she accepted it in evidence that she accepted him.

A peculiarity which we have not in England has an interest of its own sort in it. The bridegroom first gave the ring to the bride, she took it, looked on it, and gave it back—he then gave it to the clergyman, who also looked on it and returned it,—so that before the little mystic token of everlasting union was placed on her finger, it had been observed by all the three.

The finger of her glove had been previously opened on one side, so that the bridemaid had no flutter or struggle in removing the glove from her hand, but merely slipt it off the point of the finger, and thus it was uncovered ready for the ring—a method highly to be commended to all trembling or blundering bridemaids. At the close, the minister raised a hand above the head of each, and mentioning their Christian names, blessed them in the name of the Lord. It was very touching.

The emotions of congratulation were pleasantly

broken in upon by one of the nice little girls, who, holding her boy-beau with one hand, with the other presented an elegant small basket of white rosebuds, while with a sweet low voice she recited a few graceful lines of hopeful aspiration :

"Bring flowers, fresh flowers, for the bride to wear !
They were born to blush in her shining hair;
She is leaving the home of her childhood's mirth,
She hath bid farewell to her father's hearth.
Her place is now by another's side—
Bring flowers for the locks of the fair young bride !"

Then was wheeled in a table with the mighty cake, which is as much a "chieftain" at an American as at a British wedding. From it the groomsmen procured their favors, and mounted them as badges of office, and then came the old English fun about who found the ring, who the sixpence, who the scissors, and who the thimble.

At one o'clock, the pair, with their attendant damsels, arranged themselves for "the reception," while the groomsmen ushered in the guests, and presented them to the bride. They had no sinecure office till past three. The porter lost count after the number of guests had passed seven hundred, in spite of the custom for each family to give their card of invitation at the door. As a rare privilege a seat was procured for me in a place where all who entered must pass, and there, without the exertion of talking, I saw the aristocracy of New York and of many other places, glide by.

The movements were quiet and graceful, countenances beaming, many very lovely,—dresses rather elegant than gay. Amongst those that one was glad to have conversed with, even in the brief way that an introduction can produce in such a scene, were the Ex-President Van Buren, the Portuguese ambassador, who led one of his children through that lively maze, as several others did, and John Jay, grandson of the Judge, whose name has been long held in veneration as the negro's friend. It was pleasant to look on them and many more men of note in their country.

We went in groups to the dining-room, where tables were sumptuously and most elegantly spread with all the luxuries of the season,—when, having a hint that there could be no time for any other dinner, people took advantage of their opportunity. Stewed oysters, which are amongst the most nourishing and healthy luxuries of the country, with sandwiches, game, fruits, jellies, ices, and champagne, were most dutifully handed about by the gentlemen. After refreshing ourselves, we returned to the saloon with some difficulty, as the throng thickened, and the young people, who had lately begun to time their steps to the music which issued from a side-room, had at last got to dancing. The reception-callers were for a season figuring up the hall amid the circling dancers, and were almost obliged to *galope* their way into the saloon.

This hugging, and whirling with shut eyes, because of dizziness, and panting and falling on each other's shoulders, confounds people of sedate and tranquil manners. I once saw in a cursaal in Germany, through a glass door by which I passed, something similar to this, but never in Britain, though I suppose it may be seen there. A bright lady by my side quoted in my ear what Washington Irving had said at a similar scene, "Go fetch half a dozen parsons to marry these couples, for they have done all the courting already."

As the conflict thickened, the servants who had withdrawn, trooped back again. It was quite new to me to see half a dozen dark people laughing, joking, and enjoying the fun familiarly. You might see the whites within one door of the hall or hanging on the stair, and the blacks at another—and an elegant, breathless dancer, fanning and swinging in one rocking-chair, and a black child of nine or ten in the next, quite unconscious of anything like forwardness in her position. My bright friend explains the superior familiarity of the dark people in this way: "The whites are so nearly our equals, that we dare not approach nearer, but there is a bar forever between us and the colored people." There are among the colored so many "aunt" Silvas and Celias, and Sukies, old friends of the houses too, that there is a great deal of amiability in the way the superiors manage and deal with them in their visits. The white attendants are more like the French *Bonne*, than the English waiting-woman. They are all occupied about the dressings and goings to and fro, offering opinions as to what suits complexion, and hints as to what is becoming, such as only a highly indulged servant would think of giving in England.

Some of the party made their way to an upper room, where the numerous and munificent gifts to the bride had been arranged for the purpose of being shown merely to relatives. The admiration of beautiful things soon reached the ears of those below, and troop after troop ascended and exclaimed, and admired, contrary to the intention of the lord of the mansion, who, finding his instructions ill-understood, or at least, ill-obeyed, sent a messenger who most relentlessly locked the doors by which the parties had made their way into a neighboring chamber. It is the plan of most houses to have all the chambers opening into one another. This was rather a comical scrape—a whole train of ladies and gentlemen locked up as if they had been suspected of designing to carry something away. The amiable lady of the family made her way in, and apologized very handsomely for the series of mistakes, and suffered the culprits to escape without farther punishment.

"The reception" having poured out its multitude, the bride and bridegroom were at last emancipated, and made a retreat to procure some food and to dress for travelling;—and presently they slipt away by a side-door, where the drawing up of their carriage was concealed from the public gaze—and the scene of light-hearted mirth, having passed the element in which those who are equipped in perpetual sable feel at home, my friend and I, by the same private door, obtained our chariot too, and returned to town.

As a proof of the easy manner of the domestics, it may be worth while to mention that the one who opened the door for us on our returning, said—"Well, ladies, I hope you have enjoyed your day,"

—a kind of sympathy much more natural than the assumed automatonism of an English servant, who goes through all evolutions, as if he had no comprehension of what you are about, and cared as little as if you were in the bottom of the sea.

The pieces of cake which we brought home, were in pretty card-board boxes tied with white ribbons. Indeed, on occasion of two of the servants making a match, while I stayed in the house of another friend, during the winter—they presented five such boxes so tied, to the ladies of the family and their guests. People of all ranks in America do such things in a dashing style. They earn money quickly and spend it freely. We also brought home some splendid bunches of flowers, and related all our wonders, and wished the dear young people happiness, but being tolerably exhausted by the long day of excitement, went to rest, glad that we need not rise to dress for another wedding to-morrow.

The Cities.

The traveller marvels at the well-laid-out and nearly filled up streets of Buffalo, which a few years ago consisted of but a store and a hotel—and the gathering throng at Geneva, with the extensive salt-works of Salina, where lately there was only the haunt of the red hunter—and the orderly and thriving population of Rochester, loading canal-boats with pile on pile of sacks and casks, containing grain, flour, butter, cheese, and all the bountiful produce of a very rich country. He hears of Troy and Utica, and all manner of ancient names, till he is at a loss to remember in which era of time he lives, and on which quarter of the globe he stands. But he feels it is all new—the growth of yesterday. He need but go a few roods from most of these flourishing cities, to fall in with black stumps, obstinately holding their room in the fields of winter wheat; or lopped and girdled trees like so many criminals awaiting their doom; or whole acres of fir wrenched up by a machine, their once sky-pointing tops prone in the coarse and fenny grass, and their roots standing in the air, like the fangs of a strong tooth that has been drawn from its place by an engine not less stern and resolute. The forest seems ancient like mother earth, and like the deep blue sky—but the cities are like *parvenus*, all new, and smart, and bright; so that when from the Nor-west you get down to Albany, you feel as if you had reached a very ancient place, parts of it reminding one of Holland with a sort of modern square cut about it.

Washington—were the spaces filled up between its very magnificent public edifices, would be very grand. Baltimore, with its tasteful monuments and fine rivers, is filled up; its regular orderly streets giving one a little breathing of up hill and down dale; reminding Scotch folks of Jeany Dean's delight at having her legs rested by climbing Gunnerbury hill, after two or three hundred miles of plain walking. Philadelphia is full of Philanthropists and philanthropic institutions; is clean, handsome, and orderly as a young quaker's paste-board bonnet. Hartford, with its fine streets and fine trees, and all the histories attached to them—New Haven, with its avenue of Elms, like the interlacing roof of an ancient cathedral—Boston, majestic, graceful, with its beautifully laid out Common and height crowned by its noble State House—These, and many more one traverses with an ever-rising perception of the civilization, wealth, taste, and beauty of the country. But it is of New York,—the "Empire City," where traffic hastens and where shipping throngs, where wealth enjoys and poverty labors, where want is pursued by benevolence, inebriety by temperance, and vice of all sorts by Christianity,—it is of this emporium of the country that we wish to speak.

It is common to say, "New York will be a handsome city when it is finished," and so it will if that day of repose ever reaches it. One sometimes lights on a street quiet and clean, where you can stand still and enjoy it. But lo! a restless genius has bought a house. However comfortable it is he will hardly believe it his own till he has altered it. So you will see it climbing a story nearer the clouds, a conservatory bulging out on the side, a portico on the front. If it be a store, a smarter window or a deeper cellar is wanted. In short, your orderly street is quickly cumbered with all the confusion of building; and timber, bricks, and lime are spread about with little ceremony, and much incumbrance to passengers. There is wonderful forbearance on the part of the citizens, with the encroachments made on the footpaths by boxes and casks of all kinds. You must glide through them very warily, lest your clothes be rent on a corner or your foot wounded by a nail; not to mention tinctures of tar or sugary matter, which may be more easily contracted than shunned in the lower and more business parts of the city. It must be on the give and take principle that these incumbrances are suffered—"I won't complain of you to-day, for I expect my cargo in to-morrow; we must all get along"—and so they do, more at the occupiers' ease in some streets than that of the passengers. It reminded me of an indignant traveller whose horse had shied at the carcase of a dead brother at the end of a small town in Scotland,—"Why is not this nuisance removed?" "Hout, our horses are used to it, they never care." "But mine does; and if you don't have it removed, I will represent it to the Baillie." "Hout, awa, Sir—I'm Baillie myself!" Probably these cumberers of the pavement are Baillies too.

Another subject on which great forbearance is shown, is the endurance of noise in many operations, where a little care would lessen or entirely remove it. The movable sides of their long carts rattle. The loads they carry rattle. By half-past four, A. M., the milk-carts begin their clattering progress. Many of them carry six tin jars, which contain perhaps fifteen gallons apiece. These jars are slipt into six iron rings, which might be easily lined with leather, but they are not. At every motion of the cart all the six give forth their own portion of noise. Add to this the unusual quantity of rattle of the wheels on the axle, the shout or whistle or frightful Australian "Coooa" with which the milkmen summon the drowsy damsels to come forth with their empty pitchers, and you have got up a nuisance which it would require a determined anti-clatter company to put down. Woe be to the sick and wakeful who have just dropt into a slumber—it is effectually over for this morning.

Next comes the ice cart, with less commotion, its driver rings, and in his huge forceps lifts a cube of transparent solid ice; not the "rotten ice," frozen and melted, and frozen again, that we call ice in England; but the pure block cut out of the Rockland Lake, which might have been several feet thick, and frozen a couple of months before it was broken by the dealer in that frigid but important and wholesome luxury.

On the Sabbath mornings another noise is added, which inflicts not headache alone, but heartache. By six o'clock the news-boys traverse the streets shouting "The Herald, The New Yorker, &c.," furnishing half-a-day's secular reading for all who are so disposed. [These boys! lately tattered, and wan, and timid Irish emigrants]: look at them fitted out in second-hand garments, the fitting of which is not so much to be considered, as how they, destitute, earned the cash to purchase them. See them wrestling, scrambling, teasing each other in their breathing intervals. Hear their slang wit, impudence, and profanity mingled. Observe their acute calculating skill. One wants to be off home, and will "sell out" to the next, giving him the advantage of a paper or two of his "stock in trade," into the bargain. Bright fellows! what ready mother wit, what sharp adoption of trading phrases. How capable of learning something better! Poor waifs, cast on the world's unholy shore! I never saw any of them without sorrow, excepting a little party of them who had been induced to join a "boys' meeting," where their sharpened faculties seemed to enable them to apprehend meaning more easily, and more to enjoy intellectual occupation than some of their peers.

The stores are very handsome, and the reckless way in which masses of valuable goods are exposed to the sun inside, and to the dust outside, very surprising. Several of the stores occupy a whole block of buildings—a space large enough for five or six moderately sized houses. On some of these one's eye rests with peculiar complacency, as the fruit of industry united with integrity. You may be told as you pass along, "Look at that fine store. Its owner came here in debt—he and his family allowed themselves no indulgencies, but all worked hard, till he was able to return to Scotland, assemble his creditors, and pay up principal and interest. Since then they have never looked behind them—all has gone well." I worshipped repeatedly in the church with such a family, and used to turn and see them step out of their carriages with as loyal a heart to them as I have felt to our own beloved Queen, when I have stayed to see her step out of hers.

Perhaps the very purest pleasure of all the delights afforded me in that whole city, was meeting with some of my countrymen, now thriving, cheerful, hospitable, loving—who but a few years before were care-worn beings, who having strained every fibre to raise money to carry them, had crossed the ocean with much trembling. To mingle sympathies in their thankfulness, as had often been done in their cares and sorrows at home, seemed to me a treat that angels might relish. To be fanned in their rocking-chairs, refreshed by their fruits and iced water, to inquire all their histories, to play with their children, to go with them to church, and "see how like old Scotland it was," yea, even to mingle tears with them at Greenwood Cemetery, over their honored and departed dead, was a treat worth the trouble of a voyage across the Atlantic; but the citizens have made me forget the city.

Broadway is a perfect puzzle—how smaller and lighter crafts make undemolished way through that throng of omnibuses, is amazing. Many a street in London is as much crowded, but I do not suppose in any one, if you except the vicinity of the Crystal Palace at evening, you could count twenty omnibuses at a time within sight. Yet there is no pressing and driving—but cheerful, smiling courtesy, on all hands. We had occasion to cross from Jersey City on Christmas eve, when the roomy steamer could scarcely afford standing-room for the well-dressed throngs of artisans and their families who were crossing to be ready for to-morrow's holiday. How pleased they looked! How obliging! Giving way when they could, or expressing regret to one another if they could not. Not one tipsy shout,—not one staggering mortal—no wife or sister looking fearfully on her escort. Ah, Scotland! when will Temperance do for thee what it has done for these crowded cities?

My companions on that evening urged me to look in on Washington market—and it was a goodly sight. One does not care about the piles of food—such masses are to be seen in many a city in nearly equal quantity—it was the purchasers who drew my attention. The good wife laden with cheese, and beef, and ham, and vegetables, and butter, and candles. The children clustering around helping to carry her load of plum-cakes or currant loaves, and her bunch of evergreen. The men, in blue blouses or with blue trowsers over others, to preserve them from the lime or tar they had been working in all day, swinging along a huge turkey by the legs, its head knocking on the pavement as they went, while a lump of bacon filled the other hand. No wonder that brother Jonathan is vaunty and boastful, he has all the inspirations of prosperity and hope. And then to discern many an Irish countenance among these purchasers of viands, poor fellows! who never saw a turkey without its feathers in their lives, until they left "Ould Ireland,"—and to think the luxury could be had by honest working for it—it made one's heart happy.

The various devices employed for thrusting their

business into notice, strikes one as new. Pillars erected on the verge of the pavement are stuck over with instructions about oyster cellars, and barbers, and all sorts of eatables and wearables. The very boxes that protect the trees are covered with bills nailed, not pasted on. Flags under your feet have the name and trade of the occupant of the neighboring store carved on them. Movable placards against walls and lamp-posts tell of places of amusement. These, I am sorry to say, are not withdrawn, or rather new ones are put forth, on the Lord's day, and often you may see the thoughtless who have just quitted the sanctuary, turn round at the door of a theatre to read what can be had to divert them on the morrow. But the style of attracting notice, which gives a tattered and disorderly aspect to streets otherwise handsome, is the huge cotton flags stretched across the centre, in the manner the lamps are suspended in some ancient European cities. These present letters of gigantic size.

Before one of these I felt my feet arrested and my mind filled with emotions that referred to scenes and times far, far from the noise of Broadway. It was an announcement that Sir William Don would act for the public of New York every evening that week. Sir William Don! Newton Don! The scene of my children's happiest holidays. That thought came first. Mary Lundie's "Hawthorn" gathered there—

"It is the hawthorn blossom,
The fairest flower of spring;
It smiles on earth's green bosom,
And nature's minstrels sing.
A thousand happy voices
Advance to bid it hail;
Oh, how the bee rejoices
To scent it in the gale."

Has it come to this! Has this poor young man left those lovely glades to act the droll for the amusement of a foreign multitude! Then rose to mind the ancestral cups which had once for some weeks graced our sideboard, that all the pastors who came and went might see them. A pair of ancient candlesticks they were in reality, with bottoms like an inverted bowl, of workmanship so rough, that the dimple marks of the hammer that had beaten the silver into shape, were still discernible. These candlesticks had nearly three hundred years ago been inverted, and used as extempore communion-cups when Knox visited Glencairn, and for the first time dispensed the ordinance of the Supper in the Reformed Church to a group in the Castle Hall. This heirloom of an ancient house, has descended to a player! The blood of this Christian Earl of Glencairn flows still in the veins of that young actor! And has it come to this!

On festival days, when the city is afloat with frolic, you will see little flags with the stars and stripes on the heads of horses, on the roofs of carriages, flying out of windows, and at Barnum's Museum, not only all around the house, but flaunting from it across the street on cords attached to the chimney tops on the opposite side.

On a stormy day early in December, the coachmakers began to project into the street carriages with prows formed like those ships of old that carried Greece to Troy—painted, varnished, and gilded in the handsomest manner—lined and cushioned most luxuriously, in green or crimson embossed velvet. And then, for the first time, my eye rested on a sleigh. But the winter being mild, though a few times a laborious effort was made to get on in one, and one saw the thing and heard the bells tinkling like those on the leading goat or sheep on the lower Alps, yet they were not generally used. The snow, during the whole winter, turned to moisture when it did happen to fall. But they talked of the sleigh being used instead of the omnibus, and of the men adding another and another pair of horses each time they reached the point of their destination, till I was assured that twenty might be seen in one carriage. "And why do they do that?" "Oh, just for fun!" They are a lively people, always ready for a "spree;" but I question if the jaded horses would not have much preferred their stable, with their corn and hay.

The incessant and heavy traffic digs up and wears out the pavement of Broadway, so that yearly it requires to be gone over and repaired. It is surprising to see the unwieldy omnibus during the season for paving, turn down narrow side streets repeatedly in its lengthened course. Yet so attractive is this one street, which is like the spinal column of the city, that they will return to Broadway at the first block where it is passable, though they have to turn off again in the course of a few hundred yards. A comical specimen of impulsive character, I don't presume to say in the American *people*, but certainly in *one* of them, was exhibited by a gentleman in one of these omni-gatherum vehicles. He informed all whom it might concern, that he was from Buffalo—that he had never heard Jenny Lind, but would give his ears to hear her or to see her, because of the beauty of her singing and the benevolence of her character. As he could neither see nor hear her, he was resolved to go and see Tripler Hall which had been built for her, and where she had earned and charmed so many thousands. In the midst of his hearty harangue, the perverse buss turned off Broadway, the very street that contained Tripler Hall! "Ho! stop, let me out!—can I never get to Tripler Hall? This is the third buss I have been forced to jump out of, for none of them go straight up Broadway as they used to do." The enthusiast was calmed by assurances that had he sat still in the first buss he would have got to Tripler Hall, and that a fellow-passenger would show him where to alight. At last the important moment arrived. Buss had again found its way to its favorite street, and the Buffalo gentleman rushed out, and rushed into the scene of Jenny Lind's well-merited triumphs, as if he certainly expected at least—

> "A shade of song, a spirit air
> Of melodies that had been there."

More comfortable dwellings, either for ventilation in summer's heat, or for warmth in winter's cold, are nowhere to be found in the world than in New York. By means of having open doors and windows, so that the morning breeze may circulate freely through the many inlets and outlets to every chamber and hall, and then before the sun comes round in his fervor, excluding his rays by the outside green venetians, the house is kept tolerably cool; till evening breeze returns, waving the lovely trees which line the footways, and inviting its admission again into the dwelling.

The furnace in the basement warms every corner in winter, perhaps too completely for health. At least in our country we are used to feel the variation of temperature between the rooms and the hall or staircase, or between one room and another, to have rather a bracing and reviving effect. Besides, the rush of the sharp, frosty, outward air into lungs which, for too many hours of the day, have breathed nothing but the dry, hot atmosphere of the furnace, is a trial too great for so delicate a texture as lungs are made of. This, and the inadequate defence of the feet, have often been accused as the cause of the numerous victims to lung diseases—and I fear with justice.

There is much ingenuity and taste displayed in making much of little room. Even small dwellings have their neat flower knot behind, and their grapevine over a trellised arch,—and the little aviaries, conservatories, and green-houses, in very unexpected corners are innumerable. The freedom of vegetation gives encouragement to planters. It is sometimes even touching to see a tree, which has been spared in the building of five-story warehouses, alive in its dusty and dingy recess, and fulfilling all its calling of bud, blossom, smiling green leaf, and fruit-bearing. I have looked on such a tree, and compared it to a Christian choked up in worldly society and occupations, yet drinking in the pure dew of the Divine Spirit, living and refreshing the surrounding dreariness by his presence.

The seclusion of mind is a subject on which I have often mused, with admiration of the wisdom that has so constructed it. The looker-on cannot tell why one in the busy multitude that flits by him laughs and another weeps. And it is well that he cannot. The inmost heart of himself contains evil enough for each. And even its hidden joys are such as might exhale, were they open to the bystander.

Who of all the interested parties that I have happened again and again to see pressing into a "Bank for Savings," or seated on the stoop to wait their turn to enter, could guess why I should be fixed to the spot, or why my tears should flow at the sight? My mind flew back to the peaceful parish of Ruthwell, and there I saw the mild and patient pastor* calculating, and planning, and writing rules, and correcting them—and at last setting a-going his new scheme of a Bank, where as small a deposit as one shilling was to be accepted. Then I saw him smiling good cheer as he stood by his desk, with his great ledger before him, while he received the hard-earned saving from the horny hand that earned it. And again I saw him subduing his natural love of retirement, and struggling to awaken the great men of the land to the value of the scheme. And then again in London toiling to secure supporters for passing a Bill in Parliament for the protection of Savings' Banks.

And all this was past—and he who for years labored for the temporal and spiritual welfare of his people has ceased from his labors. But they have spread—and as it fell out in Solomon's day, so it befell him while "no man remembered the same wise man whose wisdom saved the city,"—cities and nations far off are profiting by it. Even so! he sought not fee nor reward here, but

"I thank Thee for the quiet rest
Thy servant taketh now,
And for the good fight foughten well,
And for his crowned brow."

* Rev. Dr. Duncan, author of the "Sacred Philosophy of the Seasons."

Hotels and Boarding-houses.

Hotels are generally well managed, and in excellent order. In frequenting the Temperance houses, the traveller is sure of society of one stamp, so that the conversation he may enter into will be of a correct, and very likely of an improving character.

The wholesome "click" of the ice against the water-pitchers has something re-assuring in its quiet sound, and the gong, giving forth its musical tone, first in the distant part of the parallelogram, then swelling nearer, till it passes along the gallery where your own chamber is situated, and then again sinking into silence at the farther end, summoning all who will to family worship, gives cheering token that you are in good society. It is very pleasant to meet three or four score of travellers in the saloon by seven in the morning, and nine at night, to join in a hymn, led perhaps by a son or daughter of the house, accompanied by an organ-toned pianoforte. Then to hear a passage of holy writ, read perhaps by the master of the hotel, and to join in a prayer by him, if no clergyman be present, or by a clergyman, without reference to his denomination, or, as I once chanced to hear, by a senator. How calm and safe the progress of a day so entered upon—and how orderly is such a household, even though it numbers at its noonday meal nearly two hundred guests. Enough has been said by English travellers about the amazing celerity with which Americans dispatch their food, and of the knife nearly going down the throat after it. Though I had no chance at the race in eating, I generally saw many persons as slow, or slower than myself. One day, being at leisure to observe the proceedings of my neighbors, I saw a very respectable-looking lady reduce one half of an oval slice of bread to the shape of a horse-shoe by one goodly bite that she took out of the middle. This lady introduced herself to me in the saloon, and—oh Dickens—oh Trollope—can ye bear the dismal truth—she told me she was a Londoner! Here ended my discoveries as to peculiarities in conduct at table. A gentleman did tell me, that he saw, at a New York hotel dinner, one person give his fork to another, with, "Just stick that fork into that potatoe for me, will you?" His surly, unneighborly neighbor did as he was requested, and *left it sticking there.* This was a most ungracious way of teaching a hasty man to apply to the waiter—yet it might be useful.

Waiters are always abundant, so that you never hear them rung for or called in an impatient tone. They are there, and know what you want as soon as you do yourself. In Gadsby's, at Washington, their mute observant attention—one black man ministering to the wants of two whites—was really too affecting. One could not eat—one wanted to get up and set them down and wait on them. They were not paid for their services. They were not volunteers in your cause. They could not go away if you ill-used them. They were slaves! They looked sleek and tranquil, however, and are in general under mild treatment in the District of Columbia.

In a country where everybody travels, the comforts and reasonable charges of hotels are important. Some of the arrangements are new to the English. There is generally, with the transient visitors, a mixture of those who make a permanent residence in the house. These are not only bachelors and young clerks, but young married people. Those who prefer to see what is going on, linger in the saloons of an evening after leaving the eating-room, when it often happens that a musical guest, or a professional person will play and sing for the entertainment of the company. You find as many newspapers as can be rescued from the reading and smoking-rooms, and a few books, and sometimes ladies have their work. It is hardly deemed courteous to write letters in the saloon, and no provision is made for that in the way of material. At best, it is an idle life. People seem waiting for something that rarely comes, in the way of disembarrassed conversation, something better than talk got up for the occasion, and one yawns and drops off, and then another, till the whole house retires to early repose.

The BOARDING HOUSE is not for the accommodation of travellers, but of those who are for some time from home, or who have no other home. In busy cities, and at watering-places, there are thousands so accommodated. It is computed that 25,000 strangers are in New York at one season of the year, some of whom may, by their affairs, be obliged to remain a considerable time. For them, at least for single gentlemen, the boarding-house may be more convenient than the English method of lodging. But for families, and for a permanency, they are not calculated to promote settled habits, or cultivate home enjoyments.

It often happens that newly-married people choose that homeless, uncomfortable method of beginning life, induced by the idea that it is more economical and less troublesome than having the responsibilities of a house. The difficulty of procuring "helps," or rather of knowing how to get any good use of them when procured, is another reason for preferring to board.

The effect of this plan on the mental and moral habits appears very unsalutary, and is silently working on the whole of society. It promotes improvident marriages, as people marry to board, who could not afford to keep house. It promotes selfishness, as persons who are all paying for everything alike, and who—the female part at least—have not much to occupy them, get jealous and watchful lest others get any advantage which they do not enjoy. It promotes epicurism, as there must be a table kept beyond the style of the real circumstances of each individual; and as they pay for it, they feel that they have a right to be fastidious and critical. It is distressing to see the children's greedy eyes roam over all the dishes, liking this and hating that, and having their plates heaped with all manner of incongruous things to prevent their disturbing the company, by crying or exclaiming. Besides the little creatures get the manners of grown persons, and talk away, polite and agreeable by the way, but forward and in an unhealthy attitude withal. I remember seeing a little fellow about five years old, who had found a shining button with a broken eye, go the round of a large saloon, in the most gentlemanly way, inquiring of each if "you had lost that, as he had found it, and it would give him pleasure to restore it to you if you could claim it."

To dwell with persons in whom you have no special interest, or whom you only, or hardly, put up with, is the reverse of improving to the heart. For a young pair to begin by living in the presence of others, when their first year is required to learn each other's peculiarities, and how to assimilate and how to forbear, seems not merely disagreeable, but dangerous. A word, a look, an unintentional neglect, may in the early stages of matrimonial union, wound deeply. To leave the wound unrevealed, or the neglect unexplained, cannot fail to make the matter worse. In such a case, there is drooping of spirits and repining, or what is still more dangerous, there is sympathy offered by some officious onlooker, and accepted, to the further alienation of the sufferer. How long in this way, may those who are really attached and fitted to cherish each other, be kept apart; and how unlike the cheerful, confiding sociality of one's own fireside, where, according to the old song,—

> "I can laugh when I'm merry,
> And sigh when I'm sad."

For the male sex the evils are not so great, as they set out early to business, and are engaged the chief hours of the day. But the females! unless they have a taste for study, what can they do in their chamber but attend a little to their garments, or gossip a little with the lady in the next room? Happy are they, if, after their toilet is made, they have a call to make, or an errand to a store, and an apology for causing the store-keepers to tumble over their goods, little to their advantage. How thus should they acquire domestic habits, or be at all more prepared to "go to housekeeping" when the time comes, than they were at the outset? They cannot know what to expect from servants, nor how to manage their tempers, nor how to show them what they do not know. One has actually heard of people returning to the boarding-house system, because they could not find any comfort in a house of their own! Anything like the domestic altar, and family order, with all the consequent and useful responsibilities are prevented by this plan. Young persons are thrown in each other's way, that had better never have met; and the children cannot be well kept apart, however averse the parents of one family may be to the manners and training of another.

The young men are driven to frequent places of public amusement, because they have no private apartment in the house, or do not like the people they meet in those which are public. For their sakes the Sermons to young men are very well devised. It was pleasant to see many hundreds of them occupying quiet, comfortable seats, and listening to saving truths, eloquently delivered.

It was the custom in earlier days, when the States were in the colonial stage of their existence, for the families, when the cares of day were over, to dress and sit upon the piazza, conversing, cooling themselves, and frolicking, as the humor took them; and rare tales are told of that olden time, when wary parents could not preserve the hearts of lovely daughters from being wounded by the archer who has slain his thousands. One that particularly took my fancy may be related. A youth saw some fair sisters in a milliner's shop, got desperate in his admiration of one of them, and there and then made up his mind that he would have her to wife, though the stars should be against him. He learnt their name, and by-and-bye discovered their residence, and the stoop that was so happy as to afford them evening refreshment. He put on his best looks—and they were very good, as his portrait indicates—and his best manners. He passed and repassed, as if in search of some one, and then with a very honest-looking apology for interrupting their pleasant conversation, inquired for Dr. Somebody. The ladies had never heard of him. "Well, but he must be thereabout;" and so he pursued his search, and presently returning, told them that it had been to no purpose. When, an evening or two after, he was passing, he could not do less than salute the fair group; and so he continued, till he was invited to mount the steps; and thus, the Rubicon being surmounted, the rest went on as it were of course, and ended "as merry as a marriage-bell." Their descendants tell the tale with as much pleasure as a hero relates his battles, or a traveller his adventures.

These evening frolics of the stoop having become out of date, something like a substitute for them has arisen. In winter, ladies who have been all day in their walking dresses, will about tea-time polish themselves a little, not knowing who may step in; but as evening is the leisure time of the young gentlemen, the belles are sure of seeing some one.

About eight o'clock one and another drops in, and the sparks of lively and gleeful repartee which are instantly kindled in the company, partake still a little of the humors of the stoop. One was glad to see the young men escaping from their desks and from the dreariness of their boarding-house to mingle for an hour among fireside harmonies, which might remind them how it was with them before they quitted the old roof-tree of home, or lead them to hope how it may be again with them when prosperous circumstances permit them in turn to become family men.

No stronger or more painful evidence exists of the migratory habits of the natives, and of the multitude of homeless emigrants, than is daily witnessed in the dead-letter-room of the General Post Office at Washington.

Weekly, columns of the newspapers in every city, contain lists of unclaimed letters, and thus they are not sacrificed without exertion to bring owners and their letters together. When that fails they are finally congregated at the centre of government, and consigned to that chamber from which, as from a condemned cell, they only come forth to suffer the extreme sentence of the laws. It was a sad sight, that spacious hall full of letters. The surrounding table behind which sat the busy gentlemen, whose irksome task it is to open them, were covered with letters—so were the desks and shelves by the walls —so was the floor, where they were heaped up like a little hay-rick, their secrets all torn open and thrown down like common things. On one side is suspended on a machine a large sack, the receiver of these opened papers; which, when it is stuffed hard and fast till it can contain no more, is succeeded by another and another, and then having sacks enough to load a cart, they are sent off to the common to be consumed. The idea of the manner in which such things are managed in my own city, arises in painful contrast to the mind. There a mis-directed order to a tradesman, or inquiry about a servant, or any trifling paper, comes back to the writer reverently sealed and enveloped with a printed "ON HER MAJESTY'S SERVICE," and a "not found," or "removed," or "dead," marked on it. The hasty inquiry, why is not this done here? rises to the lips. But it need not be uttered—a minute's reflection brings the answer. The country is vast. The States are many. Favorite names are repeated on many cities, towns, and villages, till you may find ten places known by the same name. If the letter-writer omits to add the name of the State also, there are nine chances against the letter finding its owner. Then the multitude of blundering, of illegible, of nonsensical addresses is incalculable, what can they do? If they cannot convey them as they gladly would, the next best thing is, after a competent time, to destroy them.

The heap was a sad one. Sheets overflowing in fine delicate writing. How much beautiful sentiment might be there! Sheets, out of which had been plucked pretty little stockings, boots, gloves, muffatees, collars, purses, all such small love-gages as you could imagine wrought by kind grandmothers, and loving aunts and sisters, meant for a far different destination than a transient rest on the letter-opener's shelves. In one case there was a large envelope filled with loam. What could it be? Was it the specimen of the soil of a field to be purchased? Was it sacred earth to plant some cherished flower in? Was it from Jerusalem? "Her very dust to them is dear." None could tell. The informing paper was extracted and consigned to the ever-gathering heap.

> "But should he write and I not get it,
> 'Twere but a paper lost."

True, but a paper that might relieve some home-sick heart—a paper that might reveal the truth which has for months been longed for. A paper fraught with weighty messages of joy or woe to somebody. It was not, however, the beautifully written and well-filled sheets, that one felt most disposed to be sentimental over. The active pen which wrote these will write more. The next will, perhaps, be more fortunate. But the rough uncourtly paper, the awkward, unaccustomed penmanship. The sheet bought for one penny after a month's thinking about it—the letter written with pains and much trouble, and then carefully posted in a far-off land, which was once his *home*, to tell "Sandy," or "Patrick," that his parents still live and think of him, or that "Jànet" or "Kathleen" would still be in the mind to come out and redeem her long plighted troth, as soon as he can remit the dollars—the "yours till death." Is it lost to him that all important document! Is it to perish on the common at that *auto da fè!*

Is there no means to avoid these sad inflictions? Will they not cease until all the emigrants have gone over, and all the restless dwellers in the States have settled down, and all the correspondents have learnt to write legibly? Who can tell; but probably the melancholy heap would be reduced to one half its present size if it were more the custom to live in their own houses, so that people might have homes, instead of flitting about as they do from one boarding-house to another.

The children born and brought up in boarding-houses, will never look back on the domestic hearth, and the lively nursery, as they do who are born *at home.* Regret is the deeper, when one thinks of a people so essentially Saxon, and so full of fireside charities as the Americans are, thus imperceptibly dropping into Gallican manners ; kindling many an alluring ignis fatuus, and quenching or neglecting the very light of life.

When our good ship after many days' digging and snorting her way through cross-winds, and a stormy ocean, reached smoother water, and caught the first glimpse of the Neversinks, it was delightful to observe mutual gratulations, and talk about expectant relatives who will be listening for the gunfire, or for the news-boys, and about which will wait at home, and which will fly down to the dock, &c. Every one became lively, and some musical. One gentleman sung "home, sweet home," and all seemed to sympathize. A lady who could not speak English, and whose seat was by me at dinner, had often endured such French as my benevolence induced me to inflict on her. "What is that?" she inquired, "home—home—je ne comprends pas 'home, sweet home.'" It was strange to have the conviction forced on me, that among all the elegant and copious "tournures" of the French tongue, there is no word to express the idea of *home* any more than there is that of *comfort.* "Cela veut dire," replied I, "chez soi." "Pardon, Madame, chez soi qu'est ce que cela veut dire?" "On est bien aise de rentrez chez soi. On le trouve bien doux de revenir à la maison chez soi—chez soi"—"Ah," said she with a disappointed shrug, "chez soi, et voilà tout!" Woe worth the day when its boarding-houses, however useful and pleasant an accommodation they be to strangers, have become all the "home" Americans know, and when they shrug and say "Chez soi et voilà tout" of "Home, sweet home."

The Domestics.

If the descriptions of foreign travellers be not exaggerated, and some of the scenes of domestic life to be found in periodicals, painted by native pencils, be not for effect's sake colored too highly, we must suppose that housekeepers have their own difficulties in "getting along," and that society is at present in the attitude of an inverted pyramid, the apex much in danger of being bruised flat and mingled with the superincumbent weight of its base. Nevertheless, we English are not in a condition to judge the matter unless we take in various considerations, which require to be searched about for, and hunted out of unsuspected quarters. In a newspaper account of a trial, you may see how a scavenger in the witness-box states that "when he first observed the *gentleman* he was filling the dung-cart;" or in visiting that dreary police-prison, "the Tombs," a name as dreary as itself, you will be gravely told, "The *lady* in this cell is not connected with me, we only live together for the present." You might almost think they were associated together by choice. The "lady," your informant, has huge glittering ear-rings, and jet-black ringlets, and the "lady," her "associate for the present," has an ugly black eye, however she came by it. With this view of gentlemen and ladies we may begin to suspect that it is not the pyramid of society which has suffered inversion, but the old ordering of language. Suppose this, and your astonishment ceases, when you hear that a person rings at your door and asks if "the *woman* of the house be at home, for I am the *lady* that have come to help her (to) cook."

Another circumstance we, as lookers-on, have to learn. In that country, so plentifully supplied with luxurious food, there are no distinctions made between what is consumed in the dining-room and the hall. No fruits are so costly or rare as to be treasured up to appear again on the family table. There are no viands which the domestics are prohibited to touch. A lady receives without surprise, as an explanation why her bell has been so long unanswered, that her waiting-woman had not had anything comfortable since breakfast, and was finishing a glass of jelly recommended to her by the housekeeper.

In two houses situated in cities many hundred miles apart, the following little incident has surprised me:—The children had been allowed to sit up late to see the guests. They had bid good-night and gone away, but presently returned, and when on a second or third return, mamma was troubled and inquired, she had for reason what she seemed to receive as satisfactory, that nurse was having her ice, and could not come till she was ready. That part of the company's supper would have been spoiled for nurse's taste if she first put her charge to bed. If this arises from the good-tempered indulgence of the mistress, I venture to think it is carried beyond discretion. If she cannot help herself, there is need for amendment in the order of things.

A lady told me what befel her brother in the "far West." Let it be always remembered, that the state of things there is so new and utterly different from the east, and the West seems so indefinitely far, that eastern people do not shrink from criticizing manners and notions there, and are also ready to invite the observations of strangers.

The brother was a young lawyer who had left a rising city, the scene of his labors, and gone to ruralize in his clearing, where his house and its appliances were as comfortable as is usual in such circumstances. Some of his brethren of the bar met him at the assizes and told him they were coming to see his settlement and dine with him next day. The friendly youth hastened home intent on his hospitalities, intending that never heartier dinner smoked on board, than should grace his tomorrow. He was sorely disconcerted to find that his housekeeper had gone home, without leave or warning. He rode from clearing to clearing, seeking "help." But none was to be had, as everybody was as independent and averse to servitude as himself. He was musing on his own talent for roasting turkey and boiling ham, and about to return crestfallen and discomfited to receive his friends, when a damsel compassionated his case so as to propose to "go cook" on condition of being at table with the guests, as she would be no man's servant, and had never cooked a dinner of which she had not partaken. The terms were gladly accepted. Without doubt her independent character, and the American respect for the female sex, secured her becoming treatment, but one feels persuaded that the awkwardness of her position must have produced some quarrel between the compassion and the dignity which had, when united, placed her in so new and curious a situation. This, however, it must be re-urged, was in the *far* West.

Another circumstance which never could have occurred in England may be related.

On a very stormy and cold Sunday, having caught cold at morning church, I resolved to remain by the fireside in my chamber in the afternoon, and purposely invited a young Scotch woman to come to me, when all should be gone to church. She was a stranger, and a sudden and early widow, and but for the benevolence of the friends I visited, would have been without a shelter. I wished to discuss her prospects, to let her tell her troubles, and take the great relief to a full heart, if she needed it, of having a good hearty cry beside me. I wished to try to lead her to the only consolation which will never fail, and to tell her of the faithfulness of the widow's God. She had scarcely been persuaded to take a seat, when the old housekeeper introduced herself uninvited. When asked quietly if she wanted anything, she said it was very cold, she wished to put more wood on the fire. After she had done this, she deliberately drew forward a rocking-chair, established herself in the centre of the hearth, and began to tell me of the ignorance of my young countrywoman, who, when she first came, would have dined with the colored people if she had not been there to rescue her from such a disgrace. When asked what harm it would have done her if she had, she seemed to discover that all people from Caledonia were alike savage in their ideas, and said, "She was a native American, they all knew better than to associate with *such*; keep them at a distance—if you give them an inch, they will take an ell. She had rather eat all her meals standing in her own bed-room all her life than eat with one of them." "Well, now, that seems strange to me,—cook is dark, every morsel you eat comes through colored hands; and Ben and Will that wait at table do everything for us, and I don't feel that we get any harm from them." "Wait! yes, that's another thing—keep them under, and they do well enough; but let them once look up the least bit, and there's an end of them—they won't do no more good after that." "What will you say when I tell you, I have dined at table with a colored gentleman, and found him well-bred, well-informed, and a true Christian." The old lady rose from her seat, and I expected she was going to avoid my pestilent society, but she reconsidered the matter, and, to my regret, re-seated and re-rocked herself. "Well, he might be a Christian, I believe some on them are." "If they are then our heavenly Father does not dislike darkies as you do." "No, to be sure, for He made them." "And if they get to heaven, and you get to heaven, what will you do about them there?" "Oh! that will be all settled when the time comes." With such troublesome converse did the aged domestic obtrude herself upon me in my own chamber, till I proposed to read to them, and then she fell asleep. My unbidden guest was awakened by the return from church of the rest of the family, and was, and still is, unconscious of having committed what was in my eyes a most unwonted act. It must be confessed that, though she received no invitation or encouragement, yet after she had come, my curiosity was excited to see how such a visit might turn, so that I gave no indication of annoyance at her presence.

In spite of these manners, which, though not what we are used to, we are not entitled to pronounce upon as being bad, servants seem to do all that is expected of them, at least, so far as a visitor might observe. The only thing we found difficulty about, was how to get our shoes cleaned. Mine were laid on the hearth day by day, where the housemaid in making the fire must be obliged to see and remove them. That did not procure a brushing. I have put them outside the chamber-door, and seen them kicked about and tumbled over, still the soil was left on them. I have put them on again, wondering if no ragged school-boy, with red-flannel shirt, and a blacking-box might be found in the streets as in London—and if found, how one could employ him. In short, where all besides was hospitality, comfort, and elegance, there stood your boots with the mud of yesterday in bright brown rims. When at last the favor was asked to have them brushed, you saw an expression of countenance which, it ought to be told, was never seen on any other occasion, that betrayed that something about this one service is offensive or disagreeable in a high degree. At last I inquired of a sensible lady what was wrong, and was told that shoe-cleaning is counted an office so menial, that it is beneath the dignity of freemen to condescend to such an employment,—and then it was explained why everybody wore India rubbers, or highly-polished leather, which can be washed with soap, water, and a sponge, and having acquired this knowledge, it was easy to possess oneself of the means of having comfortable feet again.

A gentleman whom I knew slightly in early days was far too much of a democrat in his notions of government to put up with such freedom as is to be had under a limited monarchy, and spurning his native shores, he took refuge in the "model republic," that he might be entirely free. After a few days' residence, when he found his boots perseveringly left untouched, he got his first lesson on the impossibility of having all things ordered to his liking even in a republic. He asked in a haughty tone, "why his boots were not cleaned," when he was told by a damsel from green Erin, that he "did not suppose she came all the way to America to clean shoes. She was as good as he was here, whatever she had been at home."

It really seems that many of the errors as to what is becoming in the several classes of society, originate more with the extravagant and unfounded expectations of the new-comers, than with those who have seen the light first under a republic. The poor Milesian, who seeing a goodly pile of hams at the door of a store, said, "This is a free country—I'm hungry—I'll take one," and shouldering it, walked off, was stopped by the policeman, to inquire how he came by it, and thus got proof that freemen have rights, peculiar and individual, as well as nations.

If we balance between this style of freedom, and the indolence and refusals to work that are born of fulness of bread, conceit, and pride, I suppose the scale will turn in favor of the wholesome though untaught aspirants after the dignity of independence rather than in favor of the pampered minions of luxury. A friend of my own, calling in London on an Earl, was admitted by the lusty porter, but having made his way thus into the outer hall, no one seemed prepared to help him onward. He saw behind a screen four powdered lackeys busily engaged at cards, and called to one to show him up to Lord ——, when presently an altercation arose about whose turn it was to go up, and who had answered the last bell. It should be stated that my friend went without equipage, his great-coat over his arm, in as simple state as did the Bishop of Ohio, when he could with difficulty find admission to the palace of the Bishop of London. The gentleman began quietly to ascend the stairs, saying, "I shall go up to the library and tell his Lordship that his people are too much engaged in gambling to have leisure to show his guests up." This produced a rush among the pampered crew, as if they all wished to share the fatigue and interruption occasioned by their master's visitor.

Is there not more of mental vigor and honesty, also, in the American struggle after independence, even where its true character is mistaken, than in this?

It has been said in explanation of the exceeding fragile and delicate appearance of the young mothers, that their health is injured by the ceaseless exertion and anxiety they undergo in consequence of not obtaining domestics, especially nurses, in whom they can confide. Certain it is, that to an eye accustomed to dwell on the vigorous aspect and rosy health of English women, there is pain in observing the pallid, languid loveliness of many of the women. The effect was such on me, that in my first voyage up the Hudson, when I saw a lady rise to cross the floor of the saloon, I felt inclined to offer her my help, under the impression that she had just recovered from a fever. But it may be fairly conjectured that the want of the habit of taking plenty of open air exercise, and the too lavish variety of foods, affect the health more than domestic exertions.

The simplicity with which intelligent and lady-like women go about their affairs at home, gave me never-ceasing pleasure. Persons of the same rank in Scotland lend a hand in domestic matters on occasion, as they do in America, but they do it secretly, as if ashamed. You may live in the house, and never suspect that the lady washes a cup, or arranges the dessert or the tea-cakes, and never see her apron. While the American, emancipated from the ceremonies and thraldoms that wind themselves by degrees around our social systems, puts on a sensible apron, that covers her all round, takes her pretty oaken pail with its shining brass hoops, her swab (a miniature of the implement with which the sailor washes his deck) and her tray, and begins operations on the breakfast table, inviting you not to withdraw, but chat with her while she puts all straight—it being Monday, her maids are in the laundry. This is common sense, and most enjoyable, putting all parties at ease. This result was produced most effectually, and in a naïve manner, on our first visit to an elegant mansion in the hill country.

A party of eight or ten had made an incursion on the hospitable family. We had finished a most capital tea-supper, consuming animal food, tarts, and preserves, together with what we call tea in England, and were amusing ourselves by hearing the histories of persons whose portraits adorned the walls of the large drawing-room. When the bright lady seemed to conclude a mental deliberation in vocal sounds, "I suspect I won't mind these English ladies; the people must be all busy to-night, it's Saturday, so I'll wash the cups." With that her page was called, who produced all the needful apparatus, and ran to and fro, disposing the china as it was washed in the closets with glass doors, which occupied the ante-room. While we were not deprived of the brilliant sallies of the washer, which doubtless were all the more lively, that she had no uneasy household care restraining her.

Whatever may exist in the interior, the difficulty with respect to servants is fast vanishing away on the seaboard, under the amazing influx of Irish people. In general, they make capital servants. They are quick at learning, obliging, and cheerful; and, if you but light on such as are trustful and honest, of which there are many, you will be very well off. I have seen two sisters and a brother, each I think having come over singly, serving in one family, all under the influence of true religon and members of a church. But the great difficulty is, that most of the Irish are Romanists. They are active and industrious, but they are under the dominion of the priests. They go to confession, and then what becomes of your family secrets if you have any? They engaged with you to attend family worship, but that has been confessed among other sins, and from that first confession begins their prohibition. They are seen no more at morn and eve bending at prayer with the rest. It is in vain that resistance is made; and one, otherwise suitable domestic is dismissed after another, with the resolution that no priest shall regulate the affairs of your family. The process goes on, and at last the wearied mistress gives in, and punishes herself no more by sending away useful helps.

There are many domestic influences silently flowing from these popish servants, which excite doubt when one hears the cheerful and confident assertions that popery must expire under free institutions,—that it is expiring,—that it never can make head in the United States. Is it doing nothing when it banishes all the servants from a share in domestic religious observances, and gets your people away at the hest of a priest to attend certain funerals and keep certain festivals, whose mysteries are unknown to Protestants? I heard of a girl complaining to her mistress that it cost her four dollars out of her last month's wages, to pay for carriages and attend funerals of people whom she did not know, but whom the priest wished to have buried *respectably*. Is it nothing to have a person in your nursery, who instead of singing to her charge a hymn about the Saviour, will teach them a "Hail Mary!" Is it nothing to have them do what I saw done by a very respectably dressed nurse in the Cathedral at Baltimore, while we were walking round to examine the paintings. She led her little girl to the holy-water font, and signed her with the cross. She led her to a pew, and taught her to kneel quietly while she recited her paternoster. She led her to the altar, and made her bend her knees before the picture of a saint; I forget if it were the Mother of Jesus or not. And again, as they went out, she crossed the dear little one with holy-water. Walking along the street beside them on coming out, the child put out her little hand confidingly to one of our party, and cheerfully trotted along when the hand was taken; the nurse explaining that the little one had recently lost her mother, and imagined that as we were in mourning we must belong to her. One did not know whether more to pity the nurse whose zeal was so true and yet so dark, or the motherless one who was under the tender training of an honest but misguided woman.

Is popery having no influence, when in accordance with its usual treachery, it insinuates female Jesuits —lay sisters—now into this family, now into that, in the guise of domestics, to learn family secrets and discover vulnerable characters? There are alarming revelations made from the confessional of William

Hogan, quondam Roman Catholic priest in Ireland and America.

Thoughtless and worldly parents who send their children to convents to procure for them cheap and elegant education, expose them without the guard of previous instruction, to the eye-attracting and sense-deluding power of popery. If there be found in the character the devotional element; and if life in its early stages is shaded by disappointment, or its occupations be found unsatisfying, how readily does thought revert to the tranquillity of the nunnery and the narratives of the sisterhood about their world-exclusive happiness. Home has taught them nothing of true religion, they naturally take refuge in all the religion they know anything of without discerning that it is false, and thus we hear of not a few of the educated classes falling into that snare.

An instance of the way this quiet, insinuating poison works, was the talk of a wide circle while we were in the United States. The story reached us but one remove from the parties acting in it, and we had reason to know its leading features to be true, from many other quarters.

An interesting young lady, who longed for more satisfying enjoyments than could be derived from a heartless round of gayety, obtained leave of her parents to retire for a short time to a convent merely to rest and be quiet. The nuns and confessors plied their vocation, and persuaded the poor child, that she would find the rest she sought in taking the vail. Her figure and the circle she moved in, rendered her vows a circumstance calculated to produce a sensation; and heartily did the vailed and black-serged sisterhood give themselves to the production of a grand *tour de théatre* at the ceremonial that was to accompany her renunciation of the world. They sent for the dressmaker who had adorned her for scenes of folly, and carefully was she measured, and minute were the descriptions of the white satin, and blond, and bows, and white roses, with which the bride of heaven was to be adorned and crowned, to make the world which she was to renounce appear the finer, and her sacrifice to the Church the greater. The intimidated dressmaker heard with wonder the volubility of the sombre sisterhood on blonds, and festoons, and rosettes, and at last inquired if she ordered all these fine things at a store, in whose name must it be done? who was responsible for the debt she was to incur? The Lady Abbess replied that the mother of the young lady, who was cognizant of and consenting to the whole affair, would discharge the bill. The order was taken, not to the store, but to the mother, who learnt for the first time the gulf on the brink of which her neglected child stood. And so, here was a bold lie told by the head of a *religious* house to aid in entrapping the seeker of true peace.

The indignant and wrathful father went to the Nunnery to claim his child. He could not see her, nor could she be given up. He then went to the Bishop, where he again met with a refusal; and it was only after he informed the Holy Father that his child, if so devoted, would become a burden on the Convent, as he would never give her a cent lest she should bestow it on them, that they unloosed their covetous grasp, and suffered her to return to the parental home.

It is very true that many, on discovering the treachery, untruthfulness, and despotism of popery, flee from it, to fall untaught into the power of Infidelity, not so superstitious, but quite as unenlightened and as bold in evil as that system from which they have escaped. Surely no true Protestant can rejoice in such falling away as this. As politicians, both parties must be equally unsound, and unfit to bear influence in the affairs of a Christian nation. If the Infidel votes for misrule, and the Papist for the dominion of Popery, they are more likely to coalesce with each other to gain their object, than with any other party in the State. The Roman Catholic Archbishop is understood to wield complete authority over the disposal of every popish vote in the city; and in New York, if I was rightly informed, the influence of Popery, not only in the municipal government, but in the returns to the Legislature and Congress, is, for the present, in the ascendant. It is so by Papists going with the party that promises most to favor them. Popery acts by no fixed rule. Its principles, its motives, and its acts alike shun the daylight of truth—and hence its power, and the danger arising from it. Its power works not only in the vicinity of the ballot-box, but in the sacred sanctuary of the homes and nurseries of the cities; and every note of caution on the subject, however feeble, ought to be deemed friendly.

The same method of hearing where servants are to be found, is used in the United States as with us. What is here called a Register, is there called an Intelligence Office. But in either case, it is not persons of the highest character that need to enter their names in such lists. The numerous strangers who are driven to extremities before they find situations adopt methods of seeking them, which are startling and new to visitors in the country. I have been repeatedly stopped in the streets of New York with the question, "Do you want any help?" followed up with, "Well, then, do you know any family that does?" And on one occasion the charm of a lovely sunset drive amid the elegant villas, and shady trees, and glancing waters of Staten Island, was destroyed for me by the address of a nice-looking young woman on that subject. She rushed out of the gate of a handsome house, almost under our horses' feet, and obtested us with all the eloquence of an Irish tongue, to stop, to listen, and to procure her a place. "She had been five days off the ocean. She had been advised to come to this Island, because it was full of respectable families. She had gone from house to house for two days. No one wanted her—no one cared for her. Och hone! she was homeless—she was penniless—she was friendless. What could she do?" She wrung her despairing hands, and her tears streamed down unwiped. We told her of Intelligence Offices—feeling that they were but poor helps. We spoke to her of hope—of asking help of the God who had brought her safely across the sea—and gave her what would secure her a few nights' lodgings, but left her where we met her, weeping on the road. If the poor stranger had had courage to leave the thronged vicinity of the city, she would doubtless soon and gladly have been engaged on a farm. Yet one does not wonder that the heart of a female should faint and shrink from such an effort. She is tempted to remain in the crowd by the likelihood of forming an engagement, and she likes to be in the midst of her own country people.

It is not only within the range of emigrant ships, that this out-of-doors and from house to house method of seeking places is followed. In the pretty town of Springfield, Mass., a very respectable looking middle-aged person addressed to me the same inquiry. Being desirous of knowing if really good servants adopt such a method, I inquired what place she desired to occupy. She replied, that she had acted as cook, and as laundress, in some of the best houses in the neighborhood.

The influx of people, which is a perpetual stream, must speedily lessen the difficulty of procuring, and also of managing "helps."

The Funerals.

Nothing in America comes over one's feelings as so unlike home, as the manner in which everything is conducted relating to the burial of the dead.

On our landing we heard that the earth was that day to receive all that remained of a venerable and excellent lady, to see whom was one of the day dreams indulged in when preparing to cross the ocean. She had been born in a house, which for many years was my happy dwelling. A degree of almost romantic sympathy, had existed between us, fostered by messages and pictures of her early home, so that the news that I should not see her, inflicted a real disappointment.

The next best thing, was to honor her memory by waiting on the last obsequies.

So much are we the children of habit, that the sight of a polished mahogany receptacle shrunk me, as if there were an absence of reverence or of sorrow in parting with her, betrayed in the very color of her coffin. It is true I had seen a colored coffin once—but it was that of a Russian Princess, covered with crimson velvet, and bedizened with all the blazoned heraldry which the death within mocks at, and holds at its true worth, a show of grandeur which is frequently the substitute for tears.

What was my amazement, nay, confusion, that very evening, while driving through the brilliant streets, to see whole stores set forth, with coffins of all sizes leaning against the walls—one black to show that they could be had in that fashion, all the others glancing in bright polish, and some with shining rows and figures of yellow nails. Coffins tall and short, for aged persons, and for babes, pattern coffins for dolls, with a stand in the centre of the room covered with glass, exhibiting fashions of last garments to choose from. Everything has its fashion.—In China it is said they mourn in yellow. With us it is all black, deep black, according to the old ballad—

"In black hung the kitchen,
In black hung the hall,
In black hung the dining-room,
Parlor and all."

Lament for Lady Jane Seymour.

In America the mourning is lighter, briefer, and

if it happens not to suit, black garments are not assumed at all. This, in certain circumstances, is very right. Many a poor Scotch family will run in debt rather than not adopt sable decencies, or they will abstain from public worship for months, rather than attend on it in colored clothes. But polished shining coffins ! a show-room of them, as smart in its way as that of a tailor or a milliner ! One must have lived a life-time in the one country, and then seen the other, before you can know how the heart shivers at the sight. One of the Broadway stores you will find still open at midnight ; its lamp still glaring and reflected from those shining surfaces into the outer darkness, and a man the watcher of the place, seated in the midst, moving his head in drowsy noddings, the dreary living thing present. Within or below the place they have accommodation for the remains that may be sent there under the clouds of night. Why such unwonted provision ? Is it not enough to prepare the narrow house when it is needed ? and may not the clay repose where the spirit left it, till the hour of its last deposit ? No, it does not suit—and here again we meet the effect of boarding-house living and dying. The living, and healthy, and gay, do not like to hear of death so near them. Many die in the house unknown to the mass of the boarders, and hence the convenience of ready-made coffins, and midnight removals of remains to the undertaker's, and of hasty funerals. Thus is death deprived of its suitable impression, and the solemn thoughts naturally associated with a spirit's entrance into the invisible world are dissipated. People seem to live in a hurry, to love, to die, to be mourned, and in too many cases to be forgotten in a hurry, which, in this dying world, when presently it will be said of each of the living, "and he died," is an unwise condition.

The little glass door opposite the face in the coffin lid, also hurts English feeling. It seems a compromise between the popish fashion of the exposure of the body dressed as in life, and the protestant custom of closing up reverently all that is left, to wait the sound of the last trumpet. Were it not usual to inter very speedily, this exposure of the countenance, which seems to me afflicting, would probably not be practised. With us it could not do at all.

In the middle ranks in New York it is usual for any neighbors that choose to enter the house of mourning, and look upon the corpse. A Scotch lady whose feelings revolted against such an exhibition, said she was forced to send the very disobliging message to the many who rung her bell, that she could not admit strangers, and allowed of no such custom. She observed very wisely, that she feared such familiarity with the aspect of death, had rather a hardening than a softening tendency, and that she had been shocked to hear young girls and boys remarking on the "natural" or "life-like," or "death-like" appearances before them, as coolly as they would criticize a picture or a doll.

In England, Christian parents have experience of the solemnizing effect on their offspring, when first conducted to look upon the frame that no longer breathes and looks lovingly on them. It is wrong to make that a light subject, which exists ever as a token of divine displeasure against human disobedience,—or that a common event which can befall each of us but once—and that once!—which kingdom may it open to us?

Invitations to funerals are frequently attached to the obituary notice in the newspaper—and the attendance depends much on the esteem in which the departed was held. The connected and the unconnected go alike, and you may see ladies in gay vestments with bright roses in their hats, mingling sincere tears with those dressed in the deepest mourning. If it is the funeral of a well-known Christian character, and a member of a church, the body is laid in front of the pulpit and the friends gather round while an act of worship is performed, and a short oration is delivered, which is not simply laudatory, or pronouncing judgment on the dead, but rather warning to the living. The service is generally simple and touching, and calculated to be useful. The Episcopal form nearly resembles that of England.

The Odd Fellows funerals are more like triumphal processions, with bands of music, flags, ribbons, and all the gaudy insignia of official people in the society, than like returning the ashes of a departed brother to the parent dust. It is said they are rendered very injurious to the morals of the community by being generally performed on the Lord's day, and during the hours of worship, and that many step in as they pass, to each place where intoxicating drinks are sold, until they return reeling from the cemetery.

As to the Irish funerals, the first I observed consisted of twenty-eight carriages, crammed with people of all ages, with laughing faces and loud jollity, dressed in red and green ribbons, rendered more conspicuous by being blown about through the open windows, by the wind. Not having observed the little modest hearse which preceded all this fun and frolic, the inquiry was not unnatural, if these people were going to a fair,—and the suprise was great to learn that they were following a funeral to the Popish burial-ground at Williamsburgh.

The hearse, in America, is a modest, low conveyance,—somewhat lower and narrower than our carriages for piano-fortes,—free from the pomp of plumes which look so like an attempt to put an air of grandeur on the most subduing event in life. The absence of escutcheons and blazonry on the house of the departed, becomes the simplicity of a republic. A more touching and simple symbol we first observed in Baltimore, and saw it afterwards in Philadelphia and elsewhere. Where death has entered, a strip of black crape is attached to the handle of the front door, the length of which indicates the age of the departed, so that no unwarned visitors can intrude on private sorrow. It is also customary in some places, to fix the outside shutters with crape in a position more than half closed, so that the inmates live in that obscured light for many weeks, or months, if it be the head of the family who is dead, or if the departed is deeply mourned.

The Americans, partaking as they do of the mixture of many nations, have caught up tastes and habits from various quarters. The German neat and tasteful arrangement of small things, shows itself in the very hanging of the empty fruit-baskets in festoons at a gardener's stall, and the arranging of small flower-pots with an eye to the undulating line of beauty. And thus, in putting the Hall of Independence, at Philadelphia, in mourning for the late President, they had drawn a long piece of crape through the beak of the eagle which floats over the figure of Washington, in such a manner, that its folds fell gracefully down, shading the statue on either side. The effect was beautiful, and suggestive of many thoughts. Men may be cut off, but institutions will remain,—a President may expire, but the Republic will survive.

Ah! what a noble country! and yet how like this blighted world. It has a dark shade mingling among its stars and stripes. One under which it sighs and groans. When will vigor, true independence and virtue, be given to it to remove that dark shade—and allow all who admire its achievements and honor its ingenious industry, to admire without a sigh, and to honor without a drawback?

That dark shade would not withdraw from the mind in the Hall of Independence, nor even at

Washington, when the heart swelled in contemplation of the magnificent Capitol and all the affairs transacted within it. It appeared in the countenance and manner of the Southerner, so different from those of the North. It hung about the figure of the shrinking *free* colored man, who seems to quail under the cold eye of the white. It trembled around the lowly quiet celerity of the slave who watched your look as if it were his duty to conjecture your wants, not from love, but from fear. It even clouded the services of the handy little boy who ran from wing to wing of the busy hotel, carrying all sorts of small wares and messages. He might be happy in his ignorance, poor boy, and he was not harshly treated, and his mother was in the house. But he was not his mother's child—he was his master's. She was not her own, nor her husband's—she also was her master's. And who was he? a humane man enough, born under providence with a white skin, otherwise he too might have become the chattel of another.

Forgive the generous wish that no tarnish should be on your country's standard. I know that millions of you hate the system which I mourn—I know that it is not foreign remark or interference which will rid you of it. You are a free people. Your own intelligence and moral energy must reclaim you—no external powers can turn you back if you go astray. You have expelled slavery from one half of your land, and live in the expectation that you will presently rid the other half of it, nay, that you will ultimately be the happy means of expelling it from the world. Yet perhaps there is some deception in your case. Can it be, as one has heard it many times stated, that, had it not been for foreign interference, Kentucky, Missouri, Maryland, and Delaware, would have ceased to hold slaves ere now? Why, if you would do right, allow your displeasure against "foreign interference" to have any power in inducing you to continue a wrong? Do you not deceive yourselves? I see our countryman James Stuart, in his "Three Years in America," adopted the idea of the friends with whom he conversed, that in ten years, slavery would be at an end in Kentucky. That was said in 1830. Twenty-one years of ill-gotten gains and woe have passed since then. The delusions of hope that tend but to prolong a system which themselves abhor, are they not most pernicious and unfounded? When did evil arise and break itself to pieces, and rejoice over its own ruins? It cannot be. The better genius of Kentucky must awake and do the work,—and rising from the wreck of its wrong, spring up to what just principles, genius, industry, and plentiful and fertile land, and free institutions, can make it. It must heal itself,—and if it does not, another ten, another twenty years may pass, and Kentucky and Delaware will be found as they are now, groaning and hating, but enduring and abetting slavery.

It was not my design to allude to this most painful subject. But in contemplating death, the termination of all our toils and all our gains, how could the depression of the colored race and its termination fail to arise in the mind: "Behold, the tears of the oppressed, and they had no comforter. Wherefore, I praised the dead which are already dead, more than the living who are yet alive." Yea—presently—haste to be just before the time comes, for presently—"The small and the great will lie down together, where the servant is free from his master."

Having fallen on this sore subject, it is right to make a remark or two to place British motives for remarking on the condition of the Africo-American race in a kinder point of view than that in which they generally first appear to an American.

We are not used to see colored people at home, though our own heavy share of the evil and responsibility of transporting them from Africa, and placing them in a state of bondage, leads us to think much of them in absence, and to be anxious about their condition when we see them and visit their haunts.

For myself, and it may truly be said of thousands besides, my observation and questions about them, are from motives the very reverse of a desire to censure, or a pleasure in remarking on what is felt by Americans to be the unsound and inconsistent part of their constitution. I wanted to know their position, social and religious, in the Free States. I wanted to know the mind of the slave-holders in the Slave States. I longed for leave to hope for good in the one, and to see good in the other. The manner in which such questions were generally met, pained me sincerely. It was the only subject on which I saw a tendency to a ruffle on the sunny surface of American temper, and reminded me of Tom Moore's anecdote of an interview he had with Byron. Byron seemed never to have forgiven the providence which had disfigured his otherwise beautiful person, by a club-foot. While the poets conversed, the eye of the Irish lyrist rested on the foot. The saturnine lord observed it, and his countenance darkened. Poor Tom became aware, and evaded a bitter burst, by making his eyes wander carelessly over the whole person, as if he had not specially marked the foot, and gradually the thunder-cloud dispersed, and sunshine returned. Every nation has its club-foot—some have two—some are perfect centipedes in deformities,—happy America, if she have but one. It is the more painfully deforming, but will be the more easily remedied. Even young ladies seem expert tacticians on this subject, and carry the war into the enemy's camp with great keenness. When a simple inquiry is made, not by an enemy, but a true friend, they accuse England of the cruelties perpetrated in Manchester on the manufacturers of cotton cloth as being worse than those inflicted on negroes who raise the raw material. They hardly believe when told that these people are free, that if they do not like one master they can engage with another, that they receive wages for their work, and if oppressed or injured they can bring the oppression before a magistrate. If, however, convinced that this is not a point where they can make a breach in the wall of the British constitution, they will assail you on the wrongs of Ireland. Should the truth that Ireland has been misgoverned by reason of its Popish preferences be conceded, they triumph and say it does not become us to criticize slavery; as if evils on one side of the Atlantic could neutralize those on the other—or as if evils in our government of Ireland—the remedy of which has cost Britain millions of gold, and more than millions of ingenuity, trouble, and disappointment—ought to seal up our hearts against every benevolent sentiment in reference to the African race, or shut us out from the natural desire of information as to the condition of one branch of the human species.

The colored people, who imitate all the respectable customs of the whites, have their funeral processions and their mourning garments, and look much more like paying respect to their dead, and feeling sympathy for the living, than the Irish do. Those of them who have any religion, are Protestants, and form the procession, not to please, or to put money in the purse of the priest, but to show kindness to the departed. I heard the minister of a colored church announce from the pulpit the death of a highly esteemed church-member, and the hour of his funeral, inviting attendance, and stating that if the choir could be spared by their employers, it would fitly assist a becoming solemnity if they would attend, and sing two appropriate hymns, which he pointed out. There was neither levity nor show,

but a becoming sentiment apparent in what the good man advised.

One custom, which at first surprised me, but afterwards commended itself as most convenient, prevails, as I found on inquiry, in many cities and villages. In cases of death, some considerate neighbor borrows for the bereaved family suitable dresses, from any one who has them, which are worn on occasion of the funeral, and then returned, thus leaving the mourners undisturbed, till their own convenience enables them to procure at leisure what they require. I have known one excellent Christian gentlewoman, in case of the death of one of the most highly esteemed pastors of her city, consider the age and size of the daughters, and who of similar figure among her acquaintance were wearing mourning at present. She then set off herself, accompanied by her maid, procured what she wanted, bonnets, shawls, and everything necessary, and carried them to the house of mourning, where they were willingly received, and used without scruple.

I also saw a dear matron, whose emotions and actions run together like parted mercury, leave the room, saying, "I think the gown I am wearing will look best for poor Mrs. —— at the funeral—will you excuse me, ladies, while I go and change it, that she may have it." Refinement that is refined away into inanity may be sqeamish at this plan, and the reserve of ancient etiquette may scorn it. To me, there was a simplicity, and heartiness, and helpfulness in the style of sympathy, which indicated real love for the neighbor. And who that has gone through the infliction of having boxes of bonnets and caps to fit on; and that has stood under the hand of a dress-maker, when ready to expire, and flung herself down, when released, in an irrepressible burst of woe, would not feel the gentle helping hand in such a place as this, to be like that of a ministering angel.

The natural and the real is always beautiful in time of sorrow, and to be preferred to the artificial and the ceremonial.

The Cemeteries and Firemen.

THE cemeteries are laid out in fine taste. Père-la-Chaise at Paris has formed the pattern, and tastefully is it imitated, and even surpassed. There are many beautiful. That on the banks of the Passaic at Newark, has a fine position in reference to the river. It was rather a delicate matter to pronounce between the claims of Mount Auburn at Boston, and Greenwood beyond Brooklyn. Not only because both are beautiful, but because there exists a degree of rivalry on the subject between Boston and New York, of which latter city, Greenwood is the principal cemetery. It contains 242 acres of the most beautifully varied grounds, and is rich in avenues of pines, elms, and yews; with fine slopes shaded by magnificent locusts, cypress, and weeping willow; and picturesque pieces of water, with fountains casting up the sparkling element to a great height, which falling, forms rainbows in the sunbeams and tranquillizes the spirit with its monotonous and stilly plash. One felt inclined to linger out the day, and yet to return again on the morrow.

There is much taste and sentiment in the monuments in both these beautiful cemeteries. Some massive, of gray granite, mingling well with the more varied forms of white marble. Mount Auburn has memorials to Fulton, Channing, and Spurzheim—the latter noble in its simplicity; the name alone in the centre of the tablet being the only epitaph. In the inscription on Channing's monument, one cannot but remark that they have evaded confessing his Unitarian principles by making mention only of the "*Christian community* to which he belonged," or a similar expression. Was the rumor then true, that in his latter days, the apostle of Unitarianism found Christ as a pattern-man, inadequate to his soul's necessities? Would that it may have been so.

At Greenwood, the lamb, the dove, the broken bud, the bursting chrysalis, the rising sun, the embraced urn, the veiled mourner, and whatever other emblem grief and faith mingled might suggest to taste, are to be seen. Nothing, however, seemed so very touching as the name alone. The sacred spot is measured out, and encircled by a light iron fence. On the locked gateway the family name is placed in large characters; but within, as each dear member occupies the place, you see on the monument, "Our Emily," "Our Henry," "Our Mother," "Our dear Parents," "Our only Son." If you will know who they are, you must look at the gate, but they who placed them there know well. They were *Ours*, the spot and the ashes are *Ours* still. With that pertinacity indicative of immortality and the resurrection, affection cleaves to the ashes; and many a rose within the rail, and many a bunch of "Forget-me-not" planted at the feet, shows that love is stronger than death, and makes its vow of constancy even to the cold clay.

The Firemen's monuments are noble and deservedly conspicuous. The cold marble erected to their memories was their country's only method of expressing its gratitude to them. And above the rest shows the statue of that brave man with the sleeping infant on his arm, to rescue whom he perilled his own life, and—lost it. As a work of art it is very beautiful; but as a testimony of his people's gratitude, it is sublime. The man who wins the battle, or raises the siege, or secures the peace, receives of course his meed of laurels, and "storied urn and monumental bust;" but the man who risks his life to save one poor little infant, who works not for fame nor for fortune, but for humanity, how worthy is he of a statue! It was bravely done! One honors the patriotic spirit that erected it. The same spirit was also shown in the erection of that other beautiful monument over the grave of the Pilot, who in saving the ship was himself drowned.

Having mentioned firemen, it may be as well to remark upon them here.

Fires are more frequent in the United States than elsewhere. "How it comes let doctors tell." Wooden houses alone will not account for it—as wood, though combustible, will not burn unless it be kindled. They have, however, become nearly as expert in extinguishing as they seem careless in kindling fires—so that a stranger learns by and by to hear the startling toll which announces the number of the district where a conflagration is going on, without any unusual beating of heart, even though it be not far off. In Philadelphia, people profess to be more afraid of the damage done by the water than by the fire.

We learned that the firemen had certain immunities, and that their enrolment originated with the Quakers. According to their principles, Friends could not go to war, but to prove themselves willing to defend the State they offered to take charge of extinguishing fires, on condition that they should not be liable to serve in the militia. They have other privileges I believe, such as not being called to sit as jurymen on trials. In return, however, they have no sinecure office. The night without a fire is the exception, and it is not uncommon during winter, to have several in one night.

One never saw a more light-built, active set of men, than those of the fire brigades. They wear dresses fit to protect the head, and leave their limber limbs unencumbered; and they have as much pride in the bright brasses and gay painting of their engine, as a sailor has in his ship, or a driver in his team. The first who with his engine reaches the scene of danger, is captain for the night; and so zealous are they of this honor, that they will remain in a room behind the engine-room, for the purpose of being ready to start on the first ring of the bell.

That they are courageous, and command often in the midst of danger with a general's eye, all their countrymen know. And that many of them are gentle as well as brave, many a deed of tender consideration for sufferers can testify. One little specimen of this came under my own knowledge, and pleased me greatly.

The house of one of my emigrant countrymen was in flames—the usual amount of agitation, racket, confusion, smoke, and hammering and tearing down were going forward amid the fire. A young daughter of the family was rushing to a picture on the wall of one of the rooms, when a fireman caught her and said she would peril her life. "Oh! but I must save it—I must. It is the picture of my home in Scotland." "Stand there then," said the kindly man, and bounding himself over the falling embers, rescued the treasure, and through the thickening cloud of smoke leapt back to present it to the agitated girl. Here was good-nature, sentiment, and sympathy, mingling with courage in the heat and hurry of the scene. The dear girl showed me her old home and the Tweed, so familiar and so dear to us both, and told me of this kindly act with sparkling eyes. She never knew her benefactor.

It has been mysteriously hinted that these fire brigades, originating in so honorable and humane a purpose, have been invaded by various evils, and made the tools of infidel encroachments, and political intrigue. How much to be lamented, if true, and how desirable that some salutary corrective be applied—some salt cast into the mass to save it from putrefaction.

They are a popular Society in every city. Courage dwells with, and protection flows from them.

Will not some of the ladies who shower nosegays on their heads when, on the anniversary, their gay procession and glittering engines pass through the streets, devise some method of exhibiting their gratitude which may infuse a moral and elevating leaven into the occupation of these men, who watch at midnight for their safety?

At the New York Fair (as they call the annual exhibition of the industry and manufactures of the whole State) the display of all the material engaged in extinguishing fires, was extensive, ingenious, and handsome, in a degree to awaken surprise in people who hear of a fire at the interval of months, and scarcely ever see a fire-engine.

The Colored Race.

THE first drive up Broadway, or turn in the Fifth Avenue, would impress the new-comer with the idea that New York is of German origin, but for the restless bustle that pervades it, and the dark coachmen mounted on the front of the carriages, and the youths seated beside them, who from their age and complexion may be their sons. When he penetrates a little further, and sees the domestic economy, he will find black cooks as well as waiters; and when he perambulates the city, he will find some streets that seem entirely inhabited by blacks, and in their vicinity a church or two of various persuasions, whose flocks and whose ministers are of the same complexion. They are generally reported to be honest, thoughtless, light-hearted, improvident people. Some of them seem very poor and desolate, especially in cold weather, which shrinks and withers them up; but in sunshine they expand, and are much more lively. They are by no means disposed to beg, or to make the most of their necessities. A gentleman connected with the "Association for Improving the Condition of the Poor," who takes charge of a district for the purpose of investigating the cases, and distributing the alms of the benevolent during winter, says his experience is, that the colored people, men and women, withdraw their claim as soon as they find employment by which they can live, while the Irish will hang on, and show plausible cause why they ought to be aided, as long as a dollar is left in the bag.

They are capable of being very industrious and useful in the community, and some of them possess both energy and mental vigor. Yet they evidently belong to a warmer clime, where prolonged or hard exertion is not necessary to supply the wants of nature; and one grieves to observe the half-developed, half-alive state they often drop into, as if chilled, when nothing occurs to arouse them.

They are not zealous to use all the means of education within their reach, yet in the "Colored Orphan Home" are to be seen children as acute and lively as in any of the white orphan houses, or Common Schools. Those who have enjoyed longer and closer means of observation can say whether the gradual dying away of this acuteness and liveliness, when they grow up, arises from constitutional causes, or from a growing conception as they advance in life of their depressed condition.

In the free States the colored children have access to the Common Schools, but if I may judge from my limited means of observation, they do not very commonly use the privilege. States that support Common Schools pay equally for black and white children. Nevertheless, in these States you will find here and there a side school, the result of private benevolence, where the children and their teacher cannot offend each other's prejudices, as all are dark.

It is too painful to look on a people who have the material in them that might do well, driven back to inertness and despondency by the ceaseless encounter of depressing obstacles. Is it true, that white children in virtue of a complexion, in the possession of which they have no merit, insult and injure children of another shade of color, for which they ought to have no disgrace? I fear it. In Albany I saw a big white boy deliberately kick a little black one who was passing along as inoffensively as myself. The poor child did not attempt to retaliate or to complain—he only fled. Is this a method in which to rear free, and generous, and just citizens?

The day and the scene were lovely as I sat on the dock at Poughkeepsie, waiting for the steamer, yet a brief exhibition of what appeared too common to draw the attention of others filled me with indignation and grief. A pleasant-looking colored youth, dressed neatly in clean summer clothing, leaned over the rail, looking down upon the water. Suddenly a dirty, ragged, vulgar fellow, perhaps jealous that a black man should look so much more respectable than himself, came up and tried to fasten a quarrel on him, which the dark man meekly evaded. The fellow struck him, and when still the injured dark man kept the peace, and turned his face to the water, the fellow kicked him and went away triumphing. No one laughed with him, as I was pleased to observe; but no one said, "Why do you insult this inoffensive man?" He saw there was none to take his part. Had I been a man, I think the insolent fellow would have got a washing in the Hudson. It would have been an honor to have been carried before a magistrate for such a trespass. O America! country of freemen, beware of laying up a store of such injuries. The God of the Black man and the White is a God of judgment, and does not forget your good deeds and your evil.

Could you but be warned before you make your responsibilities deeper and darker!

Churches for the Colored people are built by voluntary contribution in the same manner as those for the White, and often the chief part of the money is contributed by white people. Many of the pastors are dark, and, generally speaking, though they be pious, they are not intelligent or much instructed. The majority of them are Methodists—their habit of addressing the passions more than the understanding, suiting better the temperament and degree of knowledge of their flocks. These, along with Baptists, comprise almost all of the colored professors of religion. The morals of even the best colored people are said to be of a low grade, and pastors find it far easier to take care of white than of colored sheep.

These poor people feel that they live by sufferance only—their humility is quite touching in reference to white persons—and their position is so calculated to debilitate the mind, to teach them submission and dependence, rather than anything like forethought and providence, that it is not surprising to see them continue under the cloud, and rarely break out from it. It is the humor of some to indulge and spoil them, allowing in them familiarity which they would not permit in a white, while others trample on them, reproach them for being "niggers," &c. In either case they are not treated fairly. It is curious to observe them if encouraged, kindly gossiping creatures as they are—old cooks and "aunties" who have held all manner of domestic offices, never lose their claim on the family. They will call in if they fancy the lady wants her hair dressed, or if her present cook does not, perhaps, understand making the preserves so well as "Aunt Suky" does—or if they hear you have company, and will be the better of a hand to help with the ice and lemonade, and you will find an "aunt" occasionally in the lady's chamber with her little basket, and her pleasant sociable smile, as if she knows all about it; and her soft voice, and her quaint talk. Their voices are all pleasing, and a fine musical ear seems their unfailing attribute. If a street minstrel is afloat, you will be sure to see a score of little darkies hovering about him, drinking in the strains with evident delight.

Being interested in their musical powers, I gathered collections of their popular airs, and felt indignant at the ineffable nonsense of the words which are in nearly every case attached to them. If they be real, what sin attaches to enlightened men, who keep in purposed ignorance a set of immortal beings who dwell in the midst of them. If they be the invention of hired musicians, who profess to be Ethiopians, then how low is the public taste in that matter, and how insulting is it to the poor black people. Yet kind ladies told me, that much of this nonsense comes from the south, and is fostered by the owners, as the favorite singing of their pet slaves, which they like to repeat, as we do the imperfect prattle of our children. One may be allowed to question if that be the real state of the case, especially when, ever and anon, in the negro melodies you catch a strain which has been metamorphosed from some familiar Scotch or Irish tune, into somewhat of a chiming jiggish air. It is remarkable, that all their love for music and for negro melodies, if these be indeed such, has not led the dark people to seek a corner in those halls where white men with sooty faces sing their airs well, and play their favorite banjo, as well as it can be played. It is too obviously satire, and not sympathy, which these minstrels aim at. The ridicule is too broad and contemptuous to be tolerated, much less enjoyed by them. The sight of a dark complexion has long since ceased to be rare in a place of worship. Besides having churches of their own, you will, if you look well about you, find a few in a left hand gallery, or in some odd corner of many churches.

The time is happily long gone by since New York State and City, cleared themselves from the bondage and disgrace of slavery. In that unhappy time, when old Katy Fergusson was yet a girl, she was converted under the teaching of the Rev. Dr. J. M. Mason. Her examination before the session, and the purpose of admitting her to communion, excited some murmuring and much speculation amongst those whose skins God had made fair. For thus far could an evil habit of mind prevent even Christians from rejoicing, when according to His promise, "Ethiopia stretched forth her hands to God." The good and resolute doctor took no notice of these murmurings, but, with the dignity which his commanding figure and grave deportment rendered so becoming, and with the solemnity which the occasion demanded, he passed down to Katy's distant seat, led her to the table in presence of his great congregation, and exclaimed with deep emotion, "If any man be in Christ he is a new creature." "There is neither Greek nor Jew, there is neither bond nor free." "Whosoever shall do the will of my Father, the same is my brother, and sister, and mother." Prejudice in her case was disarmed and abashed, and by-and-by Katy's freedom was purchased. She, like most of her tribe, is a capital cook. They have the knack of it, and can stand any amount of heat. She has made many wedding cakes and wedding suppers, and had many young women under her training as pastry cooks, to whom she has been made useful in spiritual things.

In her house was held the first Sabbath-School of New York, and for forty years she has had a weekly prayer-meeting there. When we joined the little group, her pastor and a city missionary were present. There was a curious gathering of us—three colored, three Jewesses, and a young couple lately from Glencairn, whose amazement was unbounded at being hailed by us as fellow Dumfriesians. It touched us to sing the Scotch version of Psalms to the old airs of French and Balerma, and brought melting feelings of a quiet seat now vacant, and a voice now silent, a whole tribe of strong memories which are not read, nor even suspected by any bystander.

It is striking to observe the contrast—while some professors, drawn aside by prosperity, are one day at the Lord's table, and another introducing their offspring to crowded dancing-parties; here is an aged and now feeble and poor woman, for years keeping an altar in her house, and helping others on the way to heaven. She is a person of varied talent and much energy, still, and one day brought in to us a bouquet of waxen flowers, made by her own trembling hands, good and pretty imitations of nature.

It is to be hoped the church will care for her increasing wants, till she ceases to want any more. A friend observed to me that evening, " These Glencairn people will presently change their house, and slip out of Katy's influence." When I, uninitiated, asked the reason with surprise, I was told, " They are still in happy ignorance about the prejudice against color, but they will soon be taught, and because they will be ashamed to break off from so good a woman, they will just slip away by removing to another place." This, with many other examples, proved to me that the sentiment is not so much an instinctive aversion, as an educational prejudice, which prevents the one race from eating, or even worshipping in company with the other.

One of the leading and popular ministers in the city, stated to me that he had resided for months with a family in a Southern State, who assembled their negroes every evening while he conducted worship, including a short and simple exposition of a passage of Scripture. He said it was one of the most trying exercises he was ever engaged in, from the extreme excitability of the people. He had reasoned with them apart, against giving way to their feelings, he had rebuked them when together on the first symptom of strong emotion, he had been calm even to coldness himself, but night after night, the plainest statement of gospel truth would throw some into uncontrollable passions of tears, and others into convulsions. One woman, a nursing mother, and confided in by all on the plantation, by reason of years of Christian and prayerful consistency, fell nightly into convulsions and must be carried out. This gentleman imputed these violent emotions to a peculiarity in the negro constitution; while in my secret heart I questioned what manner of nerve-shaking events a day may produce in such a situation—or what known, and perhaps forced sins, might be then making conscience tremble. He adduced other instances of similar agitations and seizures, and specially that of a strongly built free colored man, whom he had seen, on different occasions, seized with what might be termed catalepsy. His frame would become rigid, or one limb would be as inflexible for hours as if it were a bit of timber, while the power of speech would be taken from him. The same affections seized the

South Sea Islanders, who, under convictions of their lost condition, were subject to nearly similar paroxysms. Such uncontrollable emotions, are to be deplored as very disturbing where instruction should be conveyed, besides giving the evil disposed opportunity to impute them to hypocrisy or design. Yet when we weigh the immense horrors arising from a view of dangers that refer to a never-ending condition, it is not the convulsed and the groaning, but the unconverted, who are laughing and trifling, that are more suitable subjects of wonder.

There is likely a habit, and expectation of this kind of excitement, which might explain the rising and sitting down, the utterance of groans and loud "amens," and "glorys," which we heard in one dark congregation, to which we made our way on a Sabbath evening, at Washington. All that the minister repeated and reiterated in three quarters of an hour, might have been more wisely said, at least to my taste, in fifteen minutes, and none of it was of a very arousing character. But I suppose as much response is often heard in Methodist chapels in England, though without the same bodily movement. After the service the minister mentioned that, "the church was dimly lighted, he did not see any reason why, when they enjoyed the light of the gospel, they should not have as clear light to hear it by as other churches have. The fault was in the lamps—they must have new ones. To procure these, he was commissioned by the deacons to invite the ladies and gentlemen to hold a soirée on a certain evening, their admission would cost them a small sum, when they would have tea and fruit, and addresses from gentlemen whom he named, and some sweet hymn-singing and prayer. He was the more encouraged to fall into this plan, because of the suitable and proper behavior of the ladies and gentlemen on a similar occasion, last year. Indeed, some of the ladies had begun to make preparation for the meeting already. He hoped they would all come and conduct as well as they did last year." The impression made on us by this address, is most briefly described as *very queer*. Rather exaggerated politeness, and obvious imitativeness. Thoughtless people might be disposed to laugh. For myself, its novelty amused me, but there was a better sentiment, that of gladness to see the people managing their own affairs, and struggling up to independence in that which touches themselves so nearly.

When I entered the pew at first, I asked two smart-looking young women if I should intrude on some one's room, if I sat there. "O no, Madam—

but if you *don't like to sit with us*, go into that side seat, and none of us will come near you." Having no taste for being sent to Coventry, I sat where I was.

I never conversed with a slave but once, and having written what passed at the time to a friend at home, I copy it. It showed me that very many persons in the sad condition of bondmen are tolerably well used, and not very unhappy. It also showed me more of the helplessness produced by the dependent condition, and how little they who pine for freedom, are, in the first instance, able to enjoy it. Indeed, we learned at Washington that it is by no means rare for the well-fed and clothed bondman, who is there in attendance on his Southern master, to despise the colored freeman who is poorly clothed and fed in comparison to him, and leads a laborious life. The pampered valet, however, is no true specimen of what the negro on the tobacco, cotton, or rice plantation is, even though we leave out of the comparison all that refers to morality and volition.

I had sent for the man with whom I conversed, merely to make an inquiry about the way to a place I wished to visit. His features were pleasant, beaming, and ivory black. Having obtained my information, I felt a strong desire to learn if he was free, but my heart beat so, I could not utter the question.

A companion, however, asked him. "No," said he, smiling cheerfully, "but I am buying myself; I have paid $300, I have $50 more ready, and then I want $150 more to be free." "Where is your owner?" "He is down in Georgia, but comes along about twice a year to see after me." "How long have you been in this city?" "Twelve years. I have a wife free, and God has been very kind to us in giving us but one child—so I have not much to lay out for my family, and can save the faster. Besides, I never let myself think I can't do without this, or I must have that, as some of our people do, but just do without everything, except what is necessary to make me look decent." "You can read—how did you learn?" "I used to play with my owner's children, and when they say, 'come away and play,' I say to them, 'teach me the lesson your tutor taught you this morning, first;' and so I learnt a little, and I worked hard myself." "And what are you going to do with yourself, when you have bought yourself?" "That is just what I am at a loss about." "Do you think of Liberia?" "Why, I listen as I hear gentlemen talk about it. The Society will send me and my family across—then they don't give but six months' rations after you land; and then there will be forests to clear, and stumps in the ground, and the acclimating fever, and no return for the labor at the end of six months." "But you might hire yourself to some one at odd days, and so earn a little, while your crop grows." "But I have no tools." "Oh, our 'Navvies' in England sometimes come along to a piece of work, when they have dissipated the very coat off their back; one lends a pick, and another a spade; at the week's end they can buy tools, and presently they get decently clothed." He shook his careful head. It was strange to see an acute, sensible man, using all lawful means to purchase himself, understanding how to pay by instalments, and having a regular receipt for each payment, and yet, from want of use about daily provision and self-management, more at a loss what to do with himself, than he is for the means to make the purchase. When asked why he paid $300 before he could make up the whole price, as he got no interest from his owner, I understood him to say that he could not place it out at interest, or be known to own it, and that if he died, it would not belong to his wife and child, but to his master, as a slave can own nothing.

Reverting to his grand difficulty, he said, "About Liberia, too, now that it is made independent, what if America should quarrel with us?" "America has a strong interest in keeping on good terms with Liberia." "Then if Great Britain should go to war with us, would America embroil herself with Britain for us? And which side could we take if they were at war? Britain has been always kind to Liberia." "Don't be faint-hearted, that must all come as it may. A British steamer has just reached Liberia, with an honest treaty of commerce, which both parties have signed. Besides, you are going to have a line of steamers to run between this country and that immediately. Liberia is growing in strength. You cannot here rise above a depressed condition; there you are not only free, but have equal rights." "Well, I *listen*, *listen* to the talk of the gentlemen at table, and when they notice me they say, 'What better would you be of freedom? ain't you very happy here?' and I say, 'Sir, would you like it if you had five children and I had three, if I say to you, You work and give me all your wages for my three, and let your own five do as they can? You would not like that.' 'O don't talk that way. Tom, you will stir up discontent among the colored folks.' 'Well,' says I, 'I don't speak so to them, for, poor things, they could not bear it.' But I say it to you, Sir, for it is true." "What is it," I inquired, "that enables you to bear it better than the rest, Thomas?"

"You see, I lay my case before the Lord, and just ask him to make me free or keep me slave, or to do with me just what He pleases, and that keeps me quiet, and I tell my people to be quiet, for there is no color in His presence."

The hope of salvation shed a calm and dignified sweetness and patience over his sable countenance. "Poor things," said he, again, "they could not bear it,—no, no, they could not bear it." "Do you try to do them good?" "When I was laborer here and there at riding, shingling, and farming, I taught Sabbath-school, and I never frightened the little ones about hell-fire or such things, they hear enough of that"—he did not say from whom—"but I clap their heads and love them, and tell them first to be good to their parents, and they will be always kind to them. And when they understand that, I tell them to obey God, the great Parent of us all, and He will be kind to them, and make them very happy in heaven for His dear Son's sake,—and they used all to get very fond of me." "You have very few slaves here now?" "Some—always some." "They are kindly used though, and not punished here?" This I asked trembling, for, to tell truth, at six in the morning I had quivered from head to foot at some unusual sounds which reached my chamber, that looked upon a back yard. It was the Sabbath morning—the morning, as I remembered, set apart in some places for inflicting punishment. The sounds were strange, and my heart was very full for the people all around me. "Not punished," replied Thomas, "no—not much punished. There is a whipping-post in the yard,—but we don't have the whipping now that used to be. I have been so long a time with my master, that I make free to say a word now and then. And when a servant does wrong, I venture to say, might it not be as well to change him and hire another, and not whip him, —and he rather takes that way now." "Well, Thomas, patience and prayer will conquer. The Lord knows what is best, and will provide for you when you are free."

Patient, ingenious, kind, and brave,—perhaps he will never venture to throw off the disability attached to his complexion in the land of his birth, yet he has that about him which would make him an acquisition, as a citizen, to any country.

The Colonization Society.

WHEN first we heard of this Society in England it was hailed with joy, as a wise outlet for the oppressed, and a promising method of introducing civilization to the western coast of Africa.

Those who had felt the slave-trade the most deeply as a wrong and impediment in every way to that coast, were those who gave to the agents of colonization the most ardent welcome to England. But in a year or two the prospect was clouded.

The Maryland State Colonization Society stated broadly at its seventh anniversary, that "Abolition is a curse to those it pretends to benefit, and colonization presents the only practicable plan by which the condition of the colored population can be ameliorated." And again, "That this Society hold colonization to be the antagonist of Abolition, and find the best proof of the importance of the former to the States where slavery exists, in the untiring efforts made by the latter, to defeat and prostrate it."* There was then no purpose of benefit to the whole colored family. It seemed a scheme adopted by Slave States to rid themselves of a few free negroes who were in too dangerous a proximity to their slaves. We had also hints of evil and turbulent slaves, who were an annoyance at home, receiving the gift of manumission merely that they might be got rid of. We were led to conjecture that several had been placed at Liberia against their own consent; and, as the slave-owners could never contemplate transporting three millions of people across the ocean, we were left in doubt whether the motive, held out to us, of improvement to Africa, and freedom to slaves, was the real one, or whether Liberia was not in fact a mere penal colony, or a safety valve, as a receptacle for those who could not be managed at home. The numbers sent were fewer than one would have expected from the active benevolence of Americans, who achieve great things when they are really moved, and never seem to fail in any good design for want of funds. In short, we required to investigate and to be reassured, before we dared heartily to rejoice in the plans of the Society.

* Resolutions at the public meeting held at Annapolis, Jan. 23, 1839.

After many and anxious inquiries, I am happy to come to the conclusion that the motives of the Colonization Society are purely philanthropic. It has steadily adhered to its one object—that of sending, with their own consent, people of color to Africa, and out of the accomplishment of this object is rising the good prognosticated. One free colony after another is springing up on those deadly shores once haunted by the kidnapper and the man-hunter. And the traffickers in human flesh so stupidly debased, who steeped their souls in horrors, and spent their days in watching and plotting, and their nights in rapine and cruelty, are learning that their fertile soil can enrich them by its varied and bountiful productions, while they possess just rights themselves, and allow them also to their fellow-men.

Although the idea of removing the African race from the American continent by means of Liberia is like baling out the ocean with a bucket, yet the thriving Republic, with its rising seaport towns, forms a suitable home for many of them, and exhibits a fine pattern to the uncivilized nations around them. Monrovia was the first settlement, and is the seat of government. But since then Edina is added as a seaport, and with the new colony of Maryland at Cape Palmas, is included under the general name of Liberia. Thus the Colonization Society has an average of forty miles inland, and a coast line of three hundred and fifty miles, secured from the abominable traffic in man—and fourteen thousand square miles of territory protected and ready for the free and peaceful labors of the husbandman.

The Rev. R. R. Gurley, who was sent by government to obtain information in 1850, reports "the mighty effects wrought on the intellects, hopes, and purposes of the authorities and people of Liberia by the freedom which has ever been theirs upon these shores, and the high position they have now taken of national independence. Some of the most distinguished men of the Republic are among those who went thither in childhood, have received their entire education in its schools, and bear in their manners, their whole deportment, and upon their very aspect, the signs of a just self-respect, of subdued passions, of virtuous resolutions, and of a mature and well-disciplined judgment."*

The laws of Liberia against the slave-trade are full and explicit:—"1. No vessel of their Republic is permitted to have intercourse with slave-ships, at

* Report to the Senate through the Secretary of State, Daniel Webster. Washington, September 14, 1850.

sea or elsewhere. 2. No citizen of their Republic can be permitted to act as agent for any person engaged in the slave-trade, under penalty of being six months bound to hard labor in irons—no one living there shall enter into the employ of any slave-dealer. 3. No vessel engaged in, or having connection with the slave-trade shall enter the ports of the Republic, and no foreigner residing within its jurisdiction shall have any connection with that trade." In short, the laws exhibit a determined resolve to keep such pollution far from their rising nation, and furnish a cheering prospect that, by its aid, that baleful source of crime and cruelty will finally be extinguished.

The founders of the Society, Samuel J. Mills and Dr. Finley, are men whose names are held in honor by the pious in their country. The measures adopted for the first settlement at Monrovia seemed wise, and encountered no other drawbacks than those of fever and ague, and such troubles as attend upon men who march in the van to fell the forest, and drain the swamp, and turn the wilderness and solitary place into a cultivated field.

The great obstacle to the success and popularity of the place among the colored people appears to be that they are acted for, not acting. Their depressed condition, and their ignorance render them poor judges of their own affairs, while centuries of injury deprive them of confidence in those who would now judge for them. It is easy to fill their ears with unfounded tales of the hardships and difficulties of the settlement, and not easy to excite in them a spirit of enterprise of sufficient power to raise them from their native land and native lowly position.

Having become convinced that my recent opinion of the Colonization Society was unjust, I went to its anniversary meeting during the busy week of missionary anniversaries in May—though it was so little an object of favor in my circle that I could not find a lady inclined to accompany me. The most remarkable feature of the meeting was, that in the gay and crowded Tripler Hall which blazed with light, I could see only one colored man, and he seemed a servant of the place. How strange that what may concern them so deeply, should not attract many to learn the condition of the colony erected for their sakes.

I remembered having stepped into a meeting in Edinburgh, where plans for colonizing Otago, a settlement in New Zealand, were exhibited. The company did not consist of ladies and gentlemen set down to hear speeches. The man and his young wife, the father and his two sons, sisters and brothers, and interested friends were there, of various grades of society. They advanced to the tables and examined the plans. They asked sensible questions of the knowing men whose business it was to answer them. They studied bills on the wall announcing the sailing of ships for that region. You could almost tell by the countenances in that interested assembly, who had fixed to go, and who were seeking materials for the decision. The scene had a real colonization atmosphere about it—it carried your mind to a wharf laden with packages, and a deck crowded with farewells. Not so the meeting in Tripler Hall. We heard some eloquence, some egotism, some self-defence, some wit, much irrelevance, and some nonsense. It was not a business-like audience at all. Most unlike the close attention, the ardent listening, the lively sympathy of the meetings in the Tabernacle which occupied that week. How many opportunities did the speakers fail to employ of showing the wrongs of Africa, the duty to compensate them, the means afforded by this Society to introduce the leaven of civilization and Christianity among the benighted—more darkened still by our injuries —and of describing the flourishing colony already formed, and its still brighter prospects. What eloquence might have flowed forth, on planting the standard of liberty on shores which for centuries had been haunted only by the tyrant and the slave. How insipid was the defence of a man's dear self against some petty calumny. How poor and distasteful was the most pointed wit, when it detains us on the shore, while such an ocean of spirit-rousing matter for the philanthropist lay unreached beyond!

When last of all, a sensible man with business-like information began to address them, the audience seemed to have got the laugh it came for, and in a fit of impatience rushed away. That good man sought to encourage colored people to get education and to learn trades with a view to fit them for Liberia; and mentioned one talented and educated family of his acquaintance in Baltimore who had gone to that country. One son, I think he said, had become an officer of State, and one daughter was the wife of the Governor. But much that he said which was well worth listening to, was imperfectly heard by the retiring multitude, and the meeting seemed altogether ineffective.

This exhibition had the effect of again damping my hopes from the Colonization Society, though I was told that the business was all despatched in committee. Yet surely business results, such as the state of the funds, the number gone out in the year, the number preparing to go, &c., might have been interesting to the meeting. It does not appear that many are willing to go, nor amongst them, many whose previous habits and education are of a kind calculated to strengthen or elevate the colony. Nevertheless the colony is "a true thing," and having Christianity and free institutions, we look upon it with hope, as the model of many a republic, which may yet arise on that most injured and down-trodden coast.

But turn which way we may, the question still recurs—What is to become of the American Africans? In the presence of the white man they cannot rise. It is an injury to the character of the white man, to have a people with him who is not of him, a people whom he may degrade by a false elevation of himself. He is strong and hearty. He needs no hewers of wood or drawers of water. He will be a better man when he does his lawful work himself, and when those are removed who excite his contempt or his scorn—those on whom he may vent his fit of spleen and injustice, if such fit ever happens to come upon him.

They cannot be all removed to Africa. There are enough of them already shivering in Canada, who *if every one had his own*, as some grudging

Southerners may say, would not be there. Happily for them, the fugitive slave law cannot cross that border. Still they are not in a climate that suits them. The verge of the frigid can never make a comfortable home for the denizen of the torrid zone. Why not give up to the whole race a State for themselves, at the South, and leave them to erect a standard of freedom there, and bless the bounty of the United States. Then might America raise her strain without a discord—

> " Hail Columbia, happy land,
> For all thy sons are free."

Then would the might of her influence be doubled on earth, and then could she lift up a light and glad heart to heaven.

This prejudice against complexion would begin to fade, as soon as the necessity of living mingled together was removed, and all affairs of trade, commerce, and policy could proceed naturally, as they do with other countries. At present there are perplexities and anomalies of various sorts occurring, which oblige governments to wink hard, and endure what they disapprove, or to turn corners with anything but the dignified movements of free States.

How unfit is it that England, for peace' sake, should allow her black sailors to be locked up, the hour they enter the ports of some American slave State. What an injustice to the honest, industrious tar, to deal with him as with a criminal.

Yet this is one result of the slave-ridden condition of some of the southern sea-ports; they dare not admit free blacks to company with slaves.

On the 26th of July, 1847, the Constitution of Liberia was published, and her independence proclaimed. She has thus been a free republic, exercising all the rights of free government, for nearly five years. Her claim, then, to be reckoned among the nations, ought not, and cannot with justice, be denied. She holds friendly relations with the United States, and must, like other nations, have her chargé-d'affaires at Washington. But all her people are dark. A white man cannot sit, or eat, or commune with such, on equal terms. What then must be done? Must Liberia remain unrepresented before the State that has fostered her into what she is—the State that hopes to see her grow in greatness? or must Liberia borrow a white man to stand her sponsor? Or, will America, with a magnanimity so becoming a great and a free nation, swallow down her prejudice, receive a true Liberian envoy, and show him all honor for the sake of Liberty, and of his origin.

Prisons.

Our early knowledge of prisons is commonly derived from history, and consequently, they, with too much reason, are associated in the mind with deeds of injustice, oppression, and cruelty. Dungeons where brave warriors are sighing out their existence, deep, deep, below the sympathy and the hearing of man. Towers where infant princes pay the forfeit of life to the fell usurper. Inquisitions where, for daring to think or inquire, the intelligent, liberal, and devout are tortured under the remorseless gripe of papal tyranny. Such are the images called up by the word "Prison" in the mind of the inexperienced.

After-years teach that prisoners are not necessarily oppressed, and prisons are not all scenes of injustice and cruelty. Yet it requires long habit before the steep cold stone steps of a common jail can be ascended without a trembling heart, and the hardened and careless inmates faced without strong repulsion mingling with pity. It requires a consideration of the untaught, the impoverished, and the tempted case of many a poor criminal; and also a consideration of what is in our own hearts, before we can say, as did the well-taught man, when he saw a convict passing to Tyburn, "but for the grace of God there goes John Bradford."

As the homes of America are cleaner, brighter, and of purer air than ours, so are their prisons. My means of observation were limited. It is not easy for a female to penetrate such places alone, nor easy amid the busy and obliging multitude, to meet with gentlemen who do less than marvel at your taste in sight-seeing, if you hint a wish to visit such scenes. Such observations as have come within reach, however, show me that the mistakes and experiences of old Europe have not been lost on young America. There will never then, one is led to trust, be found such dens of darkness and woe as our Howard permeated—and, even from their foundation, they have profited by such works as our Buxton's on Prison Discipline, and such operations as those of our Mrs. Fry in prison classification.

It is not for me to discuss the much debated points, between the systems of solitude in one prison, or silence in society in another. For the officials the former must be much the more easy. As to the latter, the enforcing of it—at least the enforcing of non-intercourse, seems impracticable. The temptation to break rules, and thus become an offender, is very strong, because converse with our fellows is natural. It is a pity to add to occasions of offence, where there are necessarily so many; besides, Solomon said long ago, that "a naughty person winketh with his eyes, he speaketh with his feet, he teacheth with his fingers." He has ways of insinuating his ideas though his tongue be silenced; and that it is so, seems calculated to make his feelings the more bitter. It would seem easier, more cheerful, and therefore more healthful to work alone all day, if your workshop be well aired and lighted, than to work continually under restraint in the midst of society, where the very ingenuity and cleverness exercised in outwitting the overseer, must add constantly to the temptation to do so.

It depends much on constitutional temperament how solitude will affect the spirit. We have all read with dismay the account of that brave general who, under Austrian despotism, was imprisoned seventeen years—at first with a companion. The first year they discussed political affairs, and conjectured as to the cause of their arrest. The second they related adventures and stated opinions on abstract subjects. The third they became silent; and when at the end of the fifth year his companion was removed, he felt it rather a relief to see no more through the gloom, that dim immovable countenance. Once during the remainder of the time the door was opened, and a voice, sounding to his unaccustomed ears like thunder, said he had it in command from his Imperial Majesty to inform him that Madame, his wife, had died some time last year. When liberated he had ceased almost to think or to feel. Hope had nearly ceased to linger about his heart, and the relations of life had become as nothing to him. Who that has breathed the free air of Britain or of America, does not recoil against such a deed of irresponsible power!

Neither the silent nor the solitary system in the Free States can ever expose a fellow-man to such a crying injustice; yet the effect of this dreamy solitude, on a man of strong mind, is worth deep consideration. Mind, especially uninstructed mind, cannot thrive in solitude. If it be empty of everything but its past evil associations, what can it be exercised upon that may purify or elevate. Solitude, with employment and Christian teaching, may be rendered animated and healthful, and that is the object to be aimed at in solitary prisons. Anything is better than utter loneliness. Robert the Bruce's contemplations on the perseverance of his spider, excites our interest, and we sympathize with him when it and its intricate web were swept away. And the poor Comte de Charney's very small flower, his Picciola in the court-yard of his prison, what a power of mental occupation, and of hearty sympathy was there, which, because it found no other outlet, lavished itself on a flower. Such examples of the resources of refined minds cut off from social intercourse, excite our interest; yet how unprofitable are they, and how empty do they leave the soul.

What an invaluable treasure in penal solitude is the "Moral Instructor," as he is called in the Eastern State Penitentiary of Pennsylvania. The solitary longs to hear the human voice. At last his loneliness is broken in upon. He is addressed kindly, with sage counsels, with friendly admonitions, with gospel invitations pointing to pardon, peace, and a happiness which he has never tasted. Left again alone, he pursues his work with a new leaven cast into his many musings, and he longs for the hour when the friendly teacher can return, if it be but to hear his voice again, and again to exercise his own. We do not know how many new characters this plan may send forth, but it is admirably devised. The physician's report for 1850, is wise and candid. He is no sworn partizan of the solitary plan, but exhibits its disadvantages, and points to where it is capable of improvement, with solicitude to furnish the means of a fair judgment.

One feature of the system pursued in the Pennsylvania Penitentiary is worthy of applause and imitation—it affords the reclaimed protection from being recognized hereafter by their fellow-prisoners. The Doctor advises a free intercourse between the prisoner and his friends, provided they be people of virtuous habits, both by visits and by letters, which shall pass through the hands of the Warden. He thinks it would be very useful, both to the minds and morals of the convict. He also rejoices in their rude attempts at the construction of musical instruments, and in hearing through the corridors, during the stillness of evening, the tones of various performers. He is a humane man, falling in with the design of the State, which is not simply to lock up the convict as a nuisance to society, but by wholesome restraints and mild punishment, with good instruction, to bring him out a better man and member of society.

The following extracts are from the Moral Instructor's Report:—"Here every man's cell is not only his workshop, but also his school-room and his study, where, secure from intrusive task-masters, he may calmly reflect on the consequences of evil courses, and form good resolves for the future. This, I am satisfied, is a state of feeling at present prevailing in the institution beyond comparison greater than can be hoped for under any circumstances, where prisoners pass their days in congregated labor, and return at night to cells, the arrangements of which will not admit of *private* intercourse with a religious instructor." * * * *

"We ought to remember that the measure of success is not the rule of duty, and if all is not accomplished which is desired, we must steadily and patiently pursue the onward course, in the spirit of that great apostle, who, hopeless of the conversion of his nation collectively, nevertheless continued his labor of love—'if by any means he might save *some.*' We have much reason to be grateful for the measure of success which has marked the past history of this Penitentiary. Numerous instances of a permanent change have occurred—men have been taught how to live and how to die.

"T. Larcombe, Moral Istructor."

This report is valuable in all its departments,

and most satisfactory as giving the opinion of judicious and experienced men, as to the practicability and usefulness of the solitary plan. Dr. Given is strenuous in his urgency as to some medical cautions; he advises better ventilation—more use of the large yards, and more room to carry on some of their trades. He also solicitously explains the number who were of weak intellect when admitted, lest their subsequent insanity should be imputed to their solitude. He says, "I am willing that the extreme penalty of the law should be inflicted on any offender whose guilt deserves it, but I cannot admit that a sentence of *imprisonment* justifies the community in placing the convict under any circumstances likely to injure the health of either body or mind—and with those whose consciences are tender on the score of making the situation of the prisoner more desirable than that of the honest and industrious poor man or pauper, I heartily sympathize, but would with great humility ask, if the true exercise of their philanthropy, would not consist in endeavors to alleviate the condition of the latter, and not in wishing to see the former still more wretched."

The thought expressed by their zealous physician hung on my mind all the time we followed the steps of a beloved lady through the extensive and airy wards of the prison. Her countenance beaming with hopeful love, seemed to draw a kindred beam from that even of the oldest and least susceptible female whose cell we entered. The proportion of women was very small—only eleven, I think—the males numbering upwards of 300. The female ward is on the second floor. We ascended by a light iron stairs to the gallery which surrounds it, and crossed over in the middle by an iron bridge. All the doors open into the gallery, and each has in one of the pannels a hole as large, on the outside, as the eye, but sloped inward till it becomes the size of the pupil. By this small orifice, the Matron can inspect the cell without the consciousness of the inmate. The wards run out from a circular hall in the centre, like the sticks of a fan, the doors of the cells open into them, and each cell has a yard at the back. A watchman placed at the central point can cast his eye into all the wards without shifting his position.

The manners of the matron were those of a gentlewoman. I was at first surprised, but on consideration much pleased, to observe the respect with which she treated her charge. I have seen rough wardswomen and turnkeys, who exhibited by their manner that they expected nothing good of the people, and the sure result was that their expectation was fulfilled. At Philadelphia, both matron and lady visitors expected propriety and gentleness of manners, and they created the manner by looking for it. The women welcomed us to "their poor place—hoped we would excuse a hard seat, as they had no cushion to offer," or turned up a box to sit upon "as they were not provided for so many kind friends." One old woman read a little at the request of the matron, to show our dear friend that she had acquired the art; a young one pointed out her nice writing on a slate which hung up; and a third seemed a little troubled when I asked if she had worked the curious fringe on her table cover. The matron revealed in a whisper that she was under some slight privation; some food withheld, I forget what, for her trespass in taking a towel *without leave* to exercise her fringe-making ingenuity upon. The matron encouraged them as a mother does her children, to try to do well, to recover their characters, and to be fit on going out to dwell among good people. While our friend and theirs gave them loving gospel invitations, and spoke so tenderly that one could not but feel this to be the way to melt the heart to contrition.

Down stairs we visited many men's cells. In one

we found lilliputian knives and forks, bodkins and reels for cotton, made of the bones of the beef and mutton. In another the walls and vaulted roof covered with mosaic coloring. The man was a weaver, and had contrived to extract from the yarn the colors with which he had adorned his lonely retreat. In one place we found a home-made fiddle—happily we did not hear its utterings. In another, a flute and something between a guitar and a banjo. This cell was highly decorated with bright pictures. Some of them with explanatory mottoes of capital wit, and nothing so unbecoming as to make us turn away. The inmate was a young lively colored man, whose prospect was a residence in that cell of several years. He had half covered in his airing yard, and got a small stove erected to help him in some ingenious work. I asked why he had not covered the whole yard. He said he could see and feel the sun in this corner, and at night he liked to come out and look at the stars. I observed my friend asked him gently about the trespass that had occasioned his being there, and remembering that the settled form of question at home on such subjects is not, "What did you do?" but "What *did they say* you did?" I listened with curiosity for his reply. He owned he had been engaged in a robbery, that it was very wrong; and then hinted at the circumstances of distress which led him to it. He was urged to read the Scriptures and some tracts which were in his cell, to learn all he could from the Instructor, to pray, and by all means keep himself busy; and as he clearly had a turn for drawing, my kind friend promised him some designs to copy. His frank confiding look seemed as though he could pour out all his mind to her, and it required one to look around to be reminded that, in spite of his pleasant countenance, he was shut up within these walls, and that this was a convict cell. We found ingenious implements and machines in some of the yards, which the turnkeys took pleasure in showing us. And in the hot-house of the spacious garden, we found a smart gardener, who politely regretted that he could only offer us poor flowers; February was not a favorable month, and some other ladies had been there yesterday. He had turned sickly at some house occupation, and been sent to his own employment in the garden. It required a determined belief that my informant told truth, to enable me to accept the conviction that this polite, amiable man was a convict.

It is true that a polished exterior may be but as a whited sepulchre. Yet I am persuaded that a criminal is more likely to return from his evil ways, when he is not driven to sinister and sullen looks by the impression that no eye is turned kindly on him, and that every hand is against him.

The Tombs in New York is more like a police-office, or Bridewell in England, as no one remains there, after trial, for a sentence of more than a few days. The countenances in that dismal place are dark enough. Though even there, some excited strong sympathy. One respectable German woman had the misfortune to witness a crime, and was shut up with the worthless lest she should be out of the way when wanted to give her testimony. She was a stranger, and had none to give bail for her. How she wept and beseeched, when spoken to in her native tongue, and how degrading she felt her present position! We found the white women generally shut up in pairs, but one cell was unlocked for us, rather larger than the others, where eight or ten blacks were huddled together in so small a space that it shocked me very much. Poor things, they were willing to listen, and two who could read promised to read aloud to the rest some tracts which we left. Nearly all the white women owned their being in that place arose from drinking.

Strange it is to go through another nation and find

resemblances so strong in everything between it and one's own. Virtue for virtue—invention for invention—enterprise for enterprise—principle for principle—daring for daring—crime for crime—O England! O America! you are indeed parent and child. Would that your similarities may draw you to help, and to love, and to correct each other.

There is much work carried on in the prisons. The hewing and sawing of marble is one very productive employment, and much to be prized for its healthful effects in preference to tailoring and boot and shoe making. There, however, though work is more plentiful than workmen, complaints are made, as in Britain, that such State manufactures have the effect of injuring the private mechanic. The beautiful City Hall of Brooklyn is built of white marble, every column and cornice of which came down ready for its place in the edifice from the State Prison at Auburn. While the masons, who had a personal interest in the City Hall, felt that they could have hewn all the marble without convict help. To compare small things with great, a poor sempstress in our own country told me the other day, that she had no more shirts to make from the linen warehouse that used to employ her, for the people at the "Shelter" not only made the linen, but, being expert laundresses, sent it home ready done up, fit for the counter.

It is difficult to do good in one branch of a crowded society without injuring another, or to feel at liberty to rejoice over the prosperity of an institution which opens its door to reclaim the wanderer, if thereby you impoverish and increase the hardships of the honest and industrious.

The prison of New York State is a huge factory, where enough is earned annually to clear its expenditure, and something over. Society is cleansed by its means of the profligate,—and they who would form nuisances to themselves and others are rendered productive to the State, while their own happiness is promoted.

Juvenile Delinquents and Benevolent Societies.

It has been well inquired whether it be cheaper to allow youths to become criminals, and then support them at public charge, or to control the early causes of criminality, and thereby rear up honest and useful members of society. During the formation of the character, the law-court is an idle looker-on, it is not till that formed character exhibits itself in trespass and disturbance, that law can restrain it. "Follow the embryo convict a few years, during childhood and youth. Behold the circumstances that made him what he is—circumstances (in one sense) beyond his control—circumstances which the community might, and ought to have controlled. There are hundreds of children growing up in our state, in conditions, and surrounded by circumstances that render it morally certain they will become candidates for the prison or the gallows. It is in our power to change these circumstances. Shall we do it? Yes—it is in our power to change those circumstances by placing such children in a House of Refuge; and every generous heart and reflecting mind will say we should do it."

Such were the sentiments expressed by the founders of the first Pennsylvania House of Refuge.

There are several such houses now connected with different States, partly sustained by the State, and partly by private contribution. New York has two, one in the city, and one at Rochester. Massachusetts has two—Ohio has one. New Orleans had one, authorized by the State of Louisiana, which has been destroyed by fire. It was a wooden structure, and is expected to be replaced by more appropriate buildings.

We had the pleasure of accompanying the Ladies' Committee of the House of Refuge at Philadelphia, on one of their monthly visits, and thus saw a little of the internal working of the Institution. The outset was striking to one who has plodded many a day in the mud, endeavoring to lend a little help where a great deal is needed. The carriage of the House came round and gathered up the Committee, and repeated journeys were required before all were collected. The absence of tax on carriage, coachman, and horses, allows many to drive in the United

States, whose equals in station and fortune here never attain such a relief.

Another difference, of far more weight than this to the cause of Christian charity, may be mentioned. With us, benevolent females whose influence is calculated to be useful to their own sex, obtain admission as it were by stealth, or at any rate by great favor, to prisons, Bridewells, infirmaries, &c. Nay, it is a mortifying fact, that some who desired in Christian love to enter, have been turned back from their gates, not being able to obtain orders from the proper authorities. In America the States invite the co-operation of women in such offices as become their sex, and look for their reports as guides in their management, or in making changes in the Institutions, and nobly do their women meet the wishes of the rulers, and fulfil the expectation of their country. Calm, practical, and business-like, they are able to say what they wish, exhibiting neither bashfulness nor boldness, having lost *self* in the interests of the institution. I have heard a discussion where there was much to be weighed, and a considerable difference of opinion. It was conducted with lady-like firm politeness. When put to the vote, and the "ayes had it," the "noes," without any appearance of temper, set to work on the side of the "ayes," and went on with the business. In England I have seen Quaker ladies act with equal simple decision. Perhaps their liberty arises from early training, or partly from their emancipation from some of our aristocratic trammels. But how often have I seen matters which ought to have been taken up, allowed to pass with us, merely because no one had courage to speak out, or because Mrs. or Miss So-and-so thought it was not her place to make the first move, when the Hon. Mrs., or Lady So-and-so was present—thus yielding the real interests of the institution to a matter of etiquette. One has sometimes left such a committee with pain, from the consciousness of having flinched from duty on some such petty ground, when I am pretty sure my American sisters would have had too much of the independent courage arising out of the love of the useful, to have left their scene of labor with any such pain.

It was not my lot to fall in with any discussion of this kind in the Refuge at Philadelphia. There is much to be admired in its well-aired, orderly, and beautifully clean apartments. Its bathing, and eating, and sleeping places, specially the latter, are admirably managed. The long galleries which form the dormitories are partitioned with brick, each bedroom having its own door and lock, and little window-of glass. The girls acquire habits of neatness by the encouragement given them to decorate these little chambers. Daily, after making the bed, they arrange whatever they have of pictures, pretty bags, China figures, peacock's feathers—in short, they are not particular,—anything that gives the air of pains, design, and good order, is set forth, or hung up. Happy is the girl whose lady-teacher, as a mark of approbation, gives her a gay print, or a bit of bright carpet. One would think, after examining fifty such little dormitories, that no child is born in the country without a taste for the beautiful, and that no one is so desolate as not to take pleasure in indulging it.

In some of these Institutions, one of the employments, which is in itself as dull as picking wool or teazing oakum, has arisen out of American ingenuity and thrift, and was quite new to me. It is the making of rag carpets. They cut cloths of all textures and colors into long stripes, tack them together so that they will follow the shuttle, and wind them into large balls. In this stage they are sent to the weaver, who uses them as the woof which crosses a wide warp of hempen cords, and he sends home gay, comfortable, rough-looking carpets, with which the rooms and the staircases of some institutions are covered. Such thrifty and long-lasting carpets are found in the houses of tradespeople, of all complexions, in town and country. They are also used often in the basement or kitchens of the opulent.

In the Refuge, we had the pleasure of seeing the young people promoted to higher classes according to their attainments, and after examination of the reports of the Matron and teachers as to their obedience, industry, and orderliness. They were neatly dressed, but not in uniform, the school aprons alone being all alike. When we learnt that many had been plucked from dens of dirt and wretchedness, and that some had been placed there by parents who could not manage them, it was very pleasant to consider the better path which the Christian discipline of this house opens for them. We heard them sing several hymns in a modest, agreeable manner, and saw by the glances interchanged between some of them and the ladies, that friendly relations are established and affections drawn out which cannot fail to produce a refining influence on their tempers and manners.

New York also has had for twenty-six years its Society for the Reformation of Juvenile Delinquents, in the establishment and conduct of which, both the Legislature of the State and Corporation of the City, take an interest. It has also a ladies Committee, which reports annually to the Legislature, as does the gentlemen's. Very many of its inmates have never been criminals, but are placed there as refractory, or as having fallen into bad company, by parents who cannot control them. The number received in the house last year was 380, and disposed of in that period, 371. The list of their indentures comprises nearly every imaginable trade; and it is remarkable that among so many, most of them of previous evil habits, there is not one death to record in 1850.

The managers are not content with merely training and educating the children while under their care, but keep up a knowledge of their circumstances even for years after they have passed into other positions, and long after the expiry of their term of indenture. Many of the letters from their employers, published in the reports, are of a character to cheer the managers in their labor, which is arduous. A specimen, almost the first that opens, is given. All the Reports of similar Societies contain a similar compartment:—

"John M'G. was received, April 18, 1840. He was sent to the Institution by —— County Sessions for theft. He had been running with idle, pilfering boys, refusing the admonitions of his friends for more than a year, and had acquired many bad habits. He was indentured, April 13, 1847, to a farmer, and we have received the following account of him :—

OCTOBER 25, 1850.

RESPECTED FRIEND,

John M'G. still continues with me ; he is healthy and seems contented. When I first took him, he was very troublesome, but is now doing well. He attends Church and Sabbath School, also District School during the winter, and makes good progress. He appears anxious to make something of himself, and I am trying to do all I can to encourage him. He is a smart boy, trusty and honest, so far as I know. I shall continue to do well by him, hoping he will make a useful man.

Respectfully yours, B. W."

Here is a boy who for ten years has been the child of the State, and now is "anxious to *make something of himself*." Is the State put to more expense and trouble by sustaining this Institution, than it would be by keeping up a Bridewell, where the boy might have been committed for sixty days, and dismissed a more confirmed rogue than he entered? While in the Refuge, he doubtless did something towards his own maintenance besides acquiring habits of industry and good order. At present, for want of room, they are obliged to pass the children much more quickly through the New York Institution than formerly; but to avoid that evil they are about to enlarge their accommodation, and hope soon to be located in a new position on the southern end of Ward's Island.

A circular letter of inquiry is sent annually to each person who has indentured a child from the Refuge. We give one reply in reference to a girl, to show that the females share equally with the males the care of the Institution.

September 8, 1850.

Dear Sir,

I received your communication relative to Jane M., and am happy to inform you that she still remains with me. She is industrious and much improved in her education. My family have the utmost confidence in her, she advises with them on all subjects, and seems very ambitious to do well. She has given us entire satisfaction. Her time will soon expire, and I can say that she is a respectable young woman. Her future prospects are flattering.

Yours, &c., E. B.

Answers to the inquiring circulars, though very satisfactory, are not so interesting as proofs of established character, as are the visits of former inmates, men and women, who are now free of indenture, and on their own responsibilities in life. In the superintendent's journal we find mixed up with other events as quite common, such notices as this: "April 22, Margaret F., who was indentured to Mr. T. V., of the town of ——— visited us to-day. She has served her time, as Mr. V. informs us, with credit to herself, giving him entire satisfaction. She will stay a day or two with us, and then go to Newark, with a friend of Mr. V., on good wages. She is one of the many saved by being sent to the Refuge.

"John L. also visited us, after having been absent three years; a fine-looking young man—he says he is doing well."

It is a beautiful feature in the character of these people, that they are not ashamed to own the nurse which plucked them from degradation, and placed them on the road to respectability. Their visits of gratitude, some of which I have witnessed, are very delightful, and cannot fail to encourage the laborers in their difficult way. In most of these Refuges, there is a colored department for both girls and boys—and their schools as well as meals and playgrounds are separate. I have not been able to discern any complexional distinction in the replies to their circulars of inquiry, or in any journal account of visits, and am therefore inclined to hope that the cases of colored and white are indiscriminately stated.

The Female Guardian Society or "Home for the Friendless," though not coming under the head of a Delinquent's Refuge, yet in some respects partakes of the same character. Many of its inmates find shelter there, from the misery of bad homes and wicked parents; and many seek it in consequence of other misfortunes that flesh is heir to.

The arrangement of its house is excellent. The adults find a respectable place and honest employment till they are provided for elsewhere—and a large number of nurslings, who would otherwise be exposed to every misery are educated when well, and tended when sick with maternal care. There is a house of reception at the back of the ground, to be used in case of infectious disease. Last year three hundred and thirty-three adults were received and two hundred and ninety-eight dismissed to situations. Of children, two hundred and thirty-six were received, and one hundred and forty-four provided with situations. The discipline of the house is excellent, and the kindness of the managers, shining in their careful affectionate countenances, seems to an imaginative mind like that Arabian well called the "diamond of the desert," bright, refreshing, life and love restoring to young hearts crushed by destitution, harshness, and immorality. They sometimes find places for young widows and forsaken wives, even when they carry a babe with them. This being an arrangement unknown with us, I introduce a letter which refers to a young woman, who works for small wages on condition that she may retain her infant for a considerable time.

"* * * * E. says I may tell the ladies that she does not think she could have had a better home—that she is contented and happy, and does not wish to return to the city. So far as I have seen, she is a truly worthy person. She will be well provided for here. She is decidedly the best help I ever had, and altogether better than I had any idea she would be. But I had committed my way unto the Lord, believing that he who numbers the hairs of our head would, if applied to, condescend to notice our domestic concerns, and I have not been disappointed.

"Mr. W. thinks everything of the little one. I do not know as he will ever be willing that he should leave us.

"Yours in Christian love,
"F. M. W."

Symptoms here of adoption! Good-natured, cheerful, and affectionate, the American farmer is not the man to trust with such a light in his dwelling as a pleasant child, if you do not wish it to be retained there.

The "Home for the Friendless" has quickly taken a much higher position in the estimation of the public as a place for providing servants than any of the intelligence offices. It is continually resorted to, both by citizens and country people, and makes arrangements which turn out useful and comfortable to both parties. Friends in the remote part of the State of New York send contributions of work, which are sold in a room called the Store of the Home. Much that is the fruit of taste, ingenuity, and notableness is to be procured there—specially the pretty patched quilts, lightly lined with cotton, and neatly quilted, which make a cover as light, and at the same time as warm as any eiderdown you may sleep under in Germany. Under the power of machinery, making Marseilles quilts and rugs of all colors, patterns, and dimensions so quickly, and at such moderate rates, we in Britain are losing the notable habits of our grandmothers. It would require some practice before we could produce such nice quilts as are to be seen in all the American institutions.

The Female Guardian Society has added to its other efforts at usefulness a semi-monthly paper, called the "Female Advocate." Together with moral instruction conveyed in tales and poetry, which are tasteful as well as religious, it records instances of the escapes from danger and temptation of some friendless females, and introduces salutary warnings and cautions as to hidden snares. It notices books in unison with its peculiar subjects, and gives pertinent hints on education, training of servants, and house-keeping in general. The paper is well conducted, and by its wide circulation extends an interest in the success of the plans of the Home for the Friendless many hundred miles beyond the City.

There is a common sense about American charities, which sometimes brought the towered halls and pinnacles of "mine own romantic town" to mind in rather vexatious contrast. With us, a rich man—

who may have been niggard of kindness to his poor relatives, or secretly chuckled at their procuring private aid from the society for helping decayed gentlewomen—is about to make his will. He cannot carry money to the world he is approaching. He transfers his covetousness to a new object, and now becomes desirous of posthumous fame. He bequeaths his hoard for the building of an Hospital to bear his name to posterity, and prefer in its charitable entertainment candidates who are his namesakes. His trustees come into guardianship of the hoard. Do they hasten to fulfil the last will and testament, so that the poor may have bread and the orphan education? No such thing. Those who come under the description of the will are in no pressing need. So the trustees set their thoughts on enriching with another splendid building their native city, already rich in architectural ornaments. They put the fund out to nurse for ten or twenty years, till they can make something handsome, something in keeping with *this* edifice, or that will form a grand point of view in reference to *that.* After a generation has passed, it rises a noble building, with no particularly noble name; and by and bye it is occupied; but often with children who would have learned more of domestic affection and family virtue, and thus have made better heads of families in their turn, had they remained at their father's hearth, where they might, out of his honest earnings, have been educated in the parish school, and grown stout and hearty on his homely fare.

In America the order of progress is reversed, a pressing want is felt—a man or woman with energy and a Christian heart to guide it, falls in with two or three orphans. What is to be done with them? Some compassionate friends are consulted. They join purses, hire a room, and engage a nurse. Presently another and another claimant on their humanity appears. They must hire a larger house. They must interest a wider circle, and by that means find access to their purses. Before another year passes over them, you shall find them under legislative protection, making their laws, receiving legacies, purchasing lots, and at last erecting a handsome and substantial edifice. By the time the building is finished, the inmates rejoice to enter on its more roomy and airy premises.

I believe I am correct in giving this as the history of the Orphan, the Half Orphan, and the Colored Orphan Asylums, the Home for the Friendless, and the Colored Home. It is not first a gorgeous palace, and then the inmates. It is first the cry of the widow and fatherless, then the heart stirred with compassion, and after that the house of shelter.

Edinburgh has many institutions, the result of spontaneous benevolence. But it is a contradictory state of things, that while we have magnificent asylums which are not much required, the really important places, such as the Refuge, the Night Refuge, the Maternity Hospital, the Shelter, the Delinquent's Refuges, and the Ragged Schools, can barely find funds to sustain them. One circumstance which depresses our charities is, that in our thronged population—once a claimant for external help—the aided becomes always a burden. There is no room to plant him, no hope of being rid of him. In America thousands get a *lift* when under casual pressure, and pass on. Newly-landed and newly-born emigrants are aided in their extremity, but soon find place and means of support, and are heard of no more. In a year or two they are thriving "down East," or "out West," adding to the resources of the country instead of burdening them.

In examining the report with which, without waiting for solicitation on my part, I was in every place bountifully furnished, I find evidence that necessity is invariably first proved, and then it operates as the main-spring of action. Thus the applications for a night's shelter, made at the Rosine House, Philadelphia, by women who had not the melancholy claim of its poor wanderer-inmates, led to the formation of the "Temporary Home Association," for the benefit of friendless women and children, somewhat on the plan of our House of Industry, or our Servant's and Sailor's Homes. Houses which not only alleviate present necessities, but act as preventatives against surrounding dangers.

Were it not for fear of prolixity, it would be an enjoyment to myself to describe minutely what is to be seen in many of these charitable retreats from the world's hardships. I might mention the contented expression of countenance of many a dusky woman approaching to her eightieth year, and her expressions, not of complaint in the midst of infirmities, but of gratitude that God had afforded her a comfortable bed and room, with only other three in it, to wait so quietly in till *He* calls her home. I might describe the sick-ward in the Colored Home, and the tender pity of the ladies, flitting from couch to couch, reading with one, giving a tract to another, and speaking kindly to a third. I might tell of my deep interest in the colored orphans in another house. Their lively recital of lessons, their almost lightning-look, questioning of each other in turn. Their skill in the geography of the United States—their sweet and cheerful songs, so well adapted to the country and to themselves. I might tell of little ones there, under strong spiritual influence, taking charge of putting some younger than themselves to bed, and being overheard, evening after evening, exhorting, imploring, and praying with them. I might mention their essays laid in the committee-room for inspection, quite equal to any productions of white children, whose ages and opportunities are equal.

We might go to Philadelphia and spend hours with the indigent widows and single women, in their airy house—learn their histories from themselves, and admire the plants they cherish, the wool they knit, the silken patch-work they make, and the tranquillity they enjoy. Or, with the ladies of the Nurse Society, we might inquire into the events in the district of each during the month, and learn how many lives have been saved by proper supplies of necessaries and kind attentions in the hours of nature's sorrow; or admire the economy of a charity that can succor so many at so cheap a rate. "Many poor emigrants with families of little children, have touched our country just in time to make a native of their youngest born, without the means of providing for themselves or little ones, and Providence who clothes the lilies of the field, has mercifully afforded relief through the patrons of the Moyamensing district of the Nurse Society."*

A pile of reports, a foot deep, interest, without tiring one who has the buildings, the ladies, and the objects of their charity, placed by them, afresh before her eyes, but they cannot interest others in the same way.

It is enough to say that the footsteps of Mrs. Graham—whose name is familiar and honored in Scotland—and of her friend Mrs. Hoffman, have been followed steadily by her successors. The judgment, the economy, the heathful regulations, and the Christian influences, which she was so happy as to introduce into the Orphan Asylum, her Widow's Society, and her Sabbath-schools, forty-five years since, are still the pattern of her State and city. Happy she to have fallen on a time which opened the way for the exercise of all her Christian piety and skill. Happy time, in its necessities, that had an Isabella Graham for a guide in the outset of philanthropic effort.

It is now more than thirty years since Dr. Mason saw, for the first time, an English edition of that

* Eleventh Report of the Nurse Society of Philadelphia.

good woman's life on our table. He was glad to see it, and told us of her family; so that to meet her now venerable daughter, Mrs. Bethune, still at the end of forty-five years, acting as first Directress of that same Orphan Asylum which her mother founded, was like finding a link which bound the past and the departed to the present and the useful.

How few live to see a good work advance in its useful cause, without once being turned aside for nearly half a century. How pleasant was it to stand in the noble mansion at Bloomingdale, the monument of the States' benevolence, and hear of the small beginning of the asylum, and look on the portraits of benefactors now in heaven. How pleasant to hear large and accurately taught bands of orphans examined, to look on their thriving countenances, to listen to their sweet voices as they sung; and to learn, when admiring the ingenious liveliness of many of the infant school exercises, that the dear old lady by our side was the living, sprightly inventor of all that wit, fun, and instruction, and also of many of the more sacred lessons. How quickening to the heart's throb to see a crowd of babes flock around her knees, each wishing to be noticed and caressed.

On the exhibition day, when they were brought into the city that the public might see all the children, consisting of babes of two years old to boys and girls of fifteen, we stayed to congratulate the dear First Directress on the appearance made by her blooming family. But it was not easy to approach her—she was encircled by a band of good-looking young men, well dressed, and of pleasing expression. "Who are all these, dear lady, who surround you so that one cannot reach your hand?" "Oh, these are a few of my own boys, who expect to see me here once a year. I am glad to see their faces, and to know that they are prospering." "I should think that they had grown out of your knowledge." "No—no—I know all that keep up the acquaintance. Here is one—a troublesome little fellow he was. He always thought when I went to mind my business that I had nothing to do but nurse him. I used to push him away. He was two years old." "And so you did nurse me," said the grateful man, "but I was younger than that, I was not a year and a half when you took me up."

It was a sight to make the heart sing; and one's sympathies flowed out with theirs, when the respected son of the venerated lady* made his way to her and embraced her, and their eyes were moistened as they looked on each other.

* The Rev. Dr. Bethune of Brooklyn.

The Islands.

It is a curious and rather painful sight, to watch the emptying of a newly-arrived cargo of Emigrants on the unknown shore. Squalid, thinly clad, and far from clean, you instantly distinguish the bony Irishman, with his wife, and all the children, dragging an ill-packed bundle tied with a bit of rope, which is made long enough by the help of a stripe of ticking, or a list border. They slide their bundle—their all of worldly wealth—down a plank, and having drawn it aside on the dock, they hang helplessly around it, the children tumbling on it, till the ship has disgorged her motley company, and all are ready to appear at the Emigrant Office. Next you will see a pair of stout, thickly-clothed Germans, letting down their heavy chest well nailed and corded, with a parcel of bedding on the top. And again, a rosy, round-cheeked Englishman, with his deal box, painted red. Each pours forth with a load to carry or care for, like the busy population on an ant-hill, and group after group sit on or watch by their slender store. What will become of them all? Are any of them sick? Will they all find employment? Why they will cumber the country. It will lose its American identity. How can that be preserved with such a mixed multitude flowing into it? Spare your solicitude, good stranger. Do you observe the thick, whitened waters of the Father of Rivers as they mingle with the sea? They discolor it for a little space—presently it becomes but a slight tinge, and long before the waves that meet the Mississippi have flowed back to the Reefs of Florida, the mud is deposited in the bottom of the Gulf, and the waters of the river are amalgamated with the waters of the Ocean.

Nothing convinces one more of the force and mass of the American character, than to see that the immense influx of foreigners has no power to modify it. The new-comers become modified speedily, chiefly through the political institutions. Many a mind, indolent before, perceives that it has something to do and something to obtain here, and so is roused to untried activity. Many, alas! have been roused to indignation by the treachery of selfish wretches who have boarded their vessel, promised all kinds of assistance, and sold to them so-called *railway* tickets to Buffalo; and when at Albany the poor ignorant strangers have presented them, they have found that they were tickets for canal-boats on which they must linger for very many days, providing food out of their slender funds! Such base dealings not only rouse indignation, but teach the half-passive that they must be active, or they cannot get along amidst a set of sharpers. I am happy to know that such baseness to the stranger and the poor is now put a stop to, and that the instructions obtained at the Emigrant Offices—I believe there are two—act both as guide and protector to these unfortunates. Hardship they must and do encounter; they are accustomed to that, but their hopes were high, that freedom and justice were bound together on the shores of the new world. To be met on their very first business transaction by an act of roguery, is confounding and discouraging in a high degree—the more so that, in general, it has been fellow-countrymen, feigning sympathy and acts of kindness, who have dealt the blow.

Of the multitude who come annually from Europe to try a new home, many bring education and property enough to have a plan and follow it in their future settlement. But many suffer from as great poverty of knowledge as of property, while some are also poor in health. The East River is beautifully speckled over with Islands which the wisdom of the Legislature has chosen as the receptacles of various sets of people requiring guardianship and superintendence; while its taste has caused buildings to be raised for all their purposes, which adorn the scene —already a very gem of beauties.

On WARD'S ISLAND is the great depôt where healthy Emigrants are sent to wait till they can be disposed of at work in the interior of the country. Here they rest, with light employment and under good regulations, till they recover from the effects of voyages made in crowded ships.

The Captain of the Emigrant ship is bound to produce twelve shillings currency, that is six shillings sterling, for each emigrant that he carries. This levy supports satisfactorily the immense establishment. There the German finds everything excellent, with the exception of the absence of his beer —and the astonished Irishman eats the first roast beef he ever tasted. They have a story of a Ward's man inquiring of an Irishman why, when he wrote to his brother pressing him to come out, he had told him that they had butcher's meat twice a week, when he knew they had it every day in life? "Why," said Pat, "I need not ha' been telling him that, for he would never ha' belaved it." They do not generally require to stay long on the Island.

On Blackwell's Island, we find the prison of the city of New York. The people here seem not under such close discipline as in the State Prison. But we saw bands of men gardening, terrace-making, levelling, and forcing land on their naturally sandy soil. They have made a very handsome façade of terraces, which one admires in sailing up the river. But their Island will presently be adorned to the last point, and their ingenuity will then be tasked to find other occupation.

The City Poor-House is also there. We saw about 400 women, and a nursery of babes, on the female side. Every place of this description is clean and airy. The absence of coal-smoke, the annual painting, the windows, doors, and piazzas all so well contrived for ventilation, give an air and a feeling of cheerfulness, which I have not found in similar establishments in England. We found women reading, sewing, knitting, and tending the sick, besides the stout band employed as laundresses, cooks, &c.

The Insane Asylum is also placed on Blackwell's Island. It is a very fine building, with a remarkably beautiful iron staircase, which combines beauty and strength in a high degree. The hand-rail is of dark oak; the stair is spiral, shedding gracefully off into a gallery at each landing-place. There is a fine library, in which we found a solitary German, whose delight is to work daily amongst the books, and whose humor is, as we found, not to answer any questions. We visited several wards under the guidance of one of the medical attendants, and left the place with the usual feeling of depression which the sight of remediless misery is calculated to excite.

We were rowed ashore, as we had been to the Island, by a set of stout oarsmen, whose skill, and knowledge of the strong current running up with the tide, were much needed to secure our safety. Yet not a cent was asked or expected by the men. We found this the case on visiting the other Islands, and indeed everywhere in the country. Yet the dollar is as mighty there as the sovereign is in England. I presume the explanation to be this: all government institutions belong to the community, they have a share and interest in them, and consequently means are taken to admit the people to examine them without charge.

At Washington we happened to be divided from our gentleman escort. In the Capitol we asked a watchman to admit us to the dome. He guided us up the many flights of steps, and through many galleries, and on the roof pointed out the counties and States, the rivers and cities, and the nearer public buildings and statues, and took much pains lest we should find any difficulty in the descent. I had been cogitating as we descended, whether half a dollar, or a whole one, were the right reward to present to so polite and pains-taking a guide ; when lo ! on looking round at the bottom, he had glided away, and I saw him retreating across the rotunda. They have not here any fat and lazy hangers-on of Government, who obtain, in lieu of a pension, the privilege of preying on chance visitors. No Beef-eaters, as they now call the successors of the old attendants on the Buffet, or side-board, with their jolly faces, and black velvet hats, and Elizabethan ruffs, to hurry you through the place, while they hurry through their story, and care for nothing about you, except the coin they have earned by their services.

On RANDALL'S ISLAND there is also a large establishment. To it, as to the others, we went, leaving our carriage on the opposite side, and signalling for a boat, which came for us at once, and brought us back when we had seen all we wished to see, without charge. On this island we saw upwards of 1,100 children, from two to fourteen years old. Here the foundlings, the parentless, and the offspring of the worthless and wretched are cared for. We entered our names in the Manager's book. On reading mine, he said, "You are from Scotland, I suppose. Out of these 1,100 children, nine tenths are Irish, a very few English, the remainder are German; we have little to do with your country here." So we found it on Blackwell's Island, in the Hospitals, and elsewhere. Our country-people have a name for upright industry, forethought, and economy, which obtains for them a welcome. Domestics, either male or female, are much preferred from Scotland, and repeatedly our ears were greeted with the accents of our own Doric from the coachman, when driving with friends in various cities.

Dr. Bethune gave us a characteristic anecdote, which it is pleasant to record. The people in Philadelphia were moved with pity for the Highlanders, on occasion of a severe famine, which occurred some years ago, and assembled to consult on the most efficient way to aid them. If I remember right, a cargo of flour was what they agreed to send. Whatever it was, several present cheerfully volunteered to go round the city, and raise the money from door to door. The Scotchmen present were not gratified, but troubled, by the kind proposal, and, after mutual consultation, an old gentleman stood up and asked what money would be required, and on a sum being mentioned, he said with much emotion, that "the people of his country were not used to beg, and would not like it. If the meeting would excuse them, though they were full of gratitude, they would rather raise the necessary amount among themselves"—and they did so—not, however, declining *volunteered* assistance.

But I must return to Randall's Island, where we found no countryman. It was Saturday. The children were at play. The boys with fife and drum, and banners waving marched, about twelve deep, past the front of the Centre House where we stood. Though most of them were of foreign extraction, everything in their training is calculated to naturalize or rather citizenize them. This plan we found pursued in all the institutions. It is wonderful how early they learn to feel themselves a part of the community, and to consider what becomes them in that capacity. Each banner had its motto, "Washington's body-guard," "Washington, the honest boy and friend of his country," "Are we not a band of brothers?" &c. We afterwards saw them exercise in a great open hall, shaded from the sun and heard them sing "Hail Columbia," and other patriotic songs. Then two young orators stood on a bench and harangued "right well," about the power of steam and of the uses of railways; and of the fun they should have on the 4th of July, when they would fire squibs, cry huzza, eat nice fruit and sugar-plums, drink cool iced water, and not reduce themselves below the beast with intoxicating liquors, and finally sing "Yankee Doodle." The little fellows are all embryo statesmen. The voice, enunciation, and air of one of those we heard, marked him out for an orator. What should prevent him from rising to high office in the State? We saw them at dinner. On inquiring why two boys stood on the floor looking on while the others were eating, an attendant said that was the punishment for rudeness to each other, but that they should dine when the rest had done and returned to their play. Each child had his little towel fixed to his collar. It serves as a napkin at meals, and also for washing. The plan for ablution was quite new to me, and the object of its construction is, that no one child may by possibility touch the water used by another. In the centre of the room is fixed a circular bath-tub, large enough for a child to swim in, with an aperture in the bottom which carries off its contents. Around the inside rim of the huge tub runs a pipe in which are twenty-four orifices about a foot apart. When the water is turned on it flows out at these, and each child takes his turn to occupy one of them, dabbling freely in the cooling stream, but never finding it possible twice to touch the same water, as it is all the time flowing away. Their dormitories are airy. They use iron bedsteads, and each child has a bed to himself.

The division of the extensive buildings devoted to the girls is exactly on the same plan as the other. We saw them go through various evolutions, and heard them recite and sing. We saw their nurses at dinner. Their aspect was very unpleasing to me, and when their history was explained I did not wonder. They are all taken from among the criminals on Blackwell's Island. Fierce, vulgar, and unkind, the few words that reached the ear too well suited the appearance of those who used them; and the poor orphans at their mercy seemed little likely to crowd round their knees to seek for attention. Amongst the many profuse and well-ordered charities in this generous country, which draw forth the warmest admiration, this is the solitary instance of false economy that has come under my notice. A few hundred dollars per annum would procure mild, tender, and Christian "care-takers" for these poor nurslings, some of whom looked delicate, and all of whom are capable of moral injury or improvement, according to the treatment to which they are subject.

That which seemed to me defective in the common schools, pervades this and other establishments. The fear of countenancing any denominational religion in particular, limits their religious instruction altogether. A small portion of Scripture is read daily. There is not generally any questioning upon it, and no catechisms or texts are taught. There is a service on Sunday for Protestants, and one on Wednesday for Papists. If there were real Protestant influences, the opportunity could not fail to be used to win over these poor friendless things. The only influence retained over them by their parentage is to detain them in the Church of Rome.

I asked leave to see the idiots of the place, who, considering the parentage of most of the inmates, were not so numerous as might have been expected. The amiable physician and my companions were surprised by my wish and dissuaded me. But, since seeing the unlooked-for success of Dr. Guggenbühl at the hospital of the Abendberg in catching up the slender thread of intellect, and unwinding it gently along with bracing and cheering physical treatment, I have become convinced that many are given up to hopeless idiocy, who might by proper treatment be very considerably elevated.

We found twenty-seven set around the walls of a room, like gnarled and withered plants. They were clean and well cared-for, by a kind old woman, who looks as if half her own intellect had fled, without, however, having injured her large benevolence, during the years that she has cherished her most discouraging charge. The remembrance of them is melancholy,—not a toy, a bit of twine, or a soft ball, was there to teach them the use of their poor, long, feeble, skinny fingers, or to interrupt the monotony of existence. In some of the "Homes," kind ladies have supplied this want, and the little ones trot about with horses on wheels, hoops, balls, or dolls. It would be of use in various ways if some such gifts might find their way into this doleful ward. Several of them seemed susceptible of interests,—smiling on the doctor, and watching their companions as he spoke to them in turn. Two of them proposed to sing for us "Mary in Heaven,"—they did sing, *after a fashion.* Their song, however, turned out to be "The Castle of Montgomery." As they knew the words of that song, which they had probably learned before they came there, they must have been capable of learning a hymn. After we left them, one merry little chap called over the window, "You did not hear my song." Not liking to disappoint him, we returned and heard "Old Virginia's Shore," in a very imperfect pronunciation. Several seemed greatly to enjoy the song, and the return of the company to hear it; and there were evidences that many of them might be taught something which might render life less dreary, and even awaken in them some sense of the powers of the world to come.

But who has time and patience or benevolence for so repulsive an undertaking? No one probably but some medical experimenter on matter and mind. No inmates of the huge dwelling were more tidy, or had a more airy apartment than they. It is a great thing that the State clothes, feeds, and tends these poor things—many of them victims of parental profligacy—and does not allow them to roam about like the "fool Jacks" and "daft Jamies" that we used to see a few years since hanging about inn-yards and gateways in Scotland.

This day was entirely interesting and satisfactory, in spite of the powerful sun which glared upon us. And the kind lady, whose acquaintance we made at the "Home for the Friendless," and who, out of her generous good-will, offered to conduct us, rendered it by her society still more interesting.

On Staten Island, which forms one side of the Bay of New York, is the Quarantine House, where emigrants unfit on account of sickness to be taken to Ward's Island, are cared for. Here many a patient in ship-fever is carried to be medicated and nursed—many are restored to health, but many also die.

The "Sailor's Snug Harbor" has also found its place on Staten Island; but being, as we were told, the fruit of private beneficence, it does not come into the same class with the institutions on the other islands.

Those who have buffeted with winds and waves for many a day, find in this beautiful locality a haven of repose—a kind of miniature Greenwich Hospital. To escape the tedium of being unemployed, some of them have learned the art of making baskets of a tough, reedy-looking substance, in such elegant forms that you might imagine them modelled in Greece or Etruria, rather than woven by hands that have heaved at the capstan and furled the sail.

Deaf and Blind.

THERE is a Scotch proverb, "It is easier to look on a burden than to lift it," meaning that the sympathizer does not feel so keenly as the sufferer. The result of this truth is, that many sufferers remain unaided. Yet the Christian part of our world shows varied and noble establishments, the sole object of which is to lighten, if not remove, the load of the burdened. We find it instructive to look from the institution to its source, and can generally trace it to a single bosom where the chord of compassion has been touched by a sight of distress —and from that we thankfully follow it higher, till we reach Him from whom compassions flow, and who hath the hearts of all men in his hand, and turneth them as He turneth the rivers of water. Thus was the heart of the benevolent Count Von De Reeke touched when he found naked children living on roots in a Silesian forest, whom a prolonged and bloody war had rendered parentless. Out of his emotion of pity sprung the Institution at Düsselthal Abbey, which has preserved, educated, and sent out in the world 1,400 orphans. Thus was the heart of Mrs. Tomlinson moved, by the faithfulness of a widow who rescued her children from a Popish asylum, and preferred extreme poverty with them to having them fed and perverted,—and out of this sprung the Half Orphan Asylum, beginning in a cellar, where a matron took charge of four babes. One house after another, was found too strait for them, till now they rank amongst the substantial and excellent charities of New York. Thus, too, was Dr. Guggenbühl smitten with the idea that there might exist some portion of mind under the deformity and apparent idiocy of the poor Cretin. He saw one of these miserable beings kneeling and muttering before an image of the Virgin. Compassion welled up till his heart had no repose—and out of that has sprung the cheerful and prosperous hospital of the Abendberg, which has been parent to another and another, in Switzerland; to two schools for those of feeble intellects, in England; and it is expected that more of this humble but useful family of charity are hastening to come forth vigorously in America.

But the examples are numerous, and might occupy a chapter themselves. The only one that I shall name in addition is connected closely with our present subject.

In the city of Hartford it pleased God to afflict a very lovely and intelligent young creature, Alice Cogswell, with the loss of hearing. Her father was an eminent physician. His ingenuity and inquiries for the means of instructing his beloved child were unceasing. But we prefer to quote a portion of an oration delivered by Mr. Gallaudet to the re-assembled pupils of the Asylum which sprung out of Alice's misfortune, after it has shed its benignant influence on deaf mutes for thirty-five years.

"Some of our number, both teachers and pupils, have gone to the spirit-world. She has gone, the beloved Alice, my earliest pupil, who first drew my attention to the deaf and dumb, and enkindled my sympathy for them. We will ever cherish her memory and that of her father, one of your best and long-tried friends. We will never forget that to them under the divine guidance and blessing, we owe the origin of those ample provisions which have been made for your benefit. For God saw fit to visit her at a tender age, with your common privation. And on whom else, so intelligent and lovely, could his mysterious yet benign Providence have sent this privation, to produce as it did, so deeply and extensively, the interest needed to be felt in her and her fellow-sufferers, in order to lead to prompt and effectual action on their behalf." * * *

"The same Providence cast my happy lot in this community, near to this father and daughter, herself a playmate of my younger brothers and sisters, which led to my acquaintance with her, and then to my attempting her instruction. This I did from time to time, inexperienced indeed, but with no little enthusiasm and zealous perseverance. At length, I had the privilege of being employed to carry into effect the benevolent designs of my fellow-citizens; designs, extending as they have already done, in the establishment of many kindred Institutions in various parts of our country. See in these successive links of Providence how God works out the chain of his beneficent movements."

When first the name of Gallaudet reached my ear, he was a pupil under the Abbé Sicard, at Paris, who was then teaching the highest class of deaf mutes in that city. When he returned to his native land, he succeeded in bringing with him Mr. Laurent Clerc, another élève of the French Institution, and in a brief space they were both actively engaged in Hartford, where "The American Asylum" sprung up. It is the offspring of Christian benevolence, and from it has sprung an extensive family.

An interesting and striking festival was held on Sept. 26, 1850, in the Hartford Asylum, where it is believed more persons enduring the same sad privation met, than were ever before assembled together since the world began.

Mr. Brown of New Hampshire, an early and intelligent pupil of the Asylum, stated, in his graphic language of signs, that his spirit could find no rest till he had devised some method of giving expression to his gratitude, which the lapse of years served only to increase. The idea was but suggested when it was seized and made common property. A subscription was raised, for, as he stated, the wish ran "like a prairie fire through the hearts of the whole deaf-mute band," scattered though they were all over the country. The plan was matured in secret, and resulted in presenting to MM. Gallaudet and Clerc two massive silver pitchers, accompanied by salvers, inscribed and beautifully chased with emblems.

On the festive day of presentation, upwards of two hundred deaf mutes. not then connected with the asylum, besides the two hundred inmates, were present. Let us who can express our sentiments without impediment at any time, in any society, imagine the glad recognition of old comrades, the strong delight of having their language of signs intelligible to each other, the narrative of their recent history, the love, the gladness, and then we shall perceive that the greetings of that day far surpassed those of any common assemblage of friends. There were orations delivered in the language of signs, which were interpreted in words to the rest of the company. The extent and power of this sign-language is surprising to the uninitiated, as I saw and felt when in the New York Asylum, a teacher told his class my country, and other things without writing, and they immediately wrote on their large slates what they knew of Scotland or "Caledonia," as some of them called it.

Mr. Gallaudet left the institution in 1830, to occupy the humane office of chaplain to the insane, but he is justly deemed the Father of the "American Asylum," and of all those which have sprung from it. It was a sincere gratification to be introduced to this philanthropist whom I had known by report, and honored so long, and to converse with him in the society of my dear friend Mrs. Sigourney. It was sweet to me to take shelter in her "Dove's nest," and to rest under her fostering wing, renewing our European acquaintance, and gathering, from her stores of benevolence and intelligence, much information, which adds to the interest long felt in herself and her country.

At the New York Institution for the Deaf and Dumb, happening to be in the house at dinner-time, the president with the polite hospitality which I have found everywhere in the United States, pressed us to join their party in the dining-hall. The professors and matrons, numbering about a dozen, were at a centre-table where we were placed; and there it was pleasant to find a son of Mr. Gallaudet pursuing his father's path of mercy. He told me that his father had written to him of me, and thus a friendly relation was quickly established between us. It was curious to see the keen glances of the two hundred and twenty-seven mutes who occupied the wing tables, as if they would make double use of one sense, because of the absence of another; and remarkable that their movements were all so quiet, as from their inability to hear, one might have expected an extra noise of knives and forks. They looked generally cheerful, and had pleasant interchange of sentiment in their quiet language of signs.

We were shown the daughter of a missionary in Northern India among the pupils. It is pleasing to see the interest excited by the children of missionaries. They are pointed out to strangers in all institutions, but specially if the institution be one connected with human infirmity. In the Blind Asylum at Philadelphia we were introduced to a lively little girl connected with the Chinese Mission. Well does it become us who rest at home to extend our sympathy to the offspring of our delegates, who in heathen lands, amid many hardships, have this one added to their privations and deep anxieties, that they can neither enjoy the society of their own dear children, nor superintend their mental and religious training. Many a time have I seen such children cherished in America, and been introduced to them as subjects of peculiar interest.

In August, 1850, a convention of Teachers of Deaf Mutes was held at their Institution in New York. Instructors from seven similar Asylums met there with Old Teachers and others interested in discovering the best means of improving the mental education, and the moral and social condition of the Deaf. The examination which is reported by the Rev. Mr. Day seems to have been searching and satisfactory, while the best results may be anticipated from the congregated wisdom and experience of so many zealous and practical men.

There is in the Hartford Institution an example of an individual deprived of sight as well as hearing. Julia Bliss is the child of poor parents. She lived for several years in her father's house, without any effort being made to instruct her. It is wonderful to hear how much her own sagacity had taught her. She could wash and dress little brothers and sisters; and when, in her untrained impatience, she slapped or shook any of them, as she could neither hear their cries nor see their tears, she was used to feel their eyes, and if she found them weeping, she would take pains to soothe and comfort them. She learnt the use of money, it was not distinctly known how, and if any was given to her she would hoard it till a neighbor in whom she confided came within her reach, when she would bring to her an object such as she wanted (say a comb or string of beads), show it, give her money, sign to her to go out and get it, and then not rest till she got her fairly out of the house. She was watchful about the clothing of her sisters, and very jealous if she discovered that they had new shoes or frocks, while she had old ones. Naturally of a hot temper, without any door open by which to reach her reason or conscience, she commonly managed to keep the family uncomfortable till her wishes were acceded to. She was ultimately observed by a benevolent friend, and placed under instruction. I did not see her, but was informed that she has not gained so much as she might have done, had she been earlier trained. She has one sense in great strength, of which it is thought Láura Bridgeman, her associate in misfortune, is nearly destitute. Julia discerns all persons and things by her scent, which seems of the character of that by which a dog tracks his master, or a hound his prey. She never mistakes a friend, and one of her regular occupations in the Institution, is what may sometimes have its difficulties to people with both eyes. She receives the clothes from the laundress, and sorts them in the clothes-room, never placing the property of one inmate in the pigeon-hole of another.

The idea was conceived of introducing the two girls, sisters in age, in sex, and in calamity, to each other. But it seems no proper mode of communication could be established between them, and the meeting was a failure. Laura Bridgeman at Boston, was told the history of Julia Bliss, and her romantic and sensitive mind was worked up to a passion of enthusiastic sympathy. Julia had no language by which she could be told the history of Laura, and when she found herself suddenly embraced by a person she had never felt before, and bedewed by tears, the cause of which she could not divine, she exerted a most determined resistance, much to the grief and surprise of poor Laura, whose heart, full of love, was thrown roughly back upon herself.

We had an interview with Laura Bridgeman at the noble Blind Asylum of Boston. Her first question was, "Have you seen Doctor ?" Dr. Howe, being her first link to social life, is of course to her the most interesting person in the world. A blind friend by her side, interpreted to us the hand-language of Laura, who has a pretty figure, is pale, with fair hair, neatly braided by herself, and small green shades which entirely cover the sockets once occupied by her blue eyes. Her features are animated, and her face full of sensibility. She replied sensibly to various questions, and when she was told that one of the ladies was from Scotland, she made several remarks about that country, and observed that she must have crossed 3,000 miles of ocean to come to Boston. She suddenly, without apparent explanation, made her way from behind a little table, flew across the wide hall like a bird, and must have ascended the lofty staircase with as rapid and as sure a foot as the possession of all her senses could have bestowed, for she returned in a moment. She had brought her little merchandise of watchguards woven by herself. We purchased and paid into her own delicate hand. One lady gave her a gold dollar. It was a new coin, so she had not had one before. She touched it with her tongue, carefully fingered the figures on the surface, then ran her nail round the notched edge, and said on the hand of her friend, "California." I paid her in five or six coins to make up one dollar. She fingered and counted them till she was satisfied it was right, being acquainted with the feeling and the value of half and quarter dollars, of dimes and shillings. One could not help feeling a little solicitude lest, among the few ideas which can find access to her secluded mind, that which may tend to covetousness should furnish too large a share. We were told, however, that her mother is poor, and it is for her that she exercises her industry. She inquired with curiosity whether we had chosen blue or puce color. When told that mine was to go to Scotland to be given to the physician from whom I had brought a book for Dr. Howe, she expressed great delight, smiling very pleasantly.

We were told, but not in the Institution, that Dr. H. had been greatly annoyed, after an absence, to find that a visitor had told her of the "Lamb of God, that taketh away the sin of the world." He avoids imagery, or anything like complex figures in his instructions, and she did not know what to make of this new figure. It must indeed be very difficult to tread in his steps as her instructor, yet one feels a strong sympathy with the kind friend who wished to lead her to a knowledge of the atonement.

We heard with a little surprise, that the amiable wife of Mr. Gallaudet, the benefactor of the deaf, is herself a mute. So the animated, intellectual young man, whom we met in the New York Institution, never was sung to sleep by the voice of his Mother. I was much more surprised to learn that upwards of a hundred pupils of the Hartford Asylum are married, the greater part among themselves, though some have partners who can hear and speak. The fear which we might naturally entertain with respect to their offspring, has been, by a gracious Providence, disappointed. "With a few exceptions, they are blessed with children enjoying all their faculties, which will be a great consolation to them in old age." The men are freemen, and have votes.

The reader may now be better prepared, as I am, to enter into the sentiment of the American poetess, when with her usual feeling and delicacy she describes

THE MARRIAGE OF THE DEAF AND DUMB.

"No word! no sound! But yet a solemn rite
Is consummated in yon festive hall.
Hearts are in treaty, and the soul doth take
That oath which, unabsolved, must stand, till death
With icy seal, doth stamp the scroll of life.
No word! no sound! But still a holy man,
With strong and graceful gesture, doth impose
The irrevocable vow, and with meek prayer
Present it to be registered in Heaven.
Methinks the silence heavily doth brood
Upon the spirit.—Say, thou flower-crowned bride,
What means the sigh which from that ruby lip
Doth 'scape, as if to seek some element
Which angels breathe?

Mute—mute—'tis passing strange—
Like necromancy all—and yet, 'tis well;
For the deep trust with which a maiden casts
Her all of earth, perchance her all of heaven,
Into a mortal's hand—the confidence
With which she turns in every thought to him—
Her more than brother, and her next to God,
Hath never yet been shadowed forth in sound,
Or told in language.

So, ye voiceless pair,
Pass on in hope. For ye may build as firm
Your silent altar in each other's hearts,
And catch the sunshine through the clouds of time,
As cheerily as though the pomp of speech
Did herald forth the deed. And when you dwell
Where flowers fade not, and death no treasured link

Hath power to sever more, ye need not mourn
The ear sequestrate, and the tuneless tongue,
For there the eternal dialect of love
Is the free breath of every happy soul."

Poetical Works, p. 257. MRS. L. H. SIGOURNEY.

It is of great value to the subjects of instruction, that what they are taught of Christianity, is in general sound and heartfelt; and very touching to observe that the prominent felicity of heaven dwelt on by the pupils in letters and compositions is, that their ears shall be there unstopped and their tongues loosed.

The Widow.

"Yes, there are some who sorrow's vigils keep,
Unknown that languish, undistinguished weep."

THERE is poverty everywhere in the world. In the United States there is enough of it, but it is emigrant poverty, or poverty among the depressed colored race. One heard marvels about the comfortable condition of the native people. In one small town in New England, a society of ladies, who met for devotional purposes, agreed to form a fund for the help of the poor. Having raised their means they began to look about for their objects, but they were nowhere to be found, or only found in the persons of one colored family. After the humane ladies had new-rigged all the children, and got them roused and sent to school, they added various comforts in the way of furniture, then they sent one man to repair the dripping roof, another to fill up the boards in the broken floor and—their work was done! They were obliged to turn the flow of their contributions into the wide bed of the Home Mission, for they had no poor! The gentleman who told me this was personally cognizant of it. It seems to realize the saying I have heard in my childhood, that there is but one beggar in America, and he rides on horseback. That New England village must have been happy in the absence of inebriates, "of Gin Palaces," and intoxicating drinks, for where they are found it is in vain that industry plies her diligence and the earth pours forth her stores,—there will be poverty, misery, wickedness, and degradation in their vicinity.

I had sometimes wished to see some native poor besides those to be found so comfortably provided for in the institutions, and at last I was gratified. It seems almost necessary to premise, that our visit to widow R. was entirely unpremeditated on our part, and unexpected on hers, otherwise an incident or two which occurred, might wear the air of acting in the poor woman, when it was not so. She was lonely, borne down with grief, and nearly blinded by tears with which no one sympathized.

We found, in a neat orderly room, a tall wasted figure beside a very small table, on which lay ink and paper, and two or three bright little books, very like school prizes. She was dressed in rusty black, with a cap, whose former pretensions to smartness, made its faded black lace add to the desolate appearance of the wearer.

She was writing when we entered, but on seeing strangers she laid down her pen, took out a poor muslin rag to wipe tears which were flowing fast, and without taking heed at all to who her guests might be, she began her lament, "I had one bright spot in my gloom, but God has taken it away from me. My dear R—— is gone, and I don't know where she is gone to," looking round the roof with an indescribable vague expectancy, as if she might learn from the ceiling where her daughter was. "Don't you believe in a state of happiness for those who love the Lord?" "Oh yes, I was brought up in true religion. I am a New Englander; my parents taught me about the fall of man, and salvation by Jesus Christ, about the resurrection, and the judgment, and I taught it all to my child. R—— believed in all that, but I can't see her now. I don't know where she is gone to." "If she believed in Jesus you do know, and if she is with Jesus where he is, you know she is happy." "You talk, but you never lost your one bright spot as I have done." "I have lost children, and have had very bright spots darkened. It is not because I do not feel for you that I speak, but because I know that there is consolation for those who weep." My companion hoping to turn the current of her thoughts said, "Perhaps you have heard of Mary Lundie. This is her mother." "Is it?" hardly turning her streaming eyes to me. "I have read her life many a time, and sold hundreds of it here in the streets of New York." "You sold books! how was that?" "I was born to affluence. I married and lived well with my husband, but somehow he died, and left me four children and not a dollar. I could work with my head, but not with my hands, so I wrote political articles, and tales for magazines. I wrote whatever I could get paid for, till neuralgic pains put me almost distracted, and the doctor said if I went on writing I should go out of my head." "And what did you do then?" "Then my R—— had learnt to embroider, and I sold her work, and Mr. C—— let me have books, and I hawked them from house to house, and at last, when I could not pay my rent, God sent a good spirit to help me. I never saw him, but he has paid my rent for years." "Do you not know that this lady is the wife of your good spirit?" "Is she?" looking slightly round. "No, I did not, but now she never sits on that chair at her work and talks to me, nor even lies on that bed sick.

She is gone, my bright spot, and I don't know where she is gone to," again searching the ceiling with her restless and misty eye.

Poor thing, she had employed herself in patching a pretty cushion of bits of silk during the long nights, while she watched her sick child, "to keep her poor eyes open," as she said, and was ministered to by two young ladies, real sisters of charity, without the garb and badge, and without the vow.

At last consumption, which annually nips its hundreds of the budding and blossoming, finished its work, and the widow's "one bright spot" was darkened. R—— died in her lonely arms, which clasped her an hour and a half before the poor mourner could admit the belief that she was dead; and in the morning, when the two friends came to visit her, they attended to the last claims of the departed, and left the mourner alone with her sorrow. She told us she sat alone two nights by the shell of her child, and persuaded herself when she perused her countenance at four in the morning, that she had again become rosy. Indeed her monomania turned on the idea that she had not died, but that *her spirit had just slipt away, and she didn't know where it had gone to.* Her eye invariably wandered vaguely upwards, and her voice fell into the same plaintive cadence when this afflicting thought returned in its force. She read to us some rather poetical verses, which she called "a voice from the Spirits' land," in which the daughter addresses the mourner, "Weep not for me, mother, weep not for me," and describes her present state of perfect happiness as the reason. "Who told you all those sweet things, Mrs. R.?" "My dear R——. She just came and stood by me there, and dictated it all." "Well, then, you do know where she is, for she says she is in heaven, with angels and saints, and in the presence of her Saviour. So you do know." Poor woman, she was caught by her own showing, and put to silence. Yet in a few minutes her beamless eye sought the roof, and she was repeating, "I don't know where she is gone to." I have read poetical descriptions of similar hallucinations, but never met with such before.

When we had arisen to depart, after a long visit, she said some old friends had forsaken her, because of a report that she encouraged the Romanists to come about her, but she never did. She could not protect herself from them. Sisters of Mercy had come, and after them a lady, who gave her name, and forced a book upon her poor girl, who would have avoided them, and was disturbed in mind by their talk. At last, one day, she desired this lady to go and not come again. A considerable time after she had shut the door, she was surprised to find her still lingering on the stair, and asked her why she stayed. She prolonged talk, and still seemed to have more and more to say, and by and bye the secret reason for her stay was explained. She had made an appointment with the priest, who joined them on the staircase, and offered to see the sick. The mother "honored his zeal," but politely declined. That proposal failing, he had another. He knew of a medicine that he was sure would cure the invalid. She had a regular medical attendant, and did not require to trouble his reverence. Ah, but he was so sure of the efficacy of his medicine, if he might *just go into the room*, and write the prescription. The mother said, if he was so sure, he might write it on the fly-leaf of the lady's book. This he did, and the lady undertook to procure and pay for it. It was to cost half-a-dollar. Again the priest tried to enter the sick-room, and he and the lady said, if the girl died without extreme unction, she would burn in hell-fire forever, with all heretics.

It was striking to mark, as indignation took the place of woe in the widow's heart, how her attenuated and bending form, returned to its natural height; how her voice rose, and her eyes brightened even in relating their conversatien. The dignity of becoming indignation suddenly kindled her whole frame, and you could scarcely identify the drooping creature, dying under the misery of eating grief, who had but just risen from the side of her writing table.

"I am Protestant," she said, "I don't believe in what you say, and my daughter does not wish for your services." "Then I won't get her this medicine that would cure her." "I would not give her anything you prescribe till I saw it analyzed. If I ever wish for you I will send—for the present, go away." "Then I will call again to-morrow," said the pertinacious persecutor. "You need not—I will not admit you;" and so, at last, the pair departed, having done what they could, in their view, to save the dying girl from eternal misery.

How unprotected are the poor from these bold impostors—and how unprotected are the rich from the more insidious and ensnaring measures which they adopt in their advances to them. Their perseverance in trying to compass one dying proselyte, is a rebuke to the more supine plans of Protestants. Yet this is the sect against which Protestant America can see no cause to be on its guard. The planters of which are artists, musicians, teachers, domestics, Sisters of Charity, politicians, who unweariedly put in their seed and leave it to grow while we are asleep in erroneous security.

At last, then, I had seen a really poor native. But it was not squalid—it was respectable poverty—and in the woe of a wandering mind, independence and gratitude were visible. She uttered no thanks to the "good spirit" who paid her rent—but she sent the silken pillow which she sewed by the couch of her dying child, as a gift to the "good spirit's" wife.

We went a few days after to try to procure her a room in the Home for decayed gentlewomen. But we failed at that time, though very desirous to break up the tribe of associations with that chamber and that bed, and to place the mourner within reach of a little society, if by any means the sorrow which preys on her spirit might be diverted.

The proper name of the Institution I allude to, has escaped me, and that is not to be regretted as of the numerous houses we visited, whether they were philanthropic, educational, or established for purposes of State, this was the solitary instance in which the doors were not cordially thrown open, the economy of the place described, and reports offered. Perhaps the Matron was new and unaccustomed to her office—or perhaps the person who repulsed us was a bad substitute for the Matron. However it was, it gives me great pleasure to think of the hearty reception afforded to me, a stranger without a claim, in every place with the exception of this.

We were told the number of inmates was made up at the moment—and poor Mrs. R—— was left still to imagine she held conferences with R——, though she "knew not where she was gone to."

Various Country Districts.

TRAVELLERS who pass through Virginia and Maryland tell of broken fences, unproductive fields, crumbling mills and dwellings, and the most unsightly and melancholy of all ruins—those of wooden houses. It is not easy to describe or to account for the very disagreeable impression produced by frame-house ruins. In an ancient stone wall, the fallen part makes an irregular mound on which vines and mosses grow, while that which stands has a degree of picturesque beauty in its decay. But if the ruins be that of an edifice of wood, though it were but recently smart with its correct angles and bright paint, it is ugly in decay, having none of the dignity of agedness about it. You may find one long line of planks prone on the ground, another warped and bending here out, there in, with ragged and broken boards projecting, while the roof with its forked rafters is hanging to the standing wall and seems to long to drag it down to that which is already prostrate. Mosses, lichens, mould, nettles, toad-stools—all horrid things which a witch might cull to seethe in her caldron, are springing up around. The desolate appearance of the place is painful, as you feel a persuasion that the quondam inhabitants also are in a state of decay. On those estates where human ingenuity lies prostrate at the feet of cupidity, where man does the work of the ox and the ass, and where generation after generation, the spade and the hoe have without variation worked the same earth, the fertile land is turned into barrenness. It becomes so unproductive as not to pay the labor, and is gradually left to fall out of cultivation and its buildings to drop to decay.

"What a mouldy appearance all the country we traversed this week has," I heard a lady say inquiringly, after her return from the South. A *free thinker* could have explained the cause of the mould, but it would not have been well taken to act the part of a *free speaker*. For to confess truth, brother Jonathan is not so *free* as he would like to think himself. It is marvellous to see him at the North, smother his aspirations and whisper his thoughts in subjection to the South. It is marvellous to see men who have rid themselves of dishonest gains and dishonoring institutions, submit to be made man-hunters and slave-catchers in their own free homes. It is marvellous to hear a man say he would suffer the penalty of the law, rather than obey the summons that the magistrate is entitled to give him to join in the human chase; but yet he will not dare to lift his voice against that law. He places himself in the attitude of the sufferer, and will bear fine and imprisonment rather than obey a law which oppresses his conscience. Is he in truth, and honestly, a martyr to conscience here? Would he be encroaching on the freedom of a neighbor State were he to lift up his voice against wrong? Or would he not rather be obeying the Scripture rule: "Thou shalt in any wise rebuke thy neighbor and not suffer sin upon him," or "That thou bear no sin for him."

Let us turn from this desolate landscape, and gladly survey a new scene which begins to open there. Here are some repaired houses and fields again fertile, but with other crops than those they formerly bore. These are the smiling fruits of labor stimulated by proprietorship. Look at that hearty New England farmer and his cheerful family recently settled there. See the soil turned with the plough instead of the hoe, its furrows reaching to a depth untried at least for a century. Look at its luxurious productions of fruits, vegetables, and grain. Observe that field covered with clover which will be ploughed in presently and left to manure the ground where it grew. Watch the waving crops, and inspect the early vegetables, which borne by steam to northern markets, will bring a rich return to the laborer. He has, by favor of climate, produced them six weeks sooner than they can be grown at New York, and two months earlier than at Boston. Will not such proof of the capabilities of a soil in the hand of free labor enlighten the minds of those who have worn it out and forsaken it, under the cultivation of the slave? Will not Virginia look to her mountain districts held by free men, and compare or contrast them with her lowlands? Surely the time is hastening when the children of the free shall hail another and another State freed from that yoke; a yoke that hangs on the neck of the slaveholder, and keeps his mind and conscience in bondage. Nay, it induces him to lay bonds on the necks of his free neighbors. When all things are fairly weighed, it appears that the slaveholder is as little really a freeman as is the slave. His system violates the eternal principles of justice, and consequently he dare not suffer the vicinity of the free negro, however just his claim to be there, or however it might advantage himself. Such an exhibition of liberty might spoil his *gang*. He dare not admit the instructor, lest the aurora of knowledge dawning afar should infuse into his gang some idea of a life above that of the passive brute. He dare not indulge even one favorite and promising colored man with education, lest his skill and knowledge should make the others discontented. The freedom of the press cannot exist where he is. Rome is not more exact in her expurgated lists of books and newspapers than is the legislature in a slave State. Nay, he must lord it over free States, that he may the more easily keep his own in bondage. Is he then a freeman, or is he not rather the slave of a most evil and unhappy system?

Should a young lady from a free State, without sufficient knowledge of how matters stand, become the wife of a Southerner, she, poor inexperienced child, if she carry conscience and humanity with her, may be alarmed to find herself called upon to exercise the offices and wisdom of age, being looked up to by a band of people utterly unused to confide in themselves and each other. Though a colored nurse watch by the bed of the sick domestic slave, the lady must drop the medicine. She must look upon the time-piece for the moment to administer it.

She, though at midnight or early morning hours, may be awakened to give the potion. She must not only provide clothes for her numerous family, which has no provident habit because it is untrusted, but she may find it necessary to shape them, and fix the seams for the overgrown children who can with needle and thread be taught to fasten them together. Is she free? I speak not of her moral, but of her mere physical condition. Does she not discover that she has married into bondage? Some of the most elegant, refined, intelligent, princess-like women that I have met with in the United States, were such. They have learnt to be waited upon, to have their slightest wish attended to, and withal, because they, with woman's nature, are pitiful to the sick and feeble, they have exercised much benevolence. They have, mayhap, endured much in being aware of cruelties which they had not power to mitigate. All this has refined their characters—still they are not Cornelias and Portias, fit mothers for the sons of a republic; they are refined into amiable despots, and fit mothers for the owners of slaves.

But the mouldering farms of Virginia have betrayed me into the subject which it is so unavailing for me to touch, though it never fails to oppress my heart, and I must resume my journey.

The railway which runs between Albany and Buffalo, though it passes many cities that were already made rich by possessing means of carriage on the great canal, establishes new centres of traffic, as well as greatly enhances the wealth of the old ones. Yet in some parts the country is but newly opened. The engineer goes forth in search of levels, not of fertility or beauty. And thus he has crashed his way through many a swamp inhabited by doleful creatures, and many a forest, untrodden since the Indian hunter has faded away before the white man.

We were told that we should have found plains and valleys smiling under the influence of skilful industry, if we had travelled by the high road. Yet it is only fifty years since that road was slowly piercing its way through regions as unaccustomed to man as those more recently penetrated by the iron path. In far less than fifty years more, those unsightly and tangled underwoods, those undrained marshes, and those dreary girdled trees and black stumps, will disappear from the track of the railway—and smoother fields, and comfortable dwellings, and zigzag fences take their place. These fences are the reverse of pleasing objects in the landscape; yet in a country where the quantity of wood to be cleared away forms the difficulty, it is a wiser plan to use the dead wood in forming divisions, than it would be to plant other shrubs and trees for fences. The English eye, accustomed to polished fields cultivated for centuries, chequered with beautiful hedgerows, finds this part of the country very rough, and in every part misses the hawthorn. But the circumstances are so different as to render comparison unreasonable. One is inclined to take up the prophetic strain of which the American is accused, and say what this district will presently become, when we see what it is even already in its difficult and rugged progress. Here you see a brick-field, with two or three cottages near it. A little farther on a forge, and by-and-bye a carpenter's shop, and, in a position accessible to them all, though by deep and difficult footpaths, a store partaking the character of the village shop of Scotland, known by the familiar name of, "Willie a' things." Everything you can want in a rough way is to be had there, from cheese, ham, needles, nails, tea, hammers, sugar and grindstones, down to spelling-books, butter, and Bibles, as I have seen "Willie's" *list of wares* made out.

Who that has travelled through the cultivated parts of New York or New Jersey, or that has stood on the summit of Mount Holyoke and surveyed the windings of the Connecticut river, through a valley equal in fertility and agricultural excellence to the lands that are intertwined with the links of Forth, can fail to see that time only is wanting to bring the whole of the country into the finest bearing condition. The climb to Mount Holyoke, though toilsome, is richly rewarded by the view obtained. You can trace the limits of snug farms, and see their regularly laid out ridges which could not be surpassed for accuracy of line in a Northumberland or Roxburghshire ploughing-match,—you can count their convenient farm-houses and *onsteads*, for miles, till the eye is weary, and rest it on the pretty spires among the trees that look so like Old England. Everything in the Connecticut valley is rich and regular. The land is peopled up to its capabilities, and if the sharp frosts and scorching suns would suffer the quickset hedge to grow, and that feature were added to the landscape, it would be exactly like home. We must, however, always except the giant style of everything American. The Forth with all its lovely links, even though a tide-river, lies but like a silver thread in the landscape, compared to the Connecticut. The latter river has proved the weight of its waters, by cutting its way through the neck of a peninsula around which it had flowed for centuries—so that at last it has possessed itself of a picturesque islet in its bosom consisting of several acres of the richest alluvial soil which centuries of river-laving could deposit. The contrast between this whole district and some parts of that between Albany and Buffalo, is as complete as can be between the smooth-polished and productive and the newly-possessed and wild.

For many miles the nor-western rail runs parallel with the Mohawk River; the valley is narrow and occasionally the rocks which hem it in, are precipitous and exhibit some rugged grandeur—but in no place is it so narrow as to exclude its three remarkable features. First, the Old Mohawk, which has had time enough to cut its way through these rocks since the waters of the deluge subsided. Second, the canal—a Herculean labor, which has united Lake Erie with the Hudson River for many a year, and carried many a white boat laden with produce down to the river's margin. And last, the iron way, which in that part has been put down with little trouble of blasting rocks or raising levels. One skims over scores of miles without a tunnel, and with only here and there a bridge over some mountain torrent that is skipping its way down to join the waters at the bottom of the valley.

The progress of the canal-boats, after they join the Hudson, has been much accelerated by the use of steam-tugs. Instead of tacking about and creeping down the great river, they make a steady undeviating progress, as many as half a score at a time. The persevering "Walk-on-the-Water" steamboat, like the hen in the midst of her brood, plies her onward way. They may be many and cumbrous, but she is the mother and must care for them all. They cover half an acre of water, hooked on two or three deep on each side, and dropping far behind. Many of the boats with three tiers or galleries of various merchandise, including live stock, while the central mover of them all has her freight of goods also, and the human beings who tend their several cargoes.

There is not a finer prospect in the world, either in a picturesque or soical point of view, than that to be obtained from the heights of Mount Hope, in the beautiful district which bears the name of Hyde Park, so familiar to the English ear. The trees there have all the magnificence of ancient forest denizens —a grandeur which is not to be found in the crowded and tangled wilder forest. The swells of earth, the abrupt precipices, the Catskill mountains blue and bounding the distant horizon, are all striking.

Then the Hudson, appearing in long reaches, hiding itself behind the noble banks and again coming forth in its changeless majesty—onward—onward; seeming to have but one object in its persistent flow—namely, to reach the ocean—yet all the while ministering to industry, to fertility, and to commerce.

There is a charm never to be forgotten, found on those lovely heights, fanned by the airs and scented by the roses of June, while the eye ranges from the grand to the lovely,—from the beautiful to the useful,—from the still life to the active. The lofty trees waving their proud branches to the breeze, and the graceful small sail-boats darting about like sea-fowl at play on the sparkling wavelets, contrast finely with the business-like progress of many laden barques, the gay passenger steamers, and the matronly looking mother-boat with all her chickens around her.

What a beautiful world has been given to us to dwell in—beautiful still, in spite of its moral deformities.

But I must return to the journey on the railway, towards Buffalo.

We paused at Herkimer, and there, for the first time, saw an Indian woman in the costume of her tribe. She was an Oneida, equipped in dark blue cloth petticoat and moccasins, a blanket, fastened with a kind of skewer, where the Highland brooch would have been used by our mountaineers. Her massy hair, black, till towards its roots it assumed a tinge of blue, braided and fixed up with a bunch of red worsted strings, was the only covering of her head. At the first glance one might have thought her at least fifty, as she hung on the platform of the railway, stretching out her naked, skinny arm, with a small store of Indian purses, needle-books, and pin-cushions for sale. She dropped into the inn after us, and by-and-bye we found her standing, tall, erect, and still as death, behind the door of the public room, with her long dark arm and her wares extended as before. Her long, yellow teeth, standing like stakes in an ill filled-up fence, made one think of dried heads of New Zealanders, and other unpleasant specimens of the human form in savage life that we have seen in the museums of the civilized. After subduing something in my breast that might be a mixture of timidity and repugnance, I ventured to speak to the dismal ghost, and found her willing to communicate, as far as her command of my language, which was not very extensive, enabled her. When her features relaxed a very little as she spoke, twenty years, at least, seemed taken from her age. She told me with a heavy sigh, that her people were once numerous, their hunters fleet, and their warriors brave. But they were now weak and few, and they had yielded to the white man their hunting-grounds, and gone far west. I suggested that they had room to hunt where they were settled, if they did not find it best to plant corn, and live in houses, and adopt the habits of the whites. She said they had adopted them, and now have corn, and pumpkins, and horses, and ploughs, and sheep. She said a few, about 200, still lingered here, and had a village not far off, though the mass of the tribe are gone to the west, and that here they have a minister, and schoolmaster, and can read and write. She also showed that her people have adopted the Christian creed, and that she was tolerably well-informed in the outline of Christianity. While I spoke to her, she had sat down close by me, but as soon as she perceived that our curiosity was satisfied, she slipped away with a noiseless step.

I saw in and beyond that district, many Indians, chiefly Tuscaroras, but none were equipped so fully in the ancient manner. This one adopted it, I suppose, as a flourishing sign-board is used, to attract custom. Some who were travelling by rail near the beautiful village of Canandaigua, were dressed like other people, except that their clothing seemed more voluminous and clumsy. Some that we saw making purchases in the stores at the Niagara village, had caps without bonnets, and very long blue cloth cloaks. They are so like our Scotch border gypsies, who make horn spoons and sell crockery, that I felt as if I might have hailed Will Fa' or Tibby Douglas, in our endeavors to educate whose wild-cat looking offspring, we at one time expended some energy. Who can say if they are not of the same stock of the human family? The style of figure, the hair, eyes, and skin, give indication of relationship, while those, who like Simon in America, and Borrow in England, have penetrated into those rites and habits about which they are reserved with strangers, think they can trace ceremonies originating in the ceremonial law of Moses, and indications that they must both have descended from some one of the lost tribes of Israel. Who can solve these mysteries till the great day of revealing shall come?

The poor Indian! He shares the fate too common to the aborigines. As the civilized settler increases, he decreases. Many a deed of blood have their wrongs wrought them up to, and many a time have they been made the ignorant and savage tools of the wars of those civilized foes who ought to have known better. But now they are waning away—and wide as their continent is, and unpeopled as are millions of its acres, the time may yet come when the encroaching white man may wish again to remove them, or to limit the territory in which they are now located.

Yet even in their reduced state, when they come to treat with Congress, they go through their ancient ceremonial of the council fire, the calumet, &c., and assume the dignified tone and figurative speech of their ancestors. I heard of a chief quite lately, whose presence at Washington, within the door of the hall of Congress, was indicated to the chairman. He stood leaning against the door-post as if not quite sure of his place and reception, but on receiving a courteous message from his "Great Father," inviting him to take a seat, he cast himself upon the floor, saying, "I will embrace the bosom of my Mother earth."

Times are changed with them now, compared to their condition even a quarter of a century ago, fallen as they then were. My respected friend, Dr. Sprague, with whom I gladly renewed my acquaintance at Albany, told me that twenty-five years since, as he travelled with two ladies on the way to Niagara, a large powerful Indian hailed their carriage and ordered him to carry his pack for him to Buffalo. He tried to escape from this burden, suggesting various difficulties, all of which the Indian put aside, reiterating his order, which, in view of the Indian's fowling-piece, was finally obeyed, we may guess with what emotions of satisfaction. The man kept pace with, and sometimes got ahead of the carriage, so as to find time to stop and inspire himself with a fresh dose of fire-water by the way. At the end of the journey he stood ready to recover his goods, which he did with small indication of thanks.

Buffalo has been waxing, while Indians have been waning. The solitary inn where Dr. Sprague got rid of his imposed burden and dangerous fellow-traveller, is now lost amid a crowd of smart hotels, churches, banks, docks, and every appliance that commerce requires. While the Lake which used to form the barrier to further progress, is thronged by huge steamers three stories high, which are crowded with emigrants, and their goods, merchants, and their merchandize, and with all the produce of the country.

Railways.

THE railway runs through the streets of many cities in the United States, it being always taken for granted, that the lieges can take care of themselves. In Germany the Grand Dukes treat their subjects like infants, and keep them locked within palings till the train is ready to start, lest they should hurt themselves. In England various officers are at hand to warn you off the rails and guide your erring feet, and yet ever and anon one hears of accident. In America a printed placard at all the crossings tells you, "Look out for the locomotive when the bell rings," and leaves you to be your own guardian, and that kind of care answers the purpose as well.

The superior comfort of an American railway carriage will hardly be believed by persons whose dignity or respectability demand first, second, and third class carriages. Nevertheless, it is perfectly true. Their construction with a passage down the centre of each carriage, which is long enough to contain twenty-five or thirty persons on each side, enables the conductor to pass up and down. They are so made that he or passengers can pass from one carriage to another while the train is in motion. A cord also passes along their roofs, attached to a bell, which will summon him from whatever car he may be in. Thus no unpleasant circumstance need be endured for a moment. It would be impossible for a gentleman to get himself pommelled by a flighty man waking and fancying that his single fellow-traveller wished to mesmerize him, as lately happened in one of our first class carriages. In his case there was no remedy; he must either fight or be beaten black and blue till they reached a station. If he had had fifty companions and the bell-rope to boot he would have been perfectly safe.

But say they who are accustomed to the strict social subdivisions of old monarchies, how do you do with the workmen, and the serving damsels, and all the class of people that you don't associate with in the house? Why we do very well. That is the curiosity of it. Politeness, if it do not soar to the height of refinement that it does in courts, never sinks down to rudeness or brutality in the United States. Everybody understands that everybody has rights. The "great" are more careful not to offend the "little," so that I never once heard a haughty word to an inferior; and the "little," knowing that they are in no danger of being encroached on by the "great," in their turn commit no unpleasant encroachment. People fall naturally into a classified state, so that a whole car may readily be filled with mechanics and their peers. Should two or three refined people enter it, they will find nothing to offend them. And I have travelled for hours near a knot of workmen, or an Irishwoman with her bundle, or a mechanic's wife with her baby, and felt interested in observing the propriety of their manners. I just once saw a train stopt, and a man turned out to shift for himself on a road deep with mire. Not because he had misbehaved, for he sat as dull, and heavy as strong drink could make him, but because he had no money to pay his fare. He did not seem to excite the compassion of any one, and not a word above a whisper, was uttered by the ejected man or the conductor.

In roads which have many branches, you receive a check for each article of baggage. The baggage-master, with a badge on his hat, passes through the whole train frequently in course of the journey.

The traveller gives him his checks; and at the station where he is to stay, his baggage being prepared, is popped on the platform as quickly as he can step out himself, and the train is off again. In some trains a telegraph youth enters and inquires, "Any messages to New York? Any umbrellas or shawls left at Baltimore? Will telegraph for you with pleasure," and this he will do at the rate of eighteenpence, for what in England would cost half a guinea. Boys with candies, fruits, ready-cracked butternuts, pop-corn, books, pamphlets, railway guides and newspapers pass through the cars at all stopping stations, but these have, I think, been voted a nuisance to be abated.

A lady may travel thousands of miles, and be sure of courtesy, from every one. I have found a gentleman alight, and hand you out, and inquire about your baggage, with whom your only previous intercourse has been an inquiry if the next station was that you wished to alight at. I heard a mother say, she got along better with her three children, without her husband, than she should have done with him, for when people saw she was alone, every one helped her. That gentlemen purchased cakes to feed the children, and amused them very kindly, &c.

The Conductor in passing through the carriages collects the tickets, to avoid delay at the journey's end. How impatient is the traveller in England, when, after a long day's journey, he sits within a bow-shot of the platform, while the guard pops his head into carriage after carriage with his "Tickets, please," or "Please to show your ticket"—and how impatient the friends waiting on the platform, who look upon the carriages and cannot reach them. And what a fever is he in who wants to proceed by the next train, but by wasting the quarter of an hour devoted to ticket-gathering, loses his transit. We have all seen this occur in busy, "mail-accelerating" England. It cannot occur in America.

The general cleanliness of the whole country is not departed from in the travelling conveyances. The comfortable appendage of the stove has not introduced any appearance of smoke, and the cushions, floors, and numerous windows are kept scrupulously neat. Every car has blinds for summer, and a stove in the centre for cold weather. Each velvet-cushioned seat has a movable back, so that four can turn face to face, or you may, by turning the back, be alone with one companion. Many cars have a saloon at one end, where ladies retire to nurse their babes, and where you may take a nap on a long sofa.

In such a dressing-room I had been kindly *packed* by my friends and had dropped asleep, when a change in the noise made by the carriages awaked me. It was a pale, misty moonlight, past two, A.M. I roused myself to look out, and saw water expanded as far as my eye could penetrate. Were we on the shore of the sea? I went to the other side. It was water still—not shoreless ocean, indeed, but still we were in the midst of water. I had not studied the map—no one had told me that the rails had been laid across two inlets of the Chesapeake Bay, in preference to laying them round it. So there I stood in mute surprise. These people are like the "Ancient Mariner," thought I—

> "Tramp, tramp across the land we go,
> Splash, splash across the sea."

Presently, however, we had passed the open piles, which sustain the rails, and leave the shallow tides to ebb and flow amongst them at will, and were again booming along on solid ground—and then I went to sleep again, till roused to enter a huge steamer which meets the rail at the mouth of the Susquehanna—and a busy crossing was made of it.

From the dimly-lighted carriage we found ourselves transported into a floating hotel, where cooks were frying bacon and eggs, and steaks broiling and sputtering, ladies pacifying sleepy children, and maids running with smoking tea and coffee. In a few minutes it was changed, as in a dissolving view. Cooking, eating, running about, had passed away, and we were sweeping along the rails in the dull moonlight as before, trying again to coax ourselves to sleep.

A Hill Country.

We frequently hear of colonies of settlers from the same country who have congregated together, and are long of acquiring the language and habits of their new home. Welch, German, Swedish, French, and Dutch, are to be found so united, and lately Portuguese also. The little band of Christians persecuted from Madeira by Popery fled from dungeons and pelting with stones, first to the Island of Trinidad, but not finding room there, they have finally settled in the State of Illinois. Their native tongue, in which they read the Bible and are addressed by their pastors, forms a strong bond of union, which in the meantime deprives them of the advantage to be derived from the rapid acquisition of the language which must ultimately become that of their children. Yet difficult as the English language confessedly is, I have heard an unlettered German speak it so well, that if he had not told me so, I should not have suspected he had only left his native land eleven years since. With the Dutch there is long a difficulty in mastering the *th*, and *t*, which they pronounce as *d*,—this may be observed even in their children.

We passed some very pleasant days in a settlement among the mountains, where Dutch customs are still cherished by those whose hearts never knew home-sickness, and who foster no secret longings after the land of their forefathers. Amongst the sires of these thriving families, we found aged people, whose eyes glistened when a pastor of our company addressed them in Dutch. But they had left home in childhood, and time in its ceaseless and busy flow had swept away the memories and broken the ties which once were strong and deep; their hearts and homes are now here among the Mohawk mountains, and here they desire to rest their remains.

They are a homely, honest people; industrious, but, I should say, not laborious. The people of our country, I conjecture, mingle more of the sweat of their brow with their bread than these do.

We found them the same in manner in their own farm-houses that they were in the mansion, when business called them there. It was a new sight to us to observe the tenant stand covered in the saloon of the landlord, amid a circle of ladies and gentlemen, conversing with tranquil good sense and propriety, with no perceptible consciousness of any distinction of rank.

Self-possessed, quiet independence of manner, seems common to all ranks. No one looks bold or forward, for every one is doing what it becomes him in his position to do. One never sees the supercilious stare of inquiry which seems to ask, "Who are you?" "Do you belong to our set?" "Are you one of us?" American deportment, between persons of different ranks, derives, from its republican institutions, a healthy freedom, and at the same time a wholesome restraint. There is no order of things more calculated to give native character fair play, and native dignity its due weight.

I never saw this exemplified more to my taste than in the mistress of a large dairy in one of these mountain farms. She was tall, thin, and rather delicate in appearance, yet she managed all the skilful parts of the work with her own hands. We saw many cheeses as large as those which now come to England in wooden cases. On wonder being expressed how she could manage such huge and heavy cheeses, she put on her apron, and with as much courtesy as a Countess might employ in showing her cabinet or her hot-house, she went round the great boiler and showed the machine which poured in the milk to be heated. Then we saw that which drew it off into the tub when hot, and also how it was coagulated, and afterwards worked into curd and pressed. She explained the process with precision in very melodious and complaisant tones, closing her exhibition in the cheese-room, with such grace and good-will, that she would hardly accept our acknowledgments or expressions of gratification. She was happy to have been able to gratify us. Having finished her round, she folded her apron, laid it in its place, and led us out with the air of an amiable and obliging gentlewoman.

There was much "rural felicity" enjoyed in that hill country, more pleasant in memory than capable of being conveyed by description. One may tell of the exploits performed in a long wagon, its bottom formed of loose planks, with a temporary frame laid on to hedge in the travellers. The amazing quantity of light chairs it could contain according to the number of sitters—with the children nestled in the straw at our feet. But who can convey the light-hearted merriment, the wit, the anecdote, and specially the peals of laughter when jerks in the road jumbled us all against each other. The diversion was indescribable, when one of the foreigners, ill-informed as to the construction of the conveyance, fancied, as she felt a loose plank occasionally rise and fall, yielding to the inequalities of the road, that a great boa constrictor, or some such comfortable consociate, was nestled in the straw and about to awaken.

Having left the carriages of the city, and the steamboats and railways of the low countries, we seemed also to have left the dread of bumps and bruises, and our city gravity behind us.

The object of one of these novel journeys was to visit a farmer and his family a few miles off. We found the house snug and comfortable, the rooms opening into each other, and a large centre-stove which did duty on both sides of the wall; having the chief part of the cooking apparatus on the kitchen side, and one or two places where pans or dishes might be placed on the side of the parlor. They are a sober-minded, Christian people. The great enjoyment of the large and blooming family in winter, is the practice of sacred music. The father, a man of a very beautiful countenance and good musical powers, teaches the young people and also leads the singing in the rustic church. After our arrival in the evening, we had a meeting for prayer attended by other families within reach. And then *a tea*—such a tea! for variety and ingenuity in cake-making, and "sass" as the Dutch call sweetmeats, and all good things as one may never see again except in the eye of memory. The table groaned under its load, and it must be confessed that a lively party of upwards of a dozen did their very best to relieve it of its groans. Our talk was of markets, and stock, and such country matters; of the minister whom they longed to procure to occupy the place left vacant by one who had gone to a secular occupation to find a richer pasture for his family. They reckoned the district poor, and not able to sustain a minister; though judging by the many comforts and the air of plenty in all around us, it is probable the congregation needed some enlightenment on that subject. If spiritual wants had come as keenly upon their minds, as the necessities of the body do, they could have found a way to make a minister as comfortable as they are themselves. They are the sort of people who don't much relish parting with money, but who for all that, might come out very liberally on occasion of a "bee," and feel both pride and pleasure in opening their hands lavishly when the gift is one of their own devising. They were computing how many dollars each family within range of their little church might subscribe, and feeling painfully the want of a Pastor.

We made our way on the Sabbath to the said church, a member of our party officiating. Some walked; those who were most taken care of journeyed in a kind of large open chaise, and the rest were seated on chairs in the customary wagon. We found the small edifice on the summit of a knoll, green sward all around it, and no path in particular through the field or two nearest it. It was neatly painted and clean-looking according to the custom of the country, and filled with thriving families who did lift up the voice of praise with all their might. They looked intelligently attentive, and were, I doubt not, very glad to have their closed place of worship opened once more.

There is a great difference between the aspect of the citizen and the countryman. In this fine airy region, where the thermometer does not rise in the height of summer to those prostrating fever heats to which it does in the cities, the people have enough of flesh on their bones, and roses on their cheeks, and have an air of mental repose along with good sense, good temper, and sufficient bodily activity. In the cities, it is almost distressing to look on the sharp thin faces traced too clearly with lines of care. If you walk up streets down which the merchants come at morning to their offices, you may meet a few easy loungers enjoying their cigars, but the chief part are looking keenly before them at—*nothing*. Their eyes are wide open, but what they see is some vessel due but not heard of; some venture to San Francisco, the supercargo of which they begin to suspect; some speculation to South America or China about which they are anxious; some bill to be protested; some bad debt to be pursued. Merchants pay heavily for their wealth. It is not to be wondered at that a villa in the country should be the great object in their distant vista. Nor much to be wondered at, that when it is gained, they have not the habits which enable them to relish it entirely.

Such is life! We pursue objects, and when gained we find them but shadows. We are ourselves shadows, and quickly shall have left our place to others.

When in the low country we much enjoyed the, to us, novel sounds and sights of a warm climate. The fire-flies gleaming out on all sides during the evening walk—now in the grass and again at a small height in the trees, about the bushes and among the hay-cocks, the whole air seemed luminous with their tiny, darting lights. The frogs—the little nimble, almost insect-like tree-frog, and the large still water-frog.

I remember the frog's pond of my childhood, when

life and the season alike were in their spring, and everything was a source of delight or wonder, but I never heard tones so deep and ground-shaking as in the ponds of Long Island and New Jersey. The katydids, too, were a perfect novelty. I never learned exactly of what species the mysterious disputants are, and supposed them at first to be talking-birds. I have since been told they are insects, and the dispute is carried on by the sound of their wings. The legend is, however, that Katy is accused of breaking the bottle, and the controversy about it begins at dusk. "Katy-did," in a shrill tone—"Katy-didn't," in bass. "Katy-did"—"Katy-didn't." Two such pertinacious controversialists had their home in two fine old trees in the front of a mansion, whose external beauties and internal hospitalities formed an enchanting retreat. Often in daylight I tried to find something in those trees that might be owner of such power and pertinacity of voice, but without success. They again proved their residence, however, by sunset, and all night long the discussion endured. Be awake at what hour you might, they were at it. And one was ready to cry out, "No matter whether she did, or she didn't, would you but be quiet." I unfortunately never happened to hear either the whip-poor-will or the nightingale, though both haunt those sunny glades and beautifully indented shores, so replete with all that charms the senses. They have also the humming-bird, though I never met with one except under a glass shade.

These were the beautiful and sylvan delights of the lands nearer the sea-shore. But the mountain region, with which I began my chapter, had in store for us a scene grand, as well as beautiful, giving an impression of a snow-storm, which left any experiences of heavy falls of snow in the Lammermoors far behind. When it rains in the States, it does rain, and "no mistake." No Scotch mist, or hesitating shower. And when "frost has turned the rain to snow," it comes down in the same fashion—it is quite in earnest.

We arose under a beaming winter sun among the hills of the Mohawk. But, as swift as sudden misfortune rolled the black clouds over the distant mountains, gathered over our dwelling, and burst in a whirlwind of flakes, which wrapped earth's green bosom in her shroud in ten minutes. Between gusts, when we could penetrate the hurtling air, it was strange to see the whirling pillars, at small removes from each other, which seemed to descend for many feet, apart from each other, and reminded one of the description of dreary pillars of sand in the Arabian Desert. Then a fresh swell of the gale jumbled all together again, and the thickness could not be penetrated beyond a few inches. After two or three hours of this, the clouds rolled off, and we looked forth on a wonder of tranquil, cold beauty. Every tree, fence, and house in sight was clothed minutely with a hard battered-on covering of snow on the windward side, while the side unexposed to the blast seemed quite unconscious of the storm. I thought if half of this had happened in the slower, duller snow-storms of my country, the shepherds, and all the men around, folded in plaids, with straw ropes about their legs, and hats or blue bonnets tied down, would have been laboring to drive the "silly sheep" to the windy side of the hill, to preserve them from being buried up in snow-wreaths. And so it might be, there and then. But every one took it so easily that there seemed no alarm about it.

One of the richest sunsets I ever saw, except amongst the Alps, succeeded this sudden bluster of elements, when a wide expanse of lovely clouds, rosy themselves, tinged every tree and hill-top in their own beautiful dyes.

Next morning it seemed as if a necromancer must have busied himself during our sleeping hours, in unshrouding the extensive country within our view. The snow was gone—and except a patch here and there in a northern hollow, had left no sign.

When we descended to the valley of the Mohawk, however, we found traces wide and deep, in the flowing waters which rushed down, not only in their proper beds, but in what many a farmer must have thought very improper ones. Fields were flooded for miles. Houses which yesterday had solid roads leading to them, were standing damp and dreary islands in the waste. Clumps of trees were knee deep in water. Here stood a patient cow in close and unwonted company of a pair of wild colts. There a lonely horse, holding up its limbs turn-about, on an islet of grass. Men with carts were trying their way to reach the hay-stacks, and boys, more bravely, were sculling about broad, awkward-looking boats, among the sheaves of Indian corn, picking up the floating pumpkins—the only things in the landscape, which with their large golden disks, did not seem annoyed and discomforted.

The Mohawk itself poured down; that part of its waters which made its way under the bridges threatening to bear them off in triumph on its buoyant flood. The bridges are of wood, substantially built, and many covered in, like those of Switzerland, but without the pictures of saints which adorn their more ancient and popish prototypes.

The railroad held its way on a causeway, which in various places is not high enough to escape being overflowed.

Thus was swept off our hurricane of snow. Like many a storm in the moral world—which is as dark and disturbing—in two days, the subsiding waters had carried it all away.

Manners and Customs.

Americans tell ridiculous stories of *tricks of liberty* that were played when the Republic was young, which could not last after they settled down into business-like sobriety, and can be only accounted for on the supposition that brother Jonathan felt as giddy as sailors do after a long voyage. Resembling a few merry fellows whom I saw on first treading the shore again at Holy Island advance up to the town by a game of leap-frog—a school-boy prank which they would soon get tired of.

A gentleman told me that he was leaning on the rail of a piazza at Saratoga, when President Jefferson, I think, with the Countess of Westmoreland leaning on his arm, was walking in the Saloon. Two dizzy democrats offered a dollar to a dirty, ragged fellow if he would go in, say how do you do? and shake hands with the President. The fellow being desirous of the money, proposed to go wash and make himself a little decent, but the idle wags said the dollar would only be forthcoming if he shook the hand of the President with that same unwashed paw of his. My informant saw the dollar won. Mr. Jefferson, with perfect courtesy, turned aside for a moment, returned the hail of his assailant pleasantly, and quietly resumed his walk with the lady.

Such freaks are but the effervescence of success and good spirits, and subside of themselves. It was not unnatural that the "States" should, immediately after winning their independence, couple taxation and vexations with royalty and titles, and imagine unbounded freedom in knowing all men as Tom, Dick, and Harry. It was happy that they escaped all Utopianism with regard to Socialist levelling, and have been even more in danger of hero-worship than the men of other countries. No nation more gratefully showers honors on its benefactors. It does not give Dukedoms in reward of brave generalship, nor ribbons and stars in return for limbs lost in the public service; but the Hero is enshrined in their heart of hearts. His face is to be seen in their print-shops, his name is bestowed on their Streets and Hotels, and Reading-rooms, and his arrivals are hailed with a brother's welcome.

The prejudice against titles runs high, and sometimes exhibits itself absurdly enough. I heard a gentleman seeming to congratulate himself on having made a point to address the Earl of Durham as *Mr.* Durham during his visit to New York. I suggested that an English Lord would impute that to his *ignorance* of how to manage a title. This new view of the subject seemed somewhat mortifying, seeing what he designed to exhibit, was not his ignorance, but his contempt of such kickshaws.

Nevertheless I thought I observed that the arrival of a titled man produces a degree of *empressement* in the fashionable worldly circles, though they strive to conceal it. Except, indeed, in case of such a visitor as Lord Morpeth, whose fair and impassionate views, and moral worth, recommended him to a higher style of men than those of the mere circles of fashion.

It often struck me that the desire of approbation which is so strongly marked in the American character, instead of having its source in an exacting or boasting spirit, springs from two generous sentiments. The first is the love of country. It is often amusing, but always agreeable, to see a man kindle in describing habits, properties, and inventions which are endeared to him from his having a personal honor or credit in them. The country is not worth living in, that is not worth loving; and the government that deadens instead of awakening the patriotic sentiment, must be unhealthy. I am not sure that every American who applauds his native land will coincide with or thank me for the remark, that the second seems to have its source in respect for other countries, and especially for the parent country, Great Britain. They desire their approval. They wish to be the model of all Republics. They desire to be the finest as well as the widest country in the world, and their enjoyment of its greatness is much enhanced if you admire it with them. This sentiment could not deserve to be called generous, if they only held up their country for men to admire, and closed it against strangers. But their conduct is the very reverse of this. They welcome to its homes the refugee from every country. Their soil provides a place for ex-kings, ex-generals, ex-patriots. Nay, in the energy of their patriotic welcomes, they are in danger of killing with kindness. In the case of the Ex-Governor of Hungary, it is possible that for the first time it entered the mind of Kossuth that there is some advantage in "streets bristling with bayonets," and ways cleared by *gens d'armes;* when he, weary, sea-worn, anxious, and really sick, was forced to wait two hours at the Castle Garden before room could be made for him to pass to a place of rest.

The enthusiasm is generous and inspiring, and moves all ages at once to lively demonstration. It may, however, excite expectations in Hungary which America is not prepared to meet. Individuals will give liberally of their gold, their huzzas, and speeches of welcome, and feasts, and showers of nosegays. These may seem preliminary steps towards very serious interferences with European despots, from which the nation will probably shrink back at the hour of action.

But not only do they welcome illustrious exiles. There might be some pride in sheltering them—some éclat in the eyes of the spectator-nations, in affording asylums to such as they have cast out. They receive with as free a welcome the houseless and poor—they stretch out their hands to help the landing of those who in the first instance cost them much unprofitable trouble and expense. The new-comers must be housed,—nursed, if sick, at the risk of propagating pestilence,—placed in positions where their qualifications can be made available, and often forwarded to such situations with trouble and expense to their employers. Yet you never hear the multitude of emigrants murmured against, though you often hear it wondered at. "Let them come—let them come," they say, "this is a great country—we have room and resources for them all. No industrious man or woman need starve in our country,—let them come—let them come."

Few troops of human beings could look less inviting than those that are to be seen daily making their way to the Emigration offices. But the natives look past the lean squalor of the outside to the man within, and repeat kindly, "Let them come." The wants of the country form their welcome. So many willing laborers are equivalent to so much capital.

They land without the means to purchase their first meal, but they bring a robust northern constitution. Their powers are soon found to be exactly suited to the necessity. Look on those seven hodmen on one swinging ladder, each carrying his quotum of brick or mortar. They began at morning, and now it is noon. They have not ceased to go the round up, sky high with their load, and down by another ladder, after they have laid it on the scaffold. Do they come down to stand and breathe? or sit down and rest? No,—they go on up down, up down, until evening, only pausing for meals.

Americans reared under a more enervating sun, and fed on hot cakes, and loads of butter and butcher-meat, could by no means execute those rounds, they would soon give in and rest—and so of all other laborious works. Who drain the marshes, and clear the forests, and pull the snags out of the rivers? Who dig the canals, improve the harbors, and lay the roads? It is these same shivering starving emigrants, of whom the wise in their policy and the benevolent in their pity say, "Let them come."

The God of providence, who designs to people the Western world from the East, has so inclined their hearts—and one looks through the first struggle and difficulty, and in imagination sees these starving fed, and those naked clothed, and these wild little children at common school, being taught. The mind finds such a picture charming, were it not for the fear that the poor people, bringing their empty cup, will find it difficult, according to our Scotch proverb, to "carry a full one with a steady hand." If to this smiling plenty they add the fear of God, all will be well. If they are filled only with this world, they will become heady and high-minded, and in a few years will find themselves as poorly provided for the eternal shore on which they must land, as they were for the shores of the New World when they first landed upon them.

One looks with great respect on the courage of women taking up an object and pursuing it through many difficulties and intricacies, in all manner of positions, not allowing the recollection of their sex to interfere with or impede their steps. We saw one lady seated in the library of the Capitol searching records for herself, and pointing out passages to her secretary which she desired to have extracted. Another, whose name is publicly honored, so that to mention it is not unbecoming, Miss Dix, has acted a Howard's part in searching out the cause of the neglected or ill-managed. Year after year, she has made investigations from city to city, and from state to state, and having obtained evidence of the necessities, has laid before Congress petitions for grants of land to endow and on which to build hospitals for the insane, and prisons more airy and better ordered. Her business brings her to the seat of government, as a matter of course, and she never fails to find the right man to take up her cause and plead it. Through her disinterested exertions, many sufferings have been alleviated, and many neglected ones have been made comfortable. To be thus useful members of society it is not necessary to become politicians, or to step out of a strictly feminine attitude. The American ladies who thus exert themselves do not mingle in politics.

They aim at their one object and pursue it without deviation.

An effervescence of enthusiasm for the man of the day sometimes exhibits itself among females in a manner that would alarm any British statesman, as much as it does the American gentlewoman. I do not believe it ought to be called a practice, yet in more than one city it has fallen out that Henry Clay has been called upon in his progress to submit to an amazing ordeal. I am so negligent as to have forgotten the occasion on which Mr. Clay met the gratitude of his countrywomen; or rather I was so confounded at the mode of its expression, that my attention was withdrawn from the occasion, and swallowed up in the demonstration. One impassioned female, in a tide of love and devotion, rushed forward to the hero, and contrived to reach up to his not particularly beautiful or inviting face, and—kissed him!! Did you ever see the leader-sheep of the flock leap over a rivulet, and then another, and another follow, till the whole, score upon score, in a frenzy of imitation, leaped it also? Just so followed the excited women, hundreds upon hundreds. Poor Henry Clay! Those who could not reach his head kissed his hands or his coat. As the multitude rendered it impossible that their hero should return the civility, he stood it nobly, till all who chose had saluted him,—and because of his advanced years, he probably regarded it as an act of filial reverence in his daughters.

A lady, who had entered the Hall to look upon the great statesman, assured me, with many blushes, that she stood on one side and beheld what is here stated. When I inquired as to the rank of the wonderfully grateful throng, she replied it was not possible to discriminate by means of silk gowns and fine shawls, as everybody can afford to dress well in America, but I might conjecture their rank by their method of expressing their admiration.

We must suppose that such an ebullition can occur but once in a man's life, and that it must be connected with some peculiar accessibility in the hero. One does not fancy that such an assault could be made on Daniel Webster or General Scott, or that it could be less than very unpleasing to any man.

The conduct of matters at the White House strikes every European with surprise—and, doubtless, every European blessed with a free government, with admiration. The evening we went there, the crowd of carriages and company was great, but President Fillmore had no body-guard. There were no sentinels at the gates, and no policemen peeping about to spy some one out of bounds. There was a mixture of spectators about the halls and piazzas, and probably some few were even within the saloons, who did not approach the President. Every one acquitted himself as if he were personally interested in having all pass off to advantage. Lookers-on came in to the outer apartment without tickets of admission, and on all occasions conduct themselves with propriety.

There were some magnificently-built men, such as one likes to see, holding the rank of generals and admirals. The President did not fall behind any in height and fine figure, or in pleasing intelligence of countenance. There were also some splendid women, splendidly dressed, as well as some lovely and some homely in costumes neat and elegant, but not rich. All were the same as to reception,—at least, if there were any precedence, it was not so conspicuous as to be observed by a stranger. In perambulating the circular room several times, nothing appeared calculated to scare away the cheerful simplicity of converse. The companion who chanced for the time to make the circle with us pointed out with pride the conquerors in the Mexican war, the Senators who had made eloquent appearances on the *right side*, whichever the talker happened to think such. The foreign ambassadors were distinguished, and so were the beautiful women, and those whose ancestors had suffered and made great sacrifices during the war of Independence—but all with simple heartiness. Whatever has been said or supposed in England about the aristocracy of wealth, I cannot remember that one individual was marked to me on account of his being the proprietor of millions of dollars, though doubtless there were many such present.

Politeness is the "Davy's Safety Lamp" of the country. There is a flame of ardent opinion or sentiment within, and without there may be elements of a dangerous character, which by contact, would easily kindle into hot argument, or hazardous passion. Where no more solid principle forms the protector, politeness is the surrounding guardian which prevents conflagration.

In none of the various ranks of society in which I had the means of mingling, did I meet the stiffness of etiquette, or its monotony. There is a coldness about grandeur which acts as a refrigerator on all around. It does not mingle with the general sympathies, and for want of the exercise of its own, loses the possession of them. There are many families in Europe reared in the retired state of encircling park walls and lofty gateways, whose most enlivening variety in early days is the display of the peacock's tail on the edge of the terrace, the trot of the beautiful antlered herd over the lawn, or the scud of the hare from under the shrubs. These people's sympathies are so closed out from their fellows, that the sight of a poor person within certain precincts is an offence, and the inquiry is instantly raised, how he got in. State, particularly in young people, is apt to be exacting, supercilious, and intolerant. Pride usurps the place of the kindly amenities, and groundless and idle jealousies ward off the effusion of affection which ought to spring up readily in young hearts. The enjoyment of a day, when they once come out into their own style of society, may be marred by some trifling failure in etiquette, such as one of inferior rank being placed in precedence to them. How many fine minds have been wasted on such poor stuff as this, and that which nature has made gentle and graceful, reduced to empty, self-exalting elegance, and artificial exacting refinement.

This style of consequence does not show its face in American society, though people have their own positions, and fall into and keep them naturally. When upstart wealth seeks to make its way in cultivated and refined society, unless the parties are themselves estimable and attractive, they generally find the achievement too difficult. There is much extravagance in furniture and dress in the wealthy cities, and this in many different ranks; and a rich man, or his ambitious wife, sometimes makes the show and talk of the hour by giving a splendid party—colored lamps, festoons of flowers, conservatories lighted up like moonlight groves, odors diffused from urns, dreamy music issuing from shady caves, tableaux vivans fixing the eye under Gothic arches—such are the attractions by which taste, extravagance and folly have sometimes tried to construct a path for the vulgar into the society of the refined. But the experiment generally ends in the failure of the plan, and probably you hear that the party, disappointed of the aim of all this display, has left the place in disgust, while the grand house, with its gorgeous contents, are for sale.

The absence of domestic comfort in crowded boarding-houses, exposes people to the attraction of out-door amusements, and thus many seek to pass hours in second-rate theatres, and public gardens, who could and would enjoy homes, if they possessed them. There is a levity of mind and taste thus fostered, which may pervert the character for life.

One could not remark without regret and fear, how in New York, more than in other cities, this amusement mania is breaking over old sober barriers, and Christian parents, who never themselves sought enjoyment in such pastimes, yield to the importunity of their children, and suffer them to go where the restraint of the parental eye never follows them.

On reconsidering nine months spent most agreeably amongst Christian friends, in whom my soul quietly reposed, I feel that I have acquired treasures of esteem, admiration, and love for many precious characters, which I shall cherish in memory for life. Amongst them I found no repulsive boasting, no rude comparisons, no self-exalting propositions. But whenever one enters into society of a decidedly worldly cast, you encounter something of all these. Still there is good-humor and kindness in their earnest desire to draw out the expression of your admiration of "our country."

It was delightful, and at the same time amusing, on that sunny morning when, after our very stormy voyage, we came in sight of the Neversinks, and amid a fleet of graceful white sails we entered the Narrows, to observe and participate in the varied emotions of our fellow-travellers. The joy of turning Sandy Hook, and recognizing well-known objects, mounted to enthusiasm. There being very few English on board, the lively Americans were lavish in their efforts to show me every striking object, and every fine point of view. One thought this the best position to see everything from; another hastened to remove me to that. One lent a telescope, another described a fort, another pointed out an island. All demanded approbation, admiration, nay, were not quite satisfied without ecstacy. I loved their patriotism, and felt obliged by their politeness, but their comparisons jarred against my feelings. The atmosphere was delightful, the sky deep blue, the floating clouds fleecy. It was all full of what was pleasing. But my ciceroni were not satisfied without the confession that London is "Fog Babylon," and Britain "an egg in a nest of moss." To praise the present did not satisfy their full hearts, they demanded admission of some inferiority in the absent. Such is man! It seems nearly as benevolent to abuse one's country as to say, "Madam, excuse me, but you have an ugly face." Instead of enabling one to give expression of admiration to their country, it has the effect of utterly repressing it. The whole feeling arises from inconsideration, as no one can have merit with respect to a climate in reference to which he was not consulted when he was born in it.

There is, however, another style of rivalry, which though useful to commerce and to science, is apt to stir worse feelings than those of exultation about climate or the productions of the earth, the rivalry in ship-building and sailing. We were retarded by storms. One of the Cunard line of steamers was to sail three days after us. People talked about the possibility of that ship reaching port as soon as we. The solicitude that we should be first in spite of adverse elements was immense. "If the Europa get on without meeting the skirts of our gale." "If she should enter the port by the same tide." Many were the idle "ifs," and some of them clearly accompanied with bitterness. Yet I never comprehended how deep the feeling was, till I heard our gallant captain in his deep calm voice reply to one of these "ifs," "I'd rather lose a limb."

During several days while the gale lasted, solicitude, and a degree of doubt hung on the minds of the most experienced voyagers in the cabin, as to how so huge a craft might acquit herself in such a sea. And it was not till the captain expressed his satisfaction in the brief but important sentence, "She's behaving well, sir," that an outburst of enthusiasm broke forth on the excellence of the ship, of American ship building, and of all her ships in general, and on their universal superiority to those of Britain. Our experienced captain, who knew more of maritime matters than all his passengers, sometimes put in a quiet word, which had rather a damping effect. He probably felt that, however good the vessel, the springing of a single plank could have put a stop to our boasting, and that such an event was within reach of possibility. All the discussers of ship-building did not see so far as he did.

This one national characteristic apart, the manners of the people in the United States are, taken as a whole, more frank, natural, benevolent, and lively than our own. In politeness and consideration for feminine weakness, real or supposed, they very far surpass the English. "Tell me," said a native of one of the colonies, on board the Cunard steamer by which we returned to England, "tell me what difference you observe between the manners of the Americans and ours?" "The most striking to me at the moment is their superiority in politeness. I have been leaning over this rail for half an hour, and there are six Englishmen seated on either hand, not one of whom has offered me a seat." I almost regretted my remark, for during the remainder of the voyage this amiable person never failed to fly off for a camp stool the moment he saw me ascend the stairs. Yet, had I doubted the fact before, there has been evidence enough since my return that my remark was just. Our women, though not so courageous in public acts as theirs, are left far more to their own resources in private, and are, with the public-spirited and noble exceptions, among their sisters across the ocean, more independent in thinking and acting than they.

There are a few festival days in the year, when the mechanic lays down his tools, the shopman leaves his store, and all the world has a sympathy in enjoyment.

Thanksgiving is a great day. The Governor of each State appoints it at the time most suitable. Christians flock to places of worship to offer acknowledgments for the mercies of seed-time and harvest, and all the blessings of the year, political and private. Friends flock to each other's houses, and those who have not had time to meet for many a day, eat turkey and cranberries together, while those who have the gift, recount in after-dinner speeches their blessings, and satisfactions, and submissions to the dispensations of the past months. It is a day much to be delighted in, when the prosperous "eat the fat and drink the sweet, and send portions to those who have nothing," as in the days of ancient Jewish sacrifice.

Then comes Christmas with its roast goose and plum-puddings, and its exhibitions of well-dressed Sunday-school children. In the old settlements, then comes that liberal humorsome old friend of the expecting little ones, Santa Claus. I have seen him in full equipment, a gentleman much resembling Punch in the frontispiece—only besides the hooked nose and droll, benevolent, quizzical face, he is hung round with shooting-bags, fishing-baskets, long wallets and short, all protruding in a promising manner, with pretty things, toys, and candy. He is not of such large bounty as the German Christmas-tree, on which grows sometimes a whole suit of clothes, hats, shoes, and every useful thing; but he is a more mysterious sugar-plum-loving benefactor, who particularly interests the little people in the nursery. He finds his way into their pockets, and conveniently discovers all the stockings which on Christmas eve never can rest quietly on a chair, but are hung up most invitingly, and whatever he finds of that description, he kindly stuffs with the contents of his many bags. I never could discover certainly from any child how Santa Claus gets in. Some think down the chimney, some through the key-hole, some have a shrewd suspicion that Mamma and he have some treaty about it. He is a welcome ancient guest, come how he may; and I have my own suspicion that he is a patron Saint transported from Europe, whose eastern name, Saint Nicholas, has in the hurry of western talk been abridged of a few of its letters.

But the 1st of January, which follows hard upon it, quite eclipses its predecessor. Everybody that knows anybody, must on that day pay their respects. The rushing about is amazing. The brief, graceful, pleasant congratulations are lively as they are fleeting. It is no day for a wit to expend bright things on, as no one has leisure to remember them. The hurry is so great that by common consent the word "day" is omitted in its name, and everybody calls it "New Year's."

If a pair of dove's eyes have shot through the heart of a youth, he may, without previous acquaintance with the family, call and look upon them on that day of privilege, and no one will wonder or think it intrusive. The stranger who has previously delivered his introduction, is expected to offer his salutations on that day. Old associates meet and hail each other with "auld lang syne" cordiality; and if any business misunderstanding, or any family dispute has occurred during the past year, you have but to enter, present your congratulations, shake hands all around, and it is understood that the division is henceforth to be forgotten and the wound is healed. The ladies stay at home and hold the levee, while the gentlemen run the round, sometimes of hundreds of houses. I believe the Clergy also stay to make their reception. When evening comes, those who are united by family ties pass the time together in a more quiet manner. "New-year's" is a fine specimen of the sociable and lively habits of the people, and the way of keeping it here described, is peculiar to the city of New York.

The day of days, however, is the 4th of July—that memorable and happy day of the Declaration of Independence. I had the misfortune to sail two days too soon, and cannot tell from observation how the nation exhibits its joy and exultation. But judging by the mass of fire-wheels, rockets, and squibs that I happened to see preparing, it must have been as great a day for the explosion of gunpowder, in proportion to the size of the countries, as the birthday of our much-beloved Queen, who is as popular in her monarchy as Washington was and is in his republic.

After New-year was over, I inquired of an industrious young man, when he would have another holiday. He replied, "Not till the 'fourth of July.'" It is a hard trial to bodily and mental vigor, to be so long upon the stretch, without relaxation and without variety. For they do in America cleave to their business with unremitting care. Our Father in Heaven, knowing the constitution and wants of the creatures he has made, has appointed one day in seven as a day of holy respite from toil, and of peaceful and reposing communion with Himself. Happy the man of business and of labor, who knows how to gather the manna and refreshment it is designed to shed.

There are many customs peculiar to districts, which have descended from their European progenitors, and are interesting, as heirlooms to those who inherit them. One custom, however, which I met within almost every house where I had the happiness of receiving much social enjoyment, originated in New England. The custom in the higher circles of abstinence from intoxicating drinks. The brotherly love is to be highly esteemed, which induces whole families to refuse utterly to intermeddle with that article which ensnares their neighbor, though for themselves it may have no temptation. The vigor of national character exercised by those cities,

—in one instance, I believe by a whole State—which have made for themselves a decree of total abstinence, has a grandeur in it that commands respect. In Maine, if you will have ardent spirits, you must seek them from the druggist's bottle. This is an act of the Legislature, cheerfully acceded to by the whole people. What could such a people not do, in raising the moral tone of their State, were they to adopt similar energy and self-denial in overthrowing other vices as they have in doing battle with drunkenness. Six sermons by Dr. Lyman Beecher, on the subject of Total Abstinence, published widely in Old England as well as in his own country, have had the powerful effect in urging on that important measure, which by their sound reasons and eloquent language they are well fitted to have. The cool, calm, unloaded atmosphere of the hotels is refreshing, and the table where 80 or 100 people dine, presents no liquid but cheering iced water.

I have happily nothing to do with travellers' hints about brandy and water in the bar-room, out of sight, but am satisfied that those guzzling habits are now counted dishonoring and injurious, which thirty years ago led people to drink a little half a dozen times in the day. And I must despise the taste that could induce an Englishman to try if he could not tempt a Bostonian to give him a treat of the far-famed sherry cobbler *behind the folding-doors.* Was it curiosity? he ought to have respected the motives of Boston enough to refrain from laying that snare before a friend who, to oblige him as a stranger, yielded to his temptation. Was it to discern if he who treated him, would also *in secret*, treat himself? It was basely suspicious. Or was it rather that the tempter loved to guzzle? In that case, he must hasten to become a water-drinker, lest he fall into the miserable ranks of the inebriate.

At ceremonious private dinners, coffee is often brought with the dessert—and at evening parties a beautiful variety of good things is produced, accompanied by lemonade and iced water.

Oh, those respectable china or silver jugs, a foot and a half high, with the lumps of pure ice floating in them, giving notice of their honest, wholesome presence by a knock against the sides when the vessels are moved. How often have I wished to see them established instead of Old England's nut-brown ale, and Scotland's still more ruinous whiskey.

With all the pains that have been exerted, America is not cleansed from the sin and disgrace of drunkenness, but its frequency is powerfully diminished. Now, no man puts the bottle to his neighbor, and besets him with entreaties to drink. No lady now, in making a round of calls, is in danger of coming home half tipsy, by means of the cordial at one house, the choice wine at another, and the Roman punch at a third. If people will drink, they must do it secretly. They must retreat to the bar-room, or inhale their sherry cobbler behind the folding-door. This is so much the case, that it is a fact, that some men have died of delirium tremens, who were not suspected of inebriety till betrayed by this horrid disease, which swept them into the drunkard's eternity.

The climate is of itself so exciting, that it is said, one third the quantity of liquor will carry away a man's head and feet, that would be required to produce that effect in England. The example of the clergy does them honor, and has had a powerful effect. In the house of no clergyman, of whatever denomination, did I see liquor, but I grieve to say, in some of them I heard with shame, how the habits of our Scottish clergy, their guests, had impeded their influence and shocked the abstemious people. Our clergy are all temperate men, but in the United States their pious clergymen are total abstainers for example's sake.

Niagara.

From Buffalo to Niagara the way is not altogether pleasant. The uncultured suburbs and imperfect roads of a city hasting in its growth, the ugly shanties of workmen laboring there, the trees stript of their branches, the houses for cattle without paint or any pretension to neatness, and those for men with glaring drink-inviting signs, and the ground guttered by recent rains, while the river's bank in some parts looked like the slimy edge of a tide-water canal,—such is the uninviting aspect of the first few miles of the road. It was therefore pleasing to let the eye take refuge in the deep blue, cloudless sky, effulgent in the subdued sunbeams of the balmy Indian Summer. Not a cloud remained to indicate the torrent of rain which had been emptied on the earth during the night. When, lo! while we were yet several miles from our destination a pillar of cloud appeared—white, but massy, containing an immense quantity of vapor condensed by the coolness of the surrounding air. It was not hung in the heavens a lonely cloud, revealing not whence it had been exhaled. It ascended from mother earth like the cloud from the Altar of Incense of old in the unshaded sky of the wilderness—and probably this cloud, so dense, so white, so lofty, has ascended from the altar of nature in the Indian wild for centuries before that incense sought the sky in the desert of Arabia, as it has continued to ascend 3000 years since the altar and the camp of Israel have been removed. This pillar of vapor, from the foam of Niagara, still, huge, and solemn, in the quiet air, filled the mind. Meet incense from an altar so grand and so enduring. One wanted to be alone to gaze on it and hear the accompanying boom of the mighty torrent, and feel the earth tremble around it. At length we neared the scene of this huge coil of waters, where the cloud, instead of increasing in importance, seemed to diminish. Attention was diverted. There seemed a gap between it and the surface of the foam, and the forest trees appeared to mingle in its formation. I could never recover the impression produced by my first view of the pillar of cloud.

Every one professes disappointment on the first view of the Falls. I must confess my exceeding dulness, which had excited some mirth amongst my fellow-travellers. We had unexpectedly caught a glimpse of the Genesee Falls the day before, when a brilliant sun painted a rich and perfect rainbow, which hung over the boiling volumes of the flood below, like "love watching madness with unaltered mien." In a few moments the cars stopt at Rochester, and, while we hastened back to seek the border of the Genesee, I expressed my wonder that we had already reached *Niagara!* It was but the hallucination of the moment, but made food for fun, and proved at least that I should be easily contented with my cataract. Yet in comparison with any common Falls, those of the Genesee are magnificent.

I was *not* disappointed with Niagara. And, like all the grand and noble in nature, it bears inspection. Its grandeur magnifies under contemplation, and the mind finds secret recesses of admiration, or solemn sympathies unfold to apprehend the mighty scene, and the heart's pulses learn to beat in unison with the diapason of its muffled thunders. Leisurely observation, therefore, does not exhaust, but rather enhances the interest—and weeks instead of days might glide by while the spirit would still freshly mingle with the spell of its Fall.

We took a guide from the only Hotel left open at that late season of the year, and found him useful as related to the safety of our steps, but otherwise rather an impediment than assistant. Specially—and it is the only time I was really incommoded by the much-discussed tobacco-consuming customs of the country—specially by the man's continually eating of tobacco, and obliging us to skip about and shift our places to avoid its disgusting consequences, while we wished to view the immense cascade in repose. We found this well-fed, but not well-informed person afterwards at the hotel dinner amongst the travellers.

When people on the spot are expected to describe the Falls, you generally find them gliding off from the grand theme to something that concerns man. Here such an one fell in and was carried over the precipice into the gulf below,—there another was rescued,—by such means the American flag was planted on that shelf of gravel in the midst of the rapid. And, above all, they are most apt to tell you here was a battle between the Indians and the settlers, and there between the Americans and the British. They will disturb your contemplation on the verge of that fearful gulf called the Devil's Hole, to bring forth a human jaw bleached by ninety winters, which once had belonged to an English soldier, who, with a hundred of his comrades, were by a body of Seneca Indians slain or cast down that precipice to perish. Battle, murder, or sudden death seem the subjects you cannot escape from in this vicinity, so prolific in contests between the civilized and the savage.

> "There the deer drank, and the light gale flew o'er
> The twinkling maize field rustling on the shore,
> And while that spot, so wild, and lone, and fair,
> A look of glad and innocent beauty wore,
> And peace was on the earth and in the air
> The warrior lit the pile, and bound his captive there."
>
> BRYANT.

A land, rich now in well-cultured fields and natural productions, and enshrining in its centre one of the noblest cascades of the world, has been the scene of more contests arising from pride, wrath, and cupidity, than may be found anywhere in an equal circle of miles. What is there to be feared; what of solemn and awful in these ever-rushing, and tumbling, and plunging waters, compared to that which the heart of man, boiling over in blood-thirsty rage has exhibited and executed. Not only the old Indian wars, and the war of Independence, have made this district a part of their battle-field; but in our later contests in 1813 and '14, here was the scene of most bitter conflict. Whether you will or not you must hear of warlike actions on all hands. Concealed by the woods of Goat Island, lies the battle-field of Chippewa; though concealed, you must hear of it, for there, July 5, 1814, Generals Scott and Porter drove the enemy from all his positions, and obliged him to retreat.

On the Canada side lies Lundy's Lane, where on the 25th July, 1814, after shedding much blood, both Americans and English claimed the victory. In short, the mind is disturbed and pained by endless details of strife, and forced to attend to the evil doings of the creature, when you would gladly dwell in silence on the work of the Creator.

We crossed by the Suspension Bridge to the Canada side. A bridge apparently as long and as high as Telford's great work over the Menai Strait in Wales, but much less strong. The wires are small, and the whole fabric so light that it seems scarcely designed to sustain a loaded vehicle. Indeed, we were invited to alight, and our empty carriage was driven slowly over, while we walked. Our guide cast a heavy stone from the centre, that we might watch its progress, and count the moments required for it to reach the river which rushes below. The pathway of the bridge is eight hundred feet long, and the wire cables ten thousand feet, while the columns which support them are sixty-five feet high.

We were glad to pause at the centre of the bridge and study the front view of the Horse Shoe Fall, as we could not obtain it from the trim little steam craft, the "Maid of the Mist," which plies below the Falls, it being laid up for the season. We ascended the stream to the very verge of the Great Fall—the place from whence the Table Rock plunged down into the boiling gulf a few months before. This rock had long projected forty or fifty feet over the bank, which was gradually caved out by the wasting waters. A wide and deep fissure ran across a considerable portion of it, giving warning that its period for breaking off from the side could not be distant. Yet such was the zeal of all the world to view the cataract from this fine post of observation, that the venture was made to the very last. Not two minutes before its final plunge, a lady and gentleman had stepped from it to the solid ground.

One mile above this Fall is the Burning Spring, which is covered in by a hut. After seeing the hydrogen gas, which issues from it, once lighted by a torch, I had seen enough, and retreated to the margin of the rapid. The fall of the ground here is one hundred and fifty-four feet in two miles, while the water narrows by means of Goat Island, and becomes about twenty feet in depth. It was here that the power and force of the torrent made the strongest impression on my mind. It was like hundreds of fleet steeds at full gallop, pouring on to their goal, and bearing down all before them. Irresistible, unwearying, unceasing, unchanging. Pure emerald, so that you could count the stones below, but fearful, tremendous, gigantic, as it coursed along. Its surface a little curled, but by no means indicating by superficial disturbance the might of its movements.

It may sound strange to say that, after the Rapid, the Fall itself seemed a *helpless* thing. When it reaches the edge of the precipice, what can the torrent do but fall! It must go down! The Rapid looks like a thing of life. It seems possessed of volition. The Falls like other falling things, tumbles into the boiling pool below, because it must. How can it avoid it?

Nay—more strange! I have seen smaller cascades which seemed to have more a will of their own than has this mighty Niagara. They come skipping down, stop and run about the ledge of a rock, and then skip down a little farther, as if they were at play, and would reach the bottom at their leisure. While in the Niagara river it is one fell swoop, one deadly plunge, one tumble over a precipice of 154 feet in height into a caldron of 250 feet in depth. In that caldron something like volition is recovered, for the fallen waters foam up again, as though they would re-ascend the precipice, but finding that impracticable they turn and course their way once more, like race-horse, down the rocky gorge. They meet a fresh impediment about four miles below, where a mountain crossing what would seem the natural path of the waters, forces them to bend abruptly, and seek another outlet, not, however, until they have made many a rapid turning in the whirlpool.

In that whirlpool, which we surveyed from the high bank above its margin, we saw limbs of trees, small débris of the forest, and a broken hurdle or two, wheeling round and round, seeming not likely ever to be cast out of the vortex. Yet, I presume, a natural philosopher could observe the circles as they receive fresh impulses from the ever-descending river, and calculate how many must be made before the object now in the centre shall be cast out to the border. They tell fearful tales—enough to freeze the blood—of the bodies of those who have been drowned wheeling round and round far out of reach in this never-resting caldron—now raising a limb, now half rising as if seated on the waters, again diving as if in breathless and living haste, but ever, ever refusing to near the shore or to be rescued.

A young Englishman, Francis Abbott, known as the Hermit of the Falls, built him a hut on Goat Island in 1829, where he dwelt alone till he was drowned in bathing in 1831. His history was unknown—but his collection of classical authors, his guitar, his sketch-book, all indicated the man of education, while his gentle manners excited a strong desire to learn if he were "crazed with care, or crossed in hopeless love." Mrs. Sigourney has, with her usual power and grace, told the young hermit's fate, and her description of the whirlpool will explain what sights are sometimes to be seen there more graphically than anything I can say:

He 'neath the crystal waters lay,
Luxuriant in the swimmer's play,
But now the whelming flood grew strong
And bore him like a weed along,
Though, with convulsive throes of pain
And heaving breast, he strove in vain;
Then sinking 'neath the infuriate tide,
Lone as he lived, the Hermit died.

On by the rushing current swept
The lifeless corse its voyage kept,

To where in narrow gorge comprest,
The whirling eddies never rest,
But boil with wild tumultuous sway,
The Maelstrom of Niagara.
And there within that rocky bound
In swift gyrations round and round,
Mysterious course it held;
Now springing from the torrent hoarse,
Now battling, as with maniac force
To mortal strife compelled.

Right fearful 'neath the moonbeam bright
It was to see that brow so white,
And mark the ghastly dead
Leap upward from his torture-bed
As if in passion's gust,
And tossing wild with agony,
To mock the omnipotent decree
Of dust to dust.

At length, where smoother waters flow,
Emerging from the gulf below
The hapless youth they gained, and bore
Sad to his own forsaken door.
There watched his dog with straining eye,
And scarce would let the train pass by,
Till that with instinct's rushing spell
Through the changed cheek's impurpled hue,
And stiff and stony form, he knew
The Master he had loved so well.

* * * * * * *

While strew'd around on board and chair
The last pluck'd flower, the book last read,
The ready pen, the page outspread,
The water cruse, the unbroken bread,
Revealed how sudden was the snare
That swept him to the dead.

And so he rests in foreign earth
Who drew 'mid Albion's vales his birth.

* * * * * * *

Who here his humble worship paid,
In that most glorious temple-shrine,
Where to the Majesty divine
Nature her noblest altar made.

* * * * * * *

Still with sad heart his requiem pour
Amid the cataract's ceaseless roar,
Nor grudge one tear of pitying gloom
To dew that sad enthusiast's tomb.

It would be but vain repetition to tell of the American Fall, the Cave of the Winds, the many Islets and the varied beauties of the shore, which have been so often described. There was, however, one object at the edge of the Horse-Shoe Fall, when we saw it, which had but lately been carried down the Rapid, and which excited much interest. This was a canal-boat that had broken from its moorings, and glided onward, till it came within that power which will not be impeded or robbed of its prey. Before the boat reached the fiercest part of the Rapid, a man and boy were rescued from their impending fate, by the skill and bravery of some who from the shore observed them. But the boat swept on, and the spectators expected to see her plunge down the cataract. A projecting rock, however, caught her, and there, on the very verge of that watery precipice, she lay, broadside to the fall, balanced against that small ledge of rock, and seeming almost to look down into that perilous gulf. Her fate was certain, but it was retarded. Some months after, the rock gave way under the constant pressure of those mighty waters. She plunged below, and doubtless was dashed to fragments which would join the débris in that dizzy and ceaseless whirlpool.

One might moralize, and fill a sheet with musings, on the course to ruin of many a youth who set sail in quiet waters, fell into evil, plunged on, was stopped, but not reformed, and at last plunged into a depth more dreadful far than this.

How often have I thought had the man and boy not been rescued before the boat stuck fast, what could have been done to reach them, to save them from perishing of hunger and of horror, so near two friendly banks, where hundreds would have longed to deliver them. As far as I can see, the answer must be—*nothing*. Could they have been reached by such an apparatus as Manby's?

Oh, solemn fate! So long protracted; death suspended as by a hair, yet the living moving on greensward, even within call, unless the voice of the waters conquered that of man. What a mercy they were not brought down in that boat to linger and die on that verge.

The noise of many waters is not of the astounding character expected by those unaccustomed to it. There is no deafening roar, no sound of exploding bombs arising from the Falls. It is a solemn voice of deep harmonies, plunging and profound, not splashing or dropping. In the mingled and various sounds of daylight, it may be mistaken for the rolling of heavy machinery, forming a deep bass to the lowing of cattle, the barking of dogs, and the whistle of the ploughman. It is at night, when all is still, that the noise is sensibly heard and felt. *Felt*, I say, for the concussion of the falling waters booms in the ear like an eternal thing; while, ever and anon, as the circles of trembling air float by your resting-place, so does every door, window, and movable thing jar. It is as if a giant took up the house, gave it a hasty shake, and put it down again, renewing the process at varied intervals, from two minutes to five, all the night long. It must depend on the quarter from which the wind blows, whether this ceaseless vibration is strong or weak. It is said that the sound is frequently heard on Lake Erie, at the distance of twenty-five miles, and has been heard even at Toronto, which is forty-four miles off.

Few things are more fit to teach how great is the mistake so often made by our self-complacence when we imagine that all things are made to gratify or instruct Man. Whether he wake or sleep, whether he die or never was born, the flowerets blow, the ocean roars, the brooks shine on their way, and Niagara makes the surrounding earth tremble on his.

There are eyes that we see not observing and admiring the works of creation. The eyes of watchers that wake when we sleep, and guard and prevent when we are in danger—and that give to God the glory due unto his name in everything. Oh to have every earthly admiration enjoyed with their purity, and enhanced by their holiness!

We have seen the sea breathing calmly as in slumber. We have seen the tides ebbing and flowing like a pulse. We have seen the curling wave bathing its playful crest in sunshine and pure air. We have seen old Ocean rising in his might, until billow upon billow rose and fell like the rolled hills which are formed ere the plain rises into a lofty range of mountains. We have seen wave swell after wave, and plunge along as if resolved to assail a battery of rocks, and sweep them down into the capacious bosom of the deep. We have counted their wonderful succession, till growing in power, when they reached the mystic number nine, they would rise in awful force into the very clouds when the rocks or pier stopped their headlong course, and fall in scattered foam far up on the dry land. Many a time has the mind kindled at the view of the boundless waters in all their changing moods, and felt that the hand of God was there, not more when the billows lift up themselves than when they die upon the shore.

But there is a sentiment awakened by the Falls of Niagara differing from all others. Ocean has its storms and calms—its ebbs and flows. Niagara is ever the same. It has been so for uncounted ages. Who knows how many generations of Red Men were familiar with that sullen roar before the year 1678, when a description of it was given to Europe by Father Hennepin? or how many centuries it had flowed and plunged down the steep, before the Red Man was born? Ever—ever have the waters of Lake Erie fed that powerful torrent, and ever—ever has it been flung down that precipice.

They compute that the four miles of rapids below the Falls, which are hemmed in by rocks as high and steep as those in its immediate vicinity, have all been cut through and wasted by the water. Who can tell if this be so, or at what snail's pace this mining work has been accomplished? It is not by cutting the upper rocks. They shine through the transparent water with edges as sharp as if they had just come from under the quarry-man's tool. The cascade slowly cuts its way by the revulsion of the cast-down waters caving out the earth below, making a "Cave of the Winds" between the shining liquid sheet on one side, and the dull soil on the other, till the superincumbent Rock, having lost its support, is plunged down prone. And should the deluge of fire which will ultimately turn all these waters into vapors of smoke, be so long delayed, the Niagara Falls may yet eat their way back to Lake Erie.

Time—Time—thou hast come from the bosom of Eternity, as this river comes from the bosom of the Lake. Yet the Lake is not emptied or diminished, neither is Eternity. How many rapids, and cataracts, and whirlpools have we to encounter who float for a while on thy surface! What momentous results hang on the passage. Born out of the Lake—buried in the Ocean—are we not like thee, Niagara? Born out of Eternity, and returning to Eternity, what need to prepare for it. What happiness and joy to be réconciled to the Eternal, to taste His redeeming love, to dwell in the light of His smile forever and ever.

The time is at hand when the "mighty angel clothed with a cloud, with a rainbow around his head," shall lift up his hand to Heaven, and swear by Him that liveth forever, who created all that is beautiful and grand in earth, sky, and ocean, "that there shall be time no longer." Then our opinions, our tastes, our criticisms, our books, will all be as nothing—and our interest in Christ Jesus the Lord our Righteousness will be All in All.

" The sun is but a spark of fire,
A transient meteor in the sky.
The soul, immortal as its Sire,
Shall never die."

THE END.

BONAR'S (Rev. Horatius) Night of Weeping ... 30
—— Morning of Joy, a sequel to the above ... 40
—— Story of Grace ... 30
—— Truth and Error. 18mo ... 40
—— Man, his Religion and his World ... 40
BONAR'S (Rev. Andrew) Commentary on Leviticus. 8vo ... 1 50
BONNET'S Family of Bethany. 18mo ... 40
—— Meditations on the Lord's Prayer. 18mo ... 40
BOOTH'S Reign of Grace. 12mo ... 75
BORROW'S Bible and Gipsies of Spain. 8vo, cloth ... 1 00
BOSTON'S Four-fold State. 18mo ... 50
—— Crook in the Lot. 18mo ... 30
BRETT (Rev. W. H.)—The Indian Tribes of Guiana. Illustrated. 16mo ...
BROKEN BUD; or, the Reminiscences of a Bereaved Mother. With steel Frontispiece. 16mo ... 75
BROWN'S (Rev. John, D.D.) Exposition of First Peter. 8vo .. 2 50
—— On the Sayings and Discourses of Christ. 3 vols. 8vo ....
BROWN'S Explication of the Assembly's Catechism. 12mo ... 60
BROWN (Rev. David) on the Second Advent. 12mo ... 1 25
BRIDGES on the Christian Ministry. 8vo ... 1 50
—— On the Proverbs. 8vo ... 2 00
—— On the CXIX. Psalm. New edition. 8vo ... 1 00
—— Memoir of Mary Jane Graham. 8vo ... 1 00
—— Works. 3 vols. 8vo, containing the above ... 5 00
BROWN'S Concordance. New and neat edition. 24mo ... 20
Do. Gilt edge ... 30
BUCHANAN'S Comfort in Affliction. 18mo ... 40
—— On the Holy Spirit. 18mo. Second edition ... 50
BUNBURY'S Glory, Glory, Glory, and other Narratives ... 25
BUTLER'S (Bishop) Complete Works. 8vo ... 1 50
—— Sermons, alone. 8vo ... 1 00
—— Analogy, alone. 8vo ... 75
—— and Wilson's Analogy. 8vo ... 1 25
BUNYAN'S Pilgrim's Progress, fine edition, large type. 12mo .. 1 00
Do. Gilt ... 1 50
Do. 18mo, close type ... 50
—— Jerusalem Sinner Saved. 18mo ... 50
—— Greatness of the Soul. 18mo ... 50
BURN'S (John) Christian Fragments. 18mo ... 40
BURNS' (Rev. Jabez) Parables and Miracles of Christ. 12mo .. 75
CALVIN—The Life and Times of John Calvin, the Great Reformer. By Paul Henry, D.D. 2 vols. 8vo, Portrait ... 3 00
CAMERON'S (Mrs.) Farmer's Daughter. Illustrated ... 30

CATECHISMS—The Assembly's Catechism. Per hundred.... 1 25
—— with Proofs.... 3 00
—— Brown's Short Catechism. Per hundred.... 1 25
—— Brown on the Assembly's Catechism. 18mo.... 10
CECIL'S WORKS. 3 vols. 12mo, with Portrait.... 3 00
—— Sermons, separate.... 1 00
—— Miscellanies and Remains, separate.... 1 00
—— Original Thoughts, separate.... 1 00
—— (Catharine) Memoir of Mrs. Hawks, with Portrait.... 1 00
CHARNOCK'S Choice Works.... 60
CHALMERS' Sermons. 2 vols. 8vo. With a fine Portrait.... 3 00
—— Lectures on Romans. 8vo. " " 1 50
—— Miscellanies. 8vo. " " 1 50
—— Select Works; comprising the above. 4 vols. 8vo.... 6 00
—— Evidences of Christian Revelation. 2 vols.... 1 25
—— Natural Theology. 2 vols.... 1 25
—— Moral Philosophy.... 60
—— Commercial Discourses.... 60
—— Astronomical Discourses.... 60
CHEEVER'S Lectures on the Pilgrim's Progress. Illus. 12mo.. 1 00
CHRISTIAN RETIREMENT. 12mo.... 75
—— **EXPERIENCE.** By the same author. 12mo.... 75
CLARK'S (Rev. John A.,) Walk about Zion. 12mo.... 75
—— Pastor's Testimony.... 75
—— Awake, Thou Sleeper.... 75
—— Young Disciple.... 88
—— Gathered Fragments.... 1 00
CLARKE'S Daily Scripture Promises. 32mo, gilt.... 30
COLQUHOUN'S (Lady) World's Religion. New ed., 16mo.... 50
COMMANDMENT WITH PROMISE. By the Author of "The Week," &c. Illustrated by Howland. 16mo.... 75
COWPER—The Works of William Cowper; comprising his Life, Letters and Poems, now first collected by the introduction of Cowper's Private Correspondence. Edited by the Rev. T. S. Grimshaw. With numerous illustrations on steel, and a fine Portrait by Ritchie. 1 vol. royal 8vo.... 3 00
Do. do. cloth, extra gilt.... 4 00
Do. do. morocco extra.... 5 00
—— Poetical Works, complete, separate. 2 vols. 16mo. Illus. 1 50
CUMMING'S (Rev. John, D.D.) Message from God. 18mo.... 30
—— Christ Receiving Sinners.... 30
CUNNINGHAM'S World without Souls. 18mo.... 30
CUYLER'S (Rev. T. L.) Stray Arrows.... 30
DALE (Rev. Thomas)—The Golden Psalm 16mo.... 60

DAVIES' Sermons. 3 vols. 12mo.......................... 2 00
DAVIDSON'S (Dr.) Connexions. New edition. 8vo.......... 1 50
Do. do. 3 vols. 12mo.............. 1 50
DAVID'S PSALMS, in metre. Large type. 12mo, embossed.. 75
Do. do. gilt edge......... 1 00
Do. do. Turkey morocco...... 2 00
Do. 18mo, good type, plain sheep.................... 38
Do. 48mo, very neat pocket edition, sheep.............. 20
Do. " " " morocco.......... 25
Do. " " " gilt edge.......... 31
Do. " " " tucks.............. 50
Do. with Brown's Notes. 18mo.......................... 50
Do. " " morocco gilt.......... 1 00
D'AUBIGNE'S History of the Reformation. *Carefully Revised*, with various additions not hitherto published. 4 vols. in two. 12mo, cloth.. 1 50
Do. do. 8vo, complete in 1 vol......... 1 00
—— Life of Cromwell the Protector. 12mo.................. 50
—— Germany, England and Scotland. 12mo................. 75
—— Luther and Calvin. 18mo............................. 25
—— The Authority of God the true Barrier against Infidel and Romish Aggression.......... 75
DICK'S (John, D.D.) Lectures on Theology. Fine edition, with Portrait. 2 vols. in one. Cloth............................. 2 50
Do. do sheep.............................. 3 00
Do. do. in 2 vols. Cloth................... 3 00
—— Lectures on Acts. 8vo................................ 1 50
DICKINSON'S (Rev. R. W.) Scenes from Sacred History...... 1 00
—— Responses from the Sacred Oracles..................... 1 00
DODDRIDGE'S Rise and Progress. 18mo.................. 40
—— Life of Col. Gardiner. 18mo......................... 30
DUNCAN'S Sacred Philosophy of the Seasons. 4 vols......... 3 00
—— Life. By his Son. With Portrait. 12mo................ 75
—— Tales of the Scottish Peasantry. 18mo. Illustrated....... 50
—— Cottage Fireside. 18mo. Illustrated.................. 40
—— (Mrs.) Life of Mary Lundie Duncan. 16mo.............. 75
—— —— Life of George A. Lundie. 18mo.................. 50
—— —— Memoir of George B. Phillips. 18mo............... 25
—— —— Children of the Manse........................... 1 00
—— —— America as I saw it..............................
—— (Mary Lundie) Rhymes for my Children. Illustrated.... 25
EDGAR'S Variations of Popery. 8vo........................ 1 00
EDWARD'S (Jonathan, D.D.) Charity and its Fruits. Never before published. 16mo.................................... 1 00

HAWKER'S Poor Man's Morning Portion. 12mo........... 60
Do. do. Evening Portion. " 60
—— Zion's Pilgrim. 18mo.................................. 30
HERVEY'S Meditations. 18mo.............................. 40
HETHERINGTON'S History of the Church of Scotland..... 1 50
HENGSTENBERG on the Apocalypse. 2 vols. 8vo.........
HENRY'S (Matt.) Method for Prayer......................... 40
—— Communicant's Companion. 18mo..................... 40
—— Daily Communion with God. " 30
—— Pleasantness of a Religious Life. 24mo, gilt............. 30
—— Choice Works. 12mo..................... 60
HENRY, Philip, Life of. 18mo.............................. 50
HEWITSON—Memoir of the Rev. W. H. Hewitson, Free Church Minister at Dirleton, Scotland, with Portrait. 12mo........... 85
HILL'S (George) Lectures on Divinity. 8vo.................. 2 00
—— (Rowland) Life. By Sidney. 12mo..................... 75
HISTORY OF THE PURITANS IN ENGLAND, AND THE PILGRIM FATHERS. By Stowell and Wilson. 12mo. 1 00
HISTORY OF THE REFORMATION IN EUROPE...... 40
HOUSMAN'S Life and Remains. 12mo.............. 75
HORNE'S Introduction. 2 vols. royal 8vo, half cloth.......... 3 50
Do. do. 1 vol. sheep........................ 4 00
Do. do. 2 vols. cloth........................ 4 00
Do. do. 2 vols. library style 5 00
—— (Bishop,) Commentary on the Book of Psalms........... 1 50
HOWELL'S LIFE—Perfect Peace. 18mo.................... 30
HOWE'S Redeemer's Tears, and other Essays. 18mo.......... 50
HOWARD, (John,) or the Prison World of Europe. 12mo..... 1 00
HOOKER, (Rev. H.,) The Uses of Adversity. 18mo............ 30
—— Philosophy of Unbelief................................ 75
HUSS, (John,) Life of. Translated from the German........... 25
INFANT'S PROGRESS. By the Author of "Little Henry and his Bearer." Illustrated. 16mo............................. 75
JACOBUS on Matthew. With a Harmony. Illustrated........ 75
—— Questions on do. 18mo................................. 15
—— On Mark, Luke and John, (preparing,)..................
JAMES' Anxious Inquirer. 18mo........................... 30
—— True Christian. 18mo................................. 30
—— Widow Directed. 18mo.............. 30
—— Young Man from Home................................. 30
—— Christian Professor. New edition. 12mo................ 75
—— Christian Duty. 16mo................................. 75
JAMIE GORDON; or, The Orphan. Illustrated. 16mo..... 75
JANEWAY'S Heaven upon Earth. 18mo.................... 50

JANEWAY'S Token for Children. 18mo.................... 30
JAY'S Morning Exercises. 12mo............................ 75
—— Evening " " 75
—— Christian Contemplated. 18mo......................... 40
—— Jubilee Memorial. 18mo.............................. 30
JERRAM'S Tribute to a beloved and only Daughter.......... 30
JOHNSON'S Rasselas. Elegant edition. 16mo 50
KEY TO THE SHORTER CATECHISM.................. 20
KENNEDY'S (Grace) Profession is not Principle............. 30
—— Jessy Allan, the Lame Girl. 18mo...................... 25
—— Anna Ross. 18mo. Illustrated......................... 30
—— Decision. 18mo....................................... 25
KING'S (Rev. David, LL.D.) Geology and Religion. 16mo..... 75
—— On the Eldership....................................... 50
KITTO'S (John. D.D.) Daily Bible Illustrations.

MORNING SERIES.

Vol. I. Antediluvians and Patriarchs................ 1 00
II. Moses and the Judges...................... 1 00
III. Samuel, Saul, and David.................... 1 00
IV. Solomon and the Kings..................... 1 00

EVENING SERIES.

Vol. I. Job and the Poetical Books................. 1 00
II. Isaiah and the Prophets.................... 1 00
III. The Life and Death of our Lord............ 1 00
IV. The Apostles and the Early Church......... 1 00

KRUMMACHER'S Martyr Lamb. 18mo.................... 40
—— Elijah the Tishbite. 18mo.......................... 40
—— Last Days of Elisha. New edition. 18mo............... 50
LANDS OF THE MOSLEM. By El-Mukattem. 8vo....... 1 50
LEYBURN'S Soldier of the Cross. 12mo..................... 1 00
LIFE IN NEW-YORK. 18mo.............................. 40
LIFE OF A VAGRANT. Written by himself............... 50
LIGHTED VALLEY; or, the Memoir of Miss Bolton......... 75
LOWRIE'S Letters to Sabbath-school Children............... 25
—— (Rev. John C.) Two Years in Upper India.............. 75
LOCKWOOD'S Memoir. By his Father. 18mo... 40
LUTHER'S Commentary on the Galatians. 8vo............... 1 50
MACKAY—The Wickliffites................................ 75
MARTIN'S (Sarah) Life. 18mo............................. 30
MARTYN'S (Henry) Life. 12mo. New edition............... 60
MARSHALL on Sanctification. 18mo....................... 50

MARTYRS AND COVENANTERS OF SCOTLAND..... 40
MASON'S (Dr. John) Essays on the Church.... 60
MATHEWS' Bible and Civil Government. 12mo............ 1 00
McCOSH on the Divine Government, Physical and Moral...... 2 00
McCRINDELL—The Convent. A Narrative. 18mo........... 50
McCHEYNE'S (Rev. Robert Murray) Works. 2 vols. 8vo..... 3 00
—— Life, Lectures, and Letters. Separate.................. 1 50
—— Sermons. Separate 2 00
—— Familiar Letters from the Holy Land. 18mo............ 50
McFARLANE—The Mountains of the Bible. Illustrated...... 75
McGHEE'S (Rev. R. J.) Lectures on the Ephesians. 8vo...... 2 00
McGILVRAY'S Peace in Believing......................... 25
McLEOD'S Life and Power of True Godliness............... 60
McCLELLAND (Prof. Alex.) on the Canon Interpretation of Scripture. 75
MEIKLE'S Solitude Sweetened. 12mo...................... 60
MENTEATH—Lays of the Kirk and Covenant. Illus. 16mo.. 75
MILLER (Hugh)—The Geology of the Bass Rock. Illustrated.. 75
MILLER'S (Rev. Dr. Samuel) Memoir of Rev. Dr. Nisbet...... 75
—— (Rev. John) Design of the Church. 12mo.............. 60
MICHAEL KEMP, the Farmer's Lad. 18mo................ 40
MISSIONS, the Origin and History of. 25 steel plates. 4to.... 3 50
MOFFATT'S Southern Africa. 12mo...................... 75
MONOD'S Lucilla; or, the Reading of the Bible. 18mo....... 40
MORE'S (Hannah) Private Devotion. Large type. 18mo...... 50
Do. do. do. gilt....... 75
Do. do. do. small edition. 32mo....... 20
Do. do. do. " gilt....... 30
MORELL'S History of Modern Philosophy. 8vo............... 3 00
MORNING OF LIFE. 18mo................................ 40
MURPHEY'S Bible and Geology Consistent.................. 1 00
MY SCHOOL-BOY DAYS. 18mo. Illustrated................ 30
MY YOUTHFUL COMPANIONS. 18mo. Illustrated..... 30
MY SCHOOL-BOY DAYS AND YOUTHFUL COMPANIONS, bound in one volume. Illustrated. 18mo............ 50
MY GRANDFATHER GREGORY. Illustrated........... 25
MY GRANDMOTHER GILBERT. do. 25
NEWTON'S (Rev. John) Works. 2 vols. in one. Portrait ... 2 00
—— Memoir of M. Magdalen Jasper. 18mo................ 30
NEW COBWEBS TO CATCH LITTLE FLIES. Illustrated. 16mo, square.. 50
NOEL'S Infant Piety. 18mo.............................. 25
OLMSTED'S Thoughts and Counsels for the Impenitent....... 50
OLD WHITE MEETING-HOUSE. 18mo.................. 40

OLD HUMPHREY'S Observations........................ 40
—— Addresses.. 40
—— Thoughts for the Thoughtful........................ 40
—— Walks in London.................................. 40
—— Homely Hints..................................... 40
—— Country Strolls.................................. 40
—— Old Sea Captain.................................. 40
—— Grandparents..................................... 40
—— Isle of Wight.................................... 40
—— Pithy Papers..................................... 40
—— Pleasant Tales. Illustrated........................ 40
—— North American Indians........................... 40
OPIE on Lying. New edition. 18mo, illustrated.............. 40
OSBORNE (Mrs.)—The World of Waters ; or, a Peaceful Progress o'er the Unpathed Sea. Illustrated. 16mo.............. 75
OWEN on Spiritual Mindedness. 12mo..................... 60
PALEY'S Horæ Paulinæ. 12mo............................ 75
PASCAL'S Provincial Letters. New edition. Edited by Dr. McCrie. 12mo.. 1 00
PASTOR'S DAUGHTER. By Louisa Payson Hopkins....... 40
PATTERSON on the Assembly's Shorter Catechism.......... 50
PEEP OF DAY. New edition.............................. 30
LINE UPON LINE. New edition.......................... 30
PRECEPT ON PRECEPT. New edition..................... 30
PIKE'S True Happiness. 18mo........................... 30
—— Divine Origin of Christianity. 18mo.................. 30
PHILIP'S Devotional Guides. 2 vols. 12mo................ 1 50
—— Young Man's Closet Library......................... 75
—— Marys, or the Beauty of Female Holiness.............. 40
—— Marthas, or the Varieties of Female Piety.............. 40
—— Lydias, or the Development of Female Character........ 40
—— Hannahs, or Maternal Influences on Sons............... 40
—— Love of the Spirit 40
POLLOK'S Course of Time. Elegant ed. 16mo. Portrait..... 1 00
Do. do. gilt, extra..... 1 50
Do. do. Turkey morocco, gilt............ 2 00
Do. do. 18mo. small copy, close type....... 40
—— Life, Letters, and Remains. By the Rev. Jas. Scott, D.D... 1 00
—— Tales of the Scottish Covenanters. Illustrated. 16mo.... 75
—— Helen of the Glen. 18mo. Illustrated.................. 25
—— Persecuted Family. " " 25
—— Ralph Gemmell. " " 25
PORTEUS' Lectures on Matthew. 12mo..................... 60
POWERSCOTT'S (Lady) Letters. 12mo..................... 75

PSALMS IN HEBREW. 32mo, gilt........................ 50
RETROSPECT (The). By Aliquis. 18mo.................... 40
RICHMOND'S Domestic Portraiture. Edited by Bickersteth. New and elegant edition. Illustrated. 16mo................. 75
—— Annals of the Poor. 18mo.............................. 40
ROGER MILLER; or, Heroism in Humble Life. With an Introduction, by Dr. Alexander. 18mo...................... 30
ROGER'S Jacob's Well. 18mo............................. 40
ROGERS—The Folded Lamb; or, Memorials of an Infant Son. 16mo... 60
ROMAINE on Faith. 12mo.................................. 60
—— Letters. 12mo.. 60
ROWLAND'S (Rev. H. A) Common Maxims of Infidelity..... 75
RUTHERFORD'S Letters. With Life by Bonar............ 1 50
RYLE'S Living or Dead? A Series of Home Truths. 16mo.... 75
—— Wheat or Chaff?.. 75
SCOTT'S Force of Truth. 18mo........................... 25
SCOUGAL'S Works. 18mo.................................. 40
SELECT WORKS of James, Venn, Wilson, Philip, and Jay... 1 50
SELECT CHRISTIAN AUTHORS. 2 vols. 8vo.............. 2 00
SERLE'S Christian Remembrancer. 24mo, gilt.............. 50
SINNER'S FRIEND. 18mo.................................. 25
SIGOURNEY'S (Mrs. L. H.) Water Drops. Illustrated. 16mo.. 75
—— Letters to my Pupils. With Portrait. 16mo............. 75
—— Olive Leaves. Illustrated. 16mo....................... 75
—— Boys' Book. Illustrated. 18mo......................... 40
—— Girls' Book. " " 40
—— Child's Book. " " square............................... 35
SINCLAIR'S Modern Accomplishments...................... 75
—— Modern Society... 75
—— Charlie Seymour. 18mo. Illustrated.................... 30
SIMEON'S LIFE. By Carus. With Portrait. 8vo......... 2 00
SMITH'S (Rev. James) Green Pastures for the Lord's Flock... 1 00
SMYTH'S Bereaved Parents Consoled. 12mo................ 75
SONGS IN THE HOUSE OF MY PILGRIMAGE. 16mo. 75
SORROWING YET REJOICING. 18mo........................ 30
Do. do. 32mo, gilt............... 30
SPRING'S (Rev. Dr.) Memoirs of the late Hannah L. Murray.. 1 50
STEVENSON'S Christ on the Cross. 12mo.................. 75
—— Lord our Shepherd. 12mo................................ 60
STORIES ON THE LORD'S PRAYER, AND OTHER TALES. By the Author of "Edward and Miriam.".........
SUMNER'S Exposition of Matthew and Mark. 12mo.......... 75
SUDDARDS' British Pulpit. 2 vols. 8vo.............. 3 00

WINER'S Idioms of the Language of the New Testament...... 2 50
WINSLOW on Personal Declension and Revival.............. 60
—— Midnight Harmonies; or, Thoughts for the Season of Solitude and Sorrow. 16mo.. 60
WILLISON'S Sacramental Meditations and Advices. 18mo.... 50
WYLIE'S Journey over the Region of Fulfilled Prophecy...... 30
XENOPHON'S Whole Works. Translated.................... 2 00
YOUNG'S Night Thoughts. 16mo. Large type, with Portrait... 1 00
Do. do. extra gilt........... 1 50
Do. do. Turkey morocco, gilt............ 2 00
Do. do. 18mo, close type.............. 40

ROBERT CARTER & BROTHERS,

Would invite special attention to the following New Books, which will also be found under their appropriate heads in the foregoing pages:

AMERICA AS I FOUND IT. By Mrs. Duncan, author of the Memoirs of Mary Lundie Duncan, &c. 16mo.

LECTURES ON THE EVIDENCES OF CHRISTIANITY. Delivered at the University of Virginia, by eminent Clergymen of the Presbyterian Church. 8vo. 13 portraits.

HENGSTENBERG on the Apocalypse.

MEMOIR OF WILLIAM TUTTLE.

THE FOLDED LAMB.

FRANK NETHERTON; or, the Talisman.

CHARITY AND ITS FRUITS. By Jonathan Edwards.

FAR OFF; or, Asia and Australia Described. By the Author of the "Peep of Day," &c. Illustrated.

KITTO'S Daily Bible Illustrations. Evening Series, 4 vols., uniform with the Morning Series.

WHEAT OR CHAFF? By the Rev. J. C. Ryle.

MAN—HIS RELIGION AND HIS WORLD. By Bonar. 18mo.

SONGS IN THE HOUSE OF MY PILGRIMAGE.

CHRISTIAN DUTY. By John Angel James.

www.ingramcontent.com/pod-product-compliance
Lightning Source LLC
LaVergne TN
LVHW021128110826
845150LV00005B/962

* 9 7 8 1 4 2 5 5 4 9 8 5 5 *